AF361331

THE ECCLESIASTICAL PROHIBITION OF BOOKS

CATHOLIC UNIVERSITY OF AMERICA
STUDIES IN CANON LAW
— No. 72 —

The Ecclesiastical Prohibition of Books

A DISSERTATION

Submitted to the Faculty of the School of Canon Law, Catholic University of America, in partial fulfillment of the requirements for the degree of

DOCTOR OF CANON LAW

REVEREND JOSEPH M. PERNICONE, A. B., J. U. L.
PRIEST OF THE ARCHDIOCESE OF NEW YORK

CATHOLIC UNIVERSITY OF AMERICA
WASHINGTON, D. C.
1932

NIHIL OBSTAT

ARTHUR J. SCANLAN, S. T. D.
Censor Librorum

IMPRIMATUR

† PATRICK CARDINAL HAYES
Archbishop of New York

Feast of the Conversion of Saint Paul, 1932

TO

JESUS CHRIST KING

and

HIS BLESSED MOTHER

this work is dedicated

FOREWORD

The constant increase of dangerous writings has become a matter of great concern not only to the spiritual authorities but also to the legislators of nations. This alarming situation is felt particularly by the Supreme Pontiff, who, through Peter, has been entrusted by Christ with the care of His fold. On various occasions he has expressed his preoccupation about the irreligious and immoral writings which abound today.

On May 3, 1927,[1] by his command, the Sacred Congregation of the Holy Office issued a decree to all the Bishops of the world to sound the alarm and to suggest the means against the ever growing mass of immoral literature. This decree reechoed in this country through letters or instructions issued by the Bishops, calling the attention of the faithful to the dangers of the evil press and to the laws of God and of the Church in that regard.[2]

While the Catholic Church employs every possible means for the spread of good literature, there are two principal ways in which she strives to keep dangerous literature away from the faithful; first, by examining writings of a religious or moral character before pub-

---

1. *AAS*, XIX (1927), 186, ff.

2. The Letter of His Eminence Patrick Cardinal Hayes, Archbishop of New York, of Oct. 7, 1929 (*Catholic News*, Oct. 12, 1929) may serve as a sample of the American response to the Pontiff's wishes.

lication, for the purpose of preventing the spread of what is opposed to the truths and the laws of God; secondly, by prohibiting the publication, reading and other use of evil and dangerous works. Therefore, the book legislation of the Church is divided into two parts, namely, the *Censorship of Books* and the *Prohibition of Books*. The latter is the subject of this treatise. However, due to their close connection, the treatment of Prohibition of Books often necessitates reference to Previous Censorship.

The treatise will be divided into two parts. In the first part the law of God, both natural and positive, with regard to Prohibition of Books will be stated and shown; the right of the Church to forbid books will be proven and a brief review will be given of the history of this Church legislation. In the second part, the present law of the Church on Prohibition of Books will be described and commented upon.

The writer takes this opportunity to thank the members of the faculty of the School of Canon Law and all others who have aided him towards the publication of this work.

TABLE OF CONTENTS

PART I

APOLOGETICAL AND HISTORICAL
INTRODUCTION

CHAPTER I

The Divine Law

Art. I. *The Divine Natural Law*[1]

The law of nature imposes upon all men the duty of shunning that type of literature which endangers their eternal salvation. Man is bound by nature to strive towards the attainment of his last end, God[2]. Because religion and morality are necessary means to obtain that end, man is obliged to use these means, by observing his religious and moral duties. In the search for the proper knowledge of these duties, and in his fulfillment of them, man is influenced by many factors, within and without himself, among which *literature* is a most powerful one, as will be presently seen. This influence may be useful or harmful. That kind of literature which produces harmful influence on man, that is, *hinders* him from acquiring the proper knowledge of his religious and moral duties or

---

1. St. Alphonsus, *Dissertatio De Prohibitione Librorum*, Cap. I; Arndt, *De Libris Prohibitis Commentarii*, nn. 77-82; De Meester, *Juris Canonici et Juris Canonico-civilis Compendium*, III, n. 1333; Betten, *The Roman Index of Forbidden Books*, p. 17 ff.; Bouix, *Tractatus de Curia Romana*, pp. 383-392; Raynaud, *Erotemata de Malis ac Bonis Libris, deque iusta aut iniusta eorundem confixione*, nn. 5-13; Lugo, *De Virtute Fidei*, Disputat. 21, sect. 2, n. 25; Hurley, *A Commentary on the Present Index Legislation*, p. 160 ff; Boudinhon, *La Nouvelle Legislation de l'Index*, p. 109 f; Lynk, *Twelve Talks on The Art of Right Reading*, p. 3 ff; Scott, *Religion and Common Sense*, p. 288 ff; Eymieu, *Le Government de soi-même*, p. 123 ff; Pederzini, *Ragionamento sopra il tema proposto dalla R. Accademia di Scienze, Lettere ed Arti di Modena nei seguenti termini: "Dimostrare coi migliori argomenti i mali della stampa licenziosa e i vantaggi della ben regolata; e quindi la necessità di una savia censura."*

2. St. Thomas Aquinas, *Summa Theologica*, I-II, q. 2, art. 1-8; Cronin, *The Science of Ethics*, I, p. 70, 78-79; Hull, *Man's Great Concern*, p. 1 ff.

hampers him in his fulfillment of them is *evil* because it makes
the attaining of his last end difficult and almost impossible
and, therefore, *is forbidden by the natural law.*

Does literature or the written word really influence men
for good or evil? Does it help or hinder them in their
efforts to attain their last end? The very *intention of those
who write,* the *disposition of the average reader,* the *nature
of printed works* which in truth are the constant companions
and the skillful teachers of men as well as the food of their
minds, *experience* and *history,* prove beyond doubt that books,
magazines, newspapers and *all kinds of publications wield a
tremendous power over the minds and lives of men, influ-
encing their present welfare and their future destiny.* In fact,
authors write to impart their views to others and to affect
their conduct. *Readers* unconsciously imbibe those views,
often erroneous, and make them part of their character[3]. The
ignorance and prejudices in religious and moral matters
which are so rampant today make it difficult for the average
reader to detect the venom often hidden in a most fascinating
style.[4] Books and other forms of literature, like living *companions,*[5] greatly influence those who keep their company; like

---

3. Proal, *Passion and Criminality*, p. 317. On p. 322 he states:
"With each of us there are certain authors who inspire our predilections
and feelings. We make their thoughts our own, and model ourselves on
them." And on p. 321 he writes: "The influence of literature is particularly marked in the case of persons of nervous temperament, who,
gifted as they are of more than average sensibility, sympathize more
readily with the writers. Nervosity creates a special aptitude for con-
tagion." On p. 428: "Readers borrow from their chosen heroes of fiction
language, sentiments, tastes, habits, names, costumes, even their favorite
scents."

4. Cf. preface to the *Index of Prohibited Books* (English ed.,
1930), p. VIII.

5. Ps. XVII, 26-27: "With the holy thou wilt be holy; and with
the innocent thou wilt be innocent; with the elect thou wilt be elect; and
with the perverse thou wilt be perverted." Clement XIII, encycl. *Christianae Reipublicae*, Nov. 25, 1766 (*Fontes* n. 461), writes:

> Quam vastitatem pestilentia efficiet librorum, qui apte com-
> positi, et artificii pleni, manent perpetuo, et semper nobiscum
> adsunt, nobiscum peregrinantur, nobiscum domi sedent, et
> eorum penetrant cubicula, ad quae improbo et occulto auctori
> aditus non pateret?

Proal, *Passion and Criminality*, p. 317, states: "Men reciprocally act

food[6] they enter the minds of readers and either nourish or destroy their good qualities; like *teachers*[7] they impart knowledge that will either help or hinder their readers. These are not mere theories, but truths borne out of the experience of mankind. Here reference is made to the experience not of the abnormal man, but of the average man.

There is not one of us but has had his ideals raised by the reading of a good book. Likewise most of us must confess that at some time or other in our life we read, perhaps accidentally, a book, a paper or a magazine which disconcerted our mind, tended to lower our standards of life or to shake the very basis of our religion. Such is the experience also of mankind as a whole. History gives many examples of individual or group conversions and perversions caused by reading.[8] It also tells us of many movements, good and bad, which began and grew through the same medium. For writers mould their readers in their own image, they make them participate in their own ideas, passions and sentiments. Thus the French Revolution is commonly traced to the writings of Voltaire; the Protestant Reformation took on tremendous proportions through the publications of Luther and other Prot-

---

and react on each other in way of suggestion, by their doings and words... After this, how can any one doubt as to the influence exerted by author over reader, by literature over morals?" Cf. also Scott, *Religion and Common Sense*, p. 301; Lynk *Twelve Talks on the Art of Right Reading*, p. 14; Pederzini, *Ragionamento*, p. 9.

6. Cf. St. Alphonsus, *De Prohib. Libr.* Cap. I, n. 2. He writes:

Bene S. Basilius libros appellavit cibum animarum; quia sicut cibus delectabiliter ingreditur in hominem, et deinde fit proprius hominis sanguis, sic liber, cum legitur, delectabiliter legitur (quis enim legit invitus?), et sic de facili fieri solet res propria lectoris.

7. St. Alphonsus, *De Prohib. Libr.* Cap. I, n. 2 writes:

Qui ad auctorem legendum accedit, illi pene discipulum se tradit, ipsique cor docile et benevolum offert, et ideo facile ab illo decipi potest; valde enim difficile est, quod lector aliquo amore erga Auctorem illum non afficiatur; ex quo deinde facile eveniet, ut impietas, et error latens hauriatur insensibiliter et tenaciter postea retineatur.

8. St. Alphonsus, *De Prohib. Libr.*, cap. I, n. 5; Zaccaria, *Storia Polemica delle Proibizioni dei Libri*, lib. II, diss. I, Cap. 4, n. 1. ff.; Arndt, *De Libris Prohibitis Commentarii*, nn. 35-36; Lord, *I Can Read Anything*, p. 14, ff.

estant leaders. It was principally through the medium of their written works that "Voltaire made Voltairians, Goethe Werthians, Byron Byronics, Leopardi Leopardists, Lamartine Lamartinian Romantics, Hugo worshippers of the great Victor, George Sand Sandists, Murger Bohemians, Baudelaire Baudelairians, Tolstoy Christian Socialists."[9]

The great philosopher and Father of the Church, St. Augustine, tells how a book of Cicero, *Hortensius*, now lost, helped to change his heart[10]. Even Alexander Dumas (Junior) himself, speaking of the causes of adultery, mentions an imagination "disordered by bad talk, bad books and bad example"[11].

Lest some one should object that man is no longer amenable to book influence, as he was wont to be in the past, let it be stated that no such change has taken place. The reading of Renan, Loisy, Harnack and Tyrrell has led to the spread of Modernism; many give up their belief in God after reading atheistic literature.[12] Others are firm believers in Socialism or Communism because they have read Carl Marx's works. And where is the cause to be found for all the talk about a 'new morality', free love, divorce, sex freedom, companionate marriage except in books of such writers as Ibsen, Havelock Ellis, Ellen Key and Bertrand Russell?[13] The millions spent yearly on advertising and press propaganda are proof enough of the powerful influence of the written word.

Judges, before whom harrowing experiences are daily told, assure us that literature is responsible, at least in part, for the crime wave of the day.[14] Men of letters, sound thinkers, civil rulers and spiritual leaders, highly conscious of the destructive nature of many publications, frequently protest

---

9. Proal, *o. c.*, p. 318.
10. *Conf.* lib. III, Cap. IV — *M P L*, XXXII, 685.
11. Quoted by Proal, *o. c.*, p. 428.
12. Will Durant confesses in his work *Transition*, p. 54 ff., that he lost his faith through reading.
13. Lord, *I Can Read Anything*, p. 17.
14. Proal, *Passion and Criminality*, in Chapters X and XI, presents solid arguments for that contention, together with adetailed account of some actual cases. Cf. also Ford, *Criminal Obscenity*, passim; Geisert, *The Criminal*, p. 237 ff.

and warn against them[15] The long list of enactments against
pernicious literature in all civilized countries from the time
of Pagan Rome[16] until now is another argument in favor of
the contention that bad books have a tremendous power for
evil. The State in such cases feels that, just as criminals and
dangerous persons are to be segregated from the community,
so wicked books are to be kept away from the people. This
control of literature on the part of the State, in a greater or
less degree, has always existed after the advent of Christianity in every civilized nation. Today in all codes of civil law,
including that of the United States of America[17], there are
laws against objectionable literature. In 1923 at Geneva, under the auspices of the League of Nations, an international
code was adopted for stemming effectively the spread of evil
literature[18].

---

15. No complete list of such statements by modern authorities
can be given as it would be entirely too long. A number of them from
leaders of the civil world, writers, etc., may be read in Ford's *Criminal
Obscenity*, pp. 38-51. As for statements from religious leaders, cf., among
others, the Pastoral Letter of His Em. Card. Hayes, Archbishop of New
York, Oct. 7, 1929 (*Catholic News*, Oct. 12, 1929), and another of Right
Rev. Francis C. Kelley, Bishop of Oklahoma, January 31, 1930 (*Catholic
News*, Feb. 8, 1930).

16. Many examples are cited in standard works on the subject of
Prohibition of Books. Thus, cf. St. Alphonse, *De Prohib. Libr.*, Cap. I,
n. 7; Gretser, *De Jure et More Prohibendi, Expurgandi et Abolendi Libros Haereticos et Noxios*, lib. I, Cap. XXVI; Zaccaria, *Storia Polemica*,
p. 248 ff; Heymans, *De Ecclesiastica Librorum Aliorumque Scriptorum
in Belgio Prohibitione*, n. 34. Cicero, in *Quaestiones Tusculanae*, lib. II,
n. 11 (27) writes:

> Videsne poetae quid mali afferant?... molliunt animos
> nostros... nervos omnis virtutis elidunt.

17. *U. S. Criminal Code*, sect. 245; *Tariff Act of 1930*, sect. 305;
Post Office regulations, sect. 211 and 212 of the Act of Congress approved March 4, 1909 (35 Stat. L., 1129 as amended by the Act of March
4, 1911). In Sect. 211 we read among other things: "Every obscene,
lewd, or lascivious, and every filthy book, pamphlet, picture, paper, letter,
writing, print, or other publication of an indecent character...is hereby
declared to be non-mailable matter." Cf. also Boyd-Sumner, *Debate on
Censorship of Books*, p. 33: Ford, *Criminal Obscenity*, pp. 74 ff., 108 ff.,
142, f.

18. 1911 *Supplement to the American Journal of International
Law*, V (1911), 167; XX (1926), 179-189. This international agree-

This fact is proof sufficient, if any further proof were needed, that mankind is convinced by experience of the baneful influence of a certain type of literature.

To sum up, literature undoubtedly influences men for good or for evil. The law of nature binds men to tend towards the attainment of their last end through the fulfillment of their religious and moral duties. There is a certain type of literature which hinders man from acquiring the proper knowledge of those duties or at least makes it difficult for him to comply with them. This sort of literature then, is a serious obstacle in the way of reaching one's last end and therefore is forbidden by the natural law.

Art. II. *The Divine Positive Law*[19]

God, through the law of nature, which He has implanted in the human heart, forbids man to read a book or work, which may endanger his faith or morals, because such reading would make it difficult for him to save his soul. This prohibition is more evident and more compelling in the divine positive law, as found in Revelation.

It is true that in Holy Writ there are no express references to books from which men should abstain. However, God explicitly and clearly states the principle upon which the natural prohibition of books is based, viz., that man is obliged to strive for the attainment of his last end.[20] Thus, Christ insists on the observance of the Commandments (religion and morality), as a condition of entering eternal life.[21] He warns men against

---

ment was signed and ratified by the following nations: Albania, Germany, Austria, Belgium, Brazil, the British Empire, Bulgaria, China, Colombia, Costa Rica, Cuba, Denmark, Spain, Finland, France, Greece, Haiti, Honduras, Hungary, Italy, Japan, Latvia, Lithuania, Luxemburg, Monaco, Panama, the Netherlands, Persia, Poland, Roumania, Salvador, Kingdom of the Serbs, Croates and Slovenes, Siam, Switzerland, Czechoslovakia, Turkey and Uruguay. Cf. also Ford, *Criminal Obscenity*, p. 81 ff.

19. St. Alphonsus, *De Prohib. Libr.*, Cap. I; De Meester, *Compendium*, III, n. 1334.

20. Matthew XVI, 26.

21. Matthew XIX, 16-19; XXII, 36-40.

scandals, false teachers and *other hindrances* in the way of salvation. On one occasion, He said: "Woe to the world because of scandals."[22] Evil literature is certainly a scandal i.e., a stumbling-block to many people.[23] On another occasion the Master went as far as to say: "If thy right eye scandalize thee, pluck it out and cast it from thee... And if thy right hand scandalize thee, cut it off and cast it from thee".[24] Now, if a man's salvation require that he get rid of an eye or hand, should this be an obstacle to his salvation, then, with greater reason, the same must be said of harmful publications. Our Lord warns us against *false teachers:* "Beware of false prophets who come to you in the clothing of sheep, but inwardly they are ravening wolves."[25] Bad writings are really "false prophets", and, therefore, dangerous.[26] St. Alphonsus[27] in commenting on this text writes:

> What is this clothing of sheep except the semblance of piety with which deceitful writers cleverly clothe themselves? Who are these ravening wolves but heretics who tear to pieces the fold of Christ?

Again, God implicitly, though very clearly, forbids evil books when, through His apostles, or other inspired writers, He forbids companionship or fellowship with wicked men: "I have written to you not to keep company, if any man that is named a brother, be a fornicator, or covetous, or server of idols, or a railer, or a drunkard, or an extortioner: with such a one not so much as to eat."[28] Association with evil books is at times more dangerous than fellowship with men of evil habits[29] such as those described by St. Paul.

Positive divine law, then, as expressed in these and many other similar scriptural statements, simply restates and en-

---

22. Matthew XVIII, 7.
23. Supra p. 3 ff.
24. Matthew V, 29-30.
25. Matthew VII, 15.
26. Supra p. 5.
27. *De Prohib. Libr.* Cap. I, n. 3.
28. *I Cor.* VI, 11. Cf. also II John I, 10; *Rom.* XVI, 17; *I Tim.* VI, 20.
29. Supra p. 4.

forces the natural law with regard to the proscription of bad
literature. It imposes no distinct or additional obligation.[30]
However, through Revelation, God has made known to us
many new religious truths and moral obligations. Any work
which is contrary to these and which may endanger our eternal
salvation is forbidden by the natural and positive divine law.

---

30. Hurley, *A Commentary on the Present Index Legislation*,
p. 157.

CHAPTER II

THE ECCLESIASTICAL LAW AND PROHIBITION OF BOOKS

Art. I. *Right and Duty of the Church to Forbid
Harmful Literature*[1]

The Catholic Church has the right and duty to forbid
books and publications which are opposed to faith or morals,
or which in some other way endanger man's eternal salvation.

Our Divine Lord established the Church for one supreme purpose, that she might continue throughout the centuries that work and that mission which He had received
from His Heavenly Father: "As the Father hath sent me, so
also I send you."[2] He had come into this world that "they
may have life, and may have it more abundantly[3]...that the
world may be saved by him."[4] The end, therefore, for which
Christ founded His Church is the eternal salvation of mankind.[5]

But no society can realize its end without the necessary
means. For that reason the Divine Builder of the Catholic

------

1. Bouix, *Tractatus de Curia Romana*, p. 386.; Cavagnis, *Institutiones Juris Publici Ecclesiastici*, II, p. 143 f.; Zaccaria, *Storia Polemica delle Proibizioni dei Libri*, p. 271 ff.; Heymans, *De Ecclesiastica Librorum Aliorumque Scriptorum in Belgio Prohibitione Disquisitio*, p. 99 f.; Arndt, *De Libris Prohibitis Commentarii*, pp. V-VI; Betten, *The Roman Index of Forbidden Books*, p. 9 f.

2. John XX, 21, Cf. also John XVII, 18.

3. John X, 10.

4. John III, 17, Cf. also *Acts* XIV, 12.

5. Leo XIII, Encycl. *Immortale Dei*, Nov. 1, 1885, §5 (*Fontes* n. 592); Encycl. *Satis cognitum*, June 29, 1896, §7 (*Fontes* n. 630); Encycl. *Sapientiae*, Jan. 10, 1890, §3 (*Fontes* n. 605). D'Erbigny, *Theologia de Ecclesia*, I, Thesis IV (pp. 67-89) treats this matter at length.

Church gave her all the means necessary and useful for the realization of her end.[6] Thus, He promises the earthly head of His Church: "I will give to thee the keys of the kingdom of heaven. And whatsoever thou shalt bind upon earth, it shall be bound also in heaven; and whatsoever thou shalt loose upon earth, it shall be loosed also in heaven."[7] Then He addresses all the Apostles with similar words: "Amen I say to you, whatsoever you shall bind upon earth, shall be bound also in heaven; and whatsoever you shall loose upon earth shall be loosed also in heaven."[8]

On the eve of His Ascension into Heaven, Jesus Christ explicitly and solemnly conferred upon the twelve Apostles full power to exercise their mission; "All power is given to me in heaven and in earth. Going, therefore, *teach* ye all nations; baptizing them in the name of the Father, and of the Son, and of the Holy Ghost. Teaching them *to observe* all things whatsoever I have commanded you; and behold *I am with you* all days, even to the consummation of the world."[9] "He that believeth not shall be condemned."[10] These words were addressed not only to the Apostles but to their successors[11] until the end of the world, because Christ's Church was never to die: "The gates of hell shall not prevail against it"[12] ... "I am with you all days even to the consummation of the world"[13] ... "You shall be witnesses unto me in Jerusalem and in all Judea and Samaria, and even to the uttermost parts of the earth."[14]

Thus, the Apostles and, through them, their successors throughout the centuries, the Bishops of the Catholic Church, with the Pope, the successor of St. Peter, at the head, are em-

---

6. *Index of Prohibited Books* (English ed., 1930), p. VI.
7. Matthew XVI, 19.
8. Matthew XVIII, 18.
9. Matthew XXVIII, 18-20.
10. Mark XVI, 16.
11. Tanquerey, *Synopsis Theologiae Dogmaticae*, I, nn. 633-657; D'Erbigny, *Theol. de Eccl.*, II, nn. 261-264; Dieckmann, *De Ecclesia Tractatus Historico-Dogmatici*, I, nn. 202-233.
12. Matthew XVI, 18.
13. Matthew XXVIII, 20.
14. *Acts* I, 8.

powered by Christ to use all the means necessary and useful
for the salvation of men's souls. The Church, then, has the
power *to preach and preserve the true faith and morality,*[15] to
administer the Sacraments[16] and *to rule*[17] men so that they
may reach their last end, the salvation of their souls.[18]

Christ entrusted the precious deposit of His revelation
to the Catholic Church, commanding her to guard, to preserve it intact, and to teach it to all men until the end of time.[19]
It is, therefore, within the power of the Church to use whatever means she deems necessary for the spread and defense
of Christ's revelation. Thus, she can send out missionaries all
over the world; she can establish schools for the religious
education of men; she can use the press, the radio or whatever else may foster the propagation of Christianity. On the
other hand, the Catholic Church has the right and duty to
defend the same divine treasure against all attacks in whatever form or from whomsoever they may come. For these attacks on divine revelation obscure the truth in the minds of
the faithful, lead some of them astray in faith or morals, and
render the spread of the gospel of Christ very difficult.[20] St.

---

15.   Matthew XXVIII, 18-20; *I Tim.*, VI, 20; *II Tim.*, II, 16.

16.   Matthew XXVIII, 19; Luke XXII, 19; John XX, 23.

17.   Matthew XXVIII, 18-20; Mark XVI, 16; Luke X, 16.

18.   Tanquerey, *Synopsis Theologiae Dogmaticae*, I, nn. 606-657;
834-835; Cavagnis, *Institutiones Juris Publici Ecclesiastici*, I, nn. 224 ff.;
II, lib. 2 *passim;* Pius IX, Encycl. *Vix dum a nobis*, March 7, 1874, §3
(*Fontes* n. 567); Leo XIII, Encycl. *Immortale Dei*, Nov. 1, 1885, §5
(*Fontes* n. 592); letter *Officio sanctissimo*, Dec. 22, 1887, §§6 and 13
(*Fontes* n. 596); Encycl. *Satis Cognitum*, June 29, 1896, §19 (*Fontes*
n. 630).

19.   Leo XIII, Encycl. *Satis cognitum*, June 29, 1896 (*Fontes*
n. 630).

20.   Bouix, *Tractatus de Curia Romana*, pag. 399, (Prop. IV);
Wernz, *Jus Decretalium*, III, n. 5; Tanquerey, *Syn. Theol. Dogm.*, I, n.
836; D'Erbigny, *Theologica De Ecclesia*, II, n. 388; Dieckmann, *De
Ecclesia*, II, nn. 836-839; nn. 907 and 909; Cacagnis, *Inst. Jur. Publ. Eccl.*,
II, p. 143 f.; Conc. Lateran. V, *Sessio VIII* (Denz. 738); Conc. Vatica-
num, *Sessio III*, Cap. 4 (Denz. 1797-1798); Gregory XVI, Encycl. *Mirari
vos*, Aug. 15, 1832, §8 (*Fontes* n. 485); Pius IX, Encycl. *Qui pluribus*,
Nov. 9, 1846, §6 (*Fontes* n. 504); Encycl. *Nostis et Nobiscum*, Dec. 8,
1849, §§ 6-13 (*Fontes* n. 508); letter *Tuas libenter*, Dec. 21, 1863 (*Fontes*
n. 538); Leo XIII, letter *Officio sanctissimo*, Dec. 22, 1887, §§ 6 and 13

Paul, and the other Apostles, fully aware of this duty, are very zealous in preaching and teaching God's revelation. They warn their followers against every attack made upon these truths.[21] They take strict action against heretics, seducers and false prophets.[22] They remind their disciples of the grave responsibility of guarding and defending the deposit of Faith.[23]

But, the enemies of Christianity are not satisfied with inventing errors; they are not satisfied with propagating their false beliefs by word of mouth: they do more. They preserve all their poisonous attacks upon God's revelation in books and publications of all kinds to insure their reaching a greater number of people through the long years to come.

The written onslaughts, therefore, on the revealed truths entrusted by Christ to the Church, are more harmful than the company or the spoken words of their authors. In order, then, that the Church may properly fulfill her mission and preserve intact the "Deposit of Faith" she must have the power to defend it against all written assaults. She must have the power to take necessary measures against this kind of pestilence; in other words she must have the right to condemn works which undermine faith and morals and to forbid their use to the faithful.[24]

The eternal salvation of men is imperiled not only by direct attacks upon revealed truth. Danger is not found simply

---

(*Fontes* n. 596); Pius X, Encycl. *Pascendi*, Sept. 8, 1907, *Proemium* I, 9-13; II John 9-10; Jude 3.

21.   *Acts*, xx, 28-31; *Gal.* I, 8-9; *Col.* II, 8; II *Tim.* II, 15-17; *Tit.* I, 9-13; II John 9-10; *Jude* 3.

22.   I *Cor.*, V, *passim; Gal.* I, 8-9; I *Tim.* I, 20; *Tit.* I, 10; III, 10-11.

23.   I *Tim.*, VI, 20; *Tit.* I, 9.

24.   Benedict XIV, const. *Sollicita ac provida*, July 9, 1753, *proemium* (*Fontes* n. 420); Gregory XVI, Encycl. *Mirari vos*, Aug. 15, 1832, §§ 15, 16, 22 (*Fontes* n. 485); Pius IX, Encycl. *Qui pluribus*, Nov. 9, 1846, §§ 5, 6, 9 (*Fontes* n. 504); Encycl. *Nostis et Nobiscum*, Dec. 8, 1849, §13 (*Fontes* n. 508); Leo XIII, Const. *Officiorum ac munerum*, Jan. 25, 1897, *proemium* (*Fontes* n. 632); brief *Romani Pontifices*, Sept. 17, 1900 (first document in the Leonine Index up to 1925 edition); Pius X, alloc. *Accogliamo*, Apr. 15, 1907, §§6-8 (*Fontes* n. 678); Encycl. *Pascendi*, Sept. 8, 1907 §§ 43, 44 (3-6) (*Fontes* n. 680); motu proprio *Sacrorum antistitum*, Sept. 1, 1910 (*Fontes* n. 689); Cavagnis, *o. c.*, II, p. 143 f.

in works which are purposely atheistic, materialistic and heretical. No; much poison is found in practically every form
of modern literature. Many philosophical, religious and moral
works coming from non-catholic authors; many historical publications and an unlimited number of works of fiction reek
with spiritual poison deadly to the souls of men.[25] The press
is used by many to attack or ridicule Catholic dogma and worship, to destroy the very foundations of religion and morality
and to promote errors condemned by the Church of Christ.
It is used to propound and defend heresy and schism; to undermine the discipline of the Church; to teach or recommend
superstitions of various kinds; to legalize duelling, suicide, divorce; to treat of, narrate and teach lewdness and obscenity.

In the face of this avalanche of evils and dangers, is the
Church powerless? No, Christ in giving her the mission to
save mankind gave her also the means necessary for it. And
certainly these means must include the power to condemn and
forbid all those books which in one way or another render the
salvation of souls difficult or almost impossible.[26] For, in the
words of Baronius, "the Church would labor in vain in ex-
tirpating heresies, and in promoting good morals unless she
stopped entirely the fountain from which a flood of error and
vices springs."[27]

Christ gave the Church full power to make any laws and
to take any measures necessary for the realization of her end.
This is very clear especially in His statement: "Whatsoever
you shall bind upon earth shall be bound also in heaven; and
whatsoever you shall loose upon earth shall be loosed also in
heaven."[28] This text, especially when taken in the light of
other similar texts,[29] by the very nature of the words used and
their context, shows that the most ample power legislative,
judiciary and executive, was given by Christ to His Church,

---

25. Cf. supra p. 4 ff.
26. Bouix, *o. c.*, p. 399; Cavagnis, *o. c.*, II, lib. II, nn. 12-14.
27. *Eccl. Ann.*, year 447, n. 7.
28. Matthew XVIII, 18.
29. Matthew XVI, 19; X, 40; XXVIII, 18-20; Mark XVI, 16;
Luke X, 16; John XIII, 20; XX, 21.

as far as the realization of her mission requires.[30] She has,
therefore, full right to legislate in the matter of books and
to forbid dangerous ones.[31]

Moreover, since the Church has the same mission as
Christ,[32] she, like the *good shepherd*,[33] feeds her sheep[34] and
gives her life for it.[35] "But the hireling and he that is not
the shepherd, whose own the sheep are not, seeth the wolf coming, and leaveth the sheep, and flieth: and the wolf catcheth,
and scattereth the sheep: and the hireling flieth, because he
is a hireling: and he hath no care for the sheep."[36] The Church
then, has the duty of watching her flock, mankind, of feeding
it with the pure milk and honey of God's doctrines and grace
and of protecting it from poisonous food as well as from wolves
who, though at times disguised in sheep's clothing, scatter and
kill the sheep.[37]

The Church is also, in the words of St. Paul,[38] the *spouse
of Christ*. If she is to keep faith with her bridegroom, Christ,
she must guard from destructive and dangerous elements His
Faith and His faithful for whom He shed all His blood.[39]
And it would be difficult to name anything more harmful to
Christ's doctrines and to His people than evil literature.
Therefore, as the spouse of Christ and the mother of Christians, the Church has the right to condemn and forbid such
writings.

In conclusion, the Catholic Church, in virtue of her end
to save men's souls and according to her divine constitution,

---

30. Knabenbauer, *Commentarius in Quattuor Evangelia Domini
Nostri Jesu Christi: Evangelium secundum Matthaeum*, II, 66; D'Erbigny, *o. c.*, I, n. 127 ff.; Dieckmann, *o. c.*, I, nn. 312-325.

31. D'Erbigny, *o. c.*, I, n. 128, 2, C.

32. John XX, 21.

33. John X, 2.

34. John XXI, 17.

35. John X, 11.

36. John X, 12-13.

37. These thoughts are beautifully expressed by Gregory XVI in
his Encycl. *Mirari vos*, Aug. 15, 1832 (*Fontes* n. 485). Cf. also Augustine, *A Commentary on the New Code of Canon Law*, VI, 429.

38. *Eph.* **V**, 25.

39. Dieckman, *o. c.*, II, n. 909.

has the God-given power and the sacrosanct duty to condemn and forbid whatever literature she deems dangerous.

This certainly applies to those works clearly opposed to faith or morals. It applies also to other works which are rightly suspected by the Church, such as Biblical and other religious writings which have not been subjected to her for approval.[40] For such non-approved works at times contain erroneous or otherwise dangerous statements.

The Apostles felt the responsibility of their mission most keenly and fulfilled their duty most scrupulously. They felt they had been commissioned to save mankind, and were willing to do anything so that they "might save all."[41] For that purpose they used the means placed at their disposal by Christ, namely, the administration of the sacraments, the preaching of the word of God and proper government. Above all, they were most zealous in teaching the gospel of Christ and most jealous in guarding and defending it. They warned their disciples in charge of the flock to keep intact the treasure which had been committed to their care, namely, the Deposit of Faith.[42]

Moreover they were very diligent in protecting the faith and morals of the faithful from all evil influences. Thus, they pleaded with Christians to "contend earnestly for the faith once delivered to the saints,"[43] and to "beware lest any man cheat you by philosophy, and vain deceit; according to the tradition of men, according to the elements of the world, and not according to Christ."[44] The Apostles fobade them to receive or even salute heretics[45] or to have fellowship with wicked men.[46]

Against these disseminators of unbelief, heresy or immorality, they took very drastic measures, chief among these being their exclusion from the communion of Christians, or

---

40. Can. 1399, nn. 1, 5.
41. I *Cor.* IX, 22.
42. I *Tim.* VI, 20; *Tit.* I, 9; *Acts* XX, 28-31; II *Tim.* II, 15-17.
43. Jude 3.
44. *Col.* II, 8, *Gal.* I, 8-9.
45. II John, 10.
46. I *Cor.* V, 11; II *Thess.* III, 6, 14.

excommunication,[47] for "their speech spreadeth like canker"
(II *Tim.* II, 17). No explicit condemnation of any book can be
found in the writings of the Apostles, due perhaps to the
scantiness[48] or absence of anti-Christian literature in those
early days. Yet their uncompromising attitude toward whatever was detrimental to the faith and morals of Christians
is proof enough for the assertion that the Apostles were conscious of possessing full powers to make whatever regulation
they deemed necessary for the proper fulfillment of their mission, namely, the salvation of souls. And since their regulation with regard to dangerous companions and bad teachers
was to condemn them and to forbid their company or fellowship to Christians, such must also have been their mind with
regard to bad literature which is more detrimental to men's
souls than the company or spoken word of evil men.

As a matter of fact, the *Acts of the Apostles*[49] narrate
that at Ephesus the newly converted Christians, after having
confessed their deeds, brought their books together and burned
them before St. Paul and all the others, notwithstanding their
great cost of "fifty thousand pieces of silver". This action
may have been taken by the Ephesian Christians spontane-
ously or it may have been requested by their teachers. It
seems, however, in view of the fact that the burning of the
books was immediately preceded by "confessing and declaring their deeds",[50] that the destruction of those works was
requested or ordered by their teachers or by St. Paul himself.

Be this as it may, this event narrated to us by the *Acts
of the Apostles* certainly shows what the attitude of the Apostolic Church was in those early days with regard to evil books;
it gives us the first example of the constant practice of the
Church, throughout the ages, to take away from the hands
of the faithful those books that might injure their faith or
morals and thus handicap their eternal salvation.[51]

---

47.   I *Cor.* V, *passim;* I *Tim.* I, 20; *Gal.* I, 8, 9; *Tit.* I, 10; III, 10-11.
48.   Cf. *Index of Prohibited Books* (Engl. ed., 1930), p. III.
49.   XIX, 19.
50.   *Acts* XIX, 18.
51.   Cf. Preface to the *Index of Prohibited Books* (Engl. ed., 1930),
pp. III-IV; Suarez, *De Fide Divina,* disp. 20, sect. 2, n. 5; Gretser, *De
Jure et More Prohibendi Expurgandi et Abolendi Libros Haereticos et*

The Catholic Church, conscious of the mission to save men, entrusted to her by Christ Himself, knowing also the vast powers she has received for the fulfillment of her mission, enlightened and encouraged by the example of the Apostles, has constantly throughout the nineteen centuries of her existence, in a more or less solemn manner, made regulations concerning books, forbidding some, permitting others.[52] The Church in such matters is directed and protected by the Holy Ghost and by Him who said, "I will be with you all days even to the consummation of the world".[53] Therefore, it is impossible that she did all this for so long a time without really having the right to do so.[54]

All civilized countries today have some kind of legislation with regard to literature.[55] Now, if a civil society has the right to regulate literature (and, within due bounds, no one can deny this right[56]) is it possible that the Church, the greatest of societies, and because of her spiritual nature, the most liable to be hurt by heretical, immoral or subversive writings, alone lacks that power?

Again, the State has the duty and power to ward off anything that may endanger the material, physical or moral well being of its subjects; to protect them from criminals by its prisons; to preserve them from epidemics by quarantining those who have contagious diseases; to keep them from mistaking poison for other things by laying down rules to druggists to label poisonous substances; to ward off danger on roads by posting signs which will direct the passerby; in fine, the State has the duty and right to protect its subjects from all noxious influences. The Church, an autonomous and perfect society, has subjects for whose spiritual welfare she alone has the privilege and duty to care. She alone is the

Malos, lib. I, Cap. V, (A-B), p. 28; Zaccaria, *Storia Polemica delle Proibizioni dei Libri*, pp. 1-4; Heymans, *De Eccl. Libr... Prohib.*, n. 35.

52. A brief history of book legislation in the Church will be given in the following article.

53. Matt. XXVIII, 20.

54. Suarez, *De Fide Divina*, disp. 20, sect. 2, n. 5; Bouix, *Tract. de Curia Rom.*, p. 400 ff.

55. Cf. supra p. 7 f.

56. Wernz, *Jus Decretalium*, III, n. 99; Bouix, *o. c.*, p. 426 ff.

judge in the matter of faith and morals of the faithful whether they may be endangered by this or that writing; she is an expert in the matter of the teachings of Christ, and, just like an expert in any department, she can detect and point out error and harm where the average person could see nothing wrong. The Catholic Church, therefore, must have the power, after the manner of the State, to label with "poison" or "danger" signals, writings which are harmful. After all, the prohibitions and warnings of the State have to do with the welfare of bodies which will die and decay. But the prohibitions and warnings given by the Church are of a vaster importance, because they deal with the eternal welfare of men's souls. If the former's power is granted, the latter's right must of necessity be acknowledged.

Therefore, the Catholic Church has a God-given duty and the corresponding right to forbid Christians the reading of whatever literature she judges dangerous to their spiritual welfare.

Consequently, when she proscribes a book, or gives a list or Index of books, which are not to be read, or lays down a number of rules which are to guide Christians in finding out whether a book is forbidden or not, she is not only acting within her rights, but she is performing a grave duty imposed upon her by her Founder, Christ.

Solution of Certain Difficulties

It has been said that the condemnation of harmful books is a *violation of liberty*. This common objection has been answered by Card. Merry del Val in the preface to the most recent edition of the *Index of Prohibited Books*.[57]

> No one has taught more firmly than the Catholic Church that man has been created by his Maker as a free agent, ... no one, moreover, has defended with greater vigour than She this "most excellent gift of God" against those who have had the temerity to deny, or in any way to belittle it. Only those afflicted with that moral pestilence known as liberalism can look on the barriers erected by the legitimate author-

---

57. English ed., 1930, pp. VI-VIII.

ity against license in the light of an attack on the free-will of the individual — as though man, inasmuch as he is master of his own actions, were thereby authorised always to do exactly what he wishes.

On this point that great pillar of wisdom Leo XIII has most aptly written: "There can be nothing more pernicious and nonsensical than to affirm and maintain that man, inasmuch as he is by nature created free, must be therefore above the law; for, were this so, it would indeed necessarily follow that liberty must be uncontrolled by reason; and, since this is very far from being true, it behoves man therefore to be subject to the law, because he is by nature free." (Encyclical *Libertas*, 20 June 1888).

Hence it is plain that the competent authority, when hindering by coercive measures the spread of doctrinal errors — always misleading, but lethal in the highest degree when touching on matters of religion — and when attempting to withdraw from circulation writings likely of their very nature to cause a breakdown either of faith, or of moral honesty, in no wise opposes liberty, the exercise of which consists in the choice of those means most apt to obtain eternal salvation. On the contrary, it shields it from the pitfalls into which through human frailty it might easily fall.

There is no more infringement upon liberty when the Church forbids a harmful book than there is when the State forbids swimming in polluted waters, segregates contagious diseases or by means of buoys at sea prevents ships from going to shallow, rocky or otherwise dangerous points, etc. The truth is that there is no law which does not in some way restrict the exercise of liberty. The liberty of a man is necessarily limited by the liberty of his fellow men. A judge, thus writes: "So exercise your own freedom as not to infringe the rights of others or the public peace and safety."[58] When liberty is thus properly understood, the judicious laws of the Church, condemning and forbidding books, appear to be, as they really are, a great blessing and a help to human liberty.[59]

---

58. Ford, *Criminal Obscenity*, p. 111.

59. Gregory XVI, Encycl. *Mirari Vos*, Aug. 15, 1832, §15 (*Fontes* n. 485); Leo XIII, Encycl. *Immortale Dei*, Nov. 1, 1885, §15 (*Fontes* n. 592); Encycl. *Libertas*, June 20, 1888 (*Fontes* n. 600). Cf. also Tan-

Another common accusation against the Church's prohibition of books is that she thus wages a *war against light and truth. The Church*, her enemies say, *fears that Christians may find out the truth and reject Catholicism.* Just a glance at the glorious history of the Church, especially in the field of education should convince anyone that the Church, far from being afraid of the light and truth, has left nothing undone and has stood many battles and made many sacrifices throughout the ages so that the light of truth might shine upon all men. Ignorance is considered by the Church as one of her greatest enemies. No, it is not by reason of her fear of light that the Church forbids erroneous and dangerous books, but rather by reason of her zeal for truth. For

> Impious and unclean literature is written sometimes with great charm of style; frequently it deals with subjects that excite lascivious passions, or flatter spiritual pride; always too, with specious arguments and quibbling of every kind, it aims at leaving a lasting impression in the heart and mind of the incautious reader. It is, therefore, only natural that the Church, like a provident mother, should with timely prohibitions warn the faithful lest they press their lips to deceitful cups of poison. Not, forsooth, from any fear of the light of truth does the Church forbid certain books to be read, but on account rather of the zeal of God animating Her, which does not tolerate the loss of a single soul... taught, too, by age-long experience that man, fallen from an original state of grace, is strongly prone to evil and is consequently in dire need of protection and defense.[60]

The Catholic Church has with her the truths of God which, through the ever living presence of Christ within her[61] and the continuous assistance of the Holy Ghost[62] remain always intact. When she, therefore, brands a book as pernicious and forbids it, she is simply showing the light to humanity

---

querey, *o. c.*, I, n. 931 ff.; Heymans, *o. c.*, nn. 79-85; Wernz, *o. c.*, n. 112; Bouix, *o. c.*, p. 435 ff.; Moureau, *La Nouvelle Legislation de l'Index*, p. 5; Lugo, *De Virtute Fidei*, disp. 21, sect. 2, n. 26; Scott, *Religion and Common Sense*, pp. 289, 298, 301, 304.

60. *Index of Prohibited Books* (English ed., 1930), pp. VIII-IX.
61. Matt. XXVIII, 20.
62. John XIV, 16; XVI, 13.

so that they may abandon the dangerous darkness of evil literature, follow the beacon light of the Church, and thus be saved.

But, the enemies of the Church argue, by forbidding Christians to read whatever is contrary to the Catholic faith, *the Catholic Church does not give them a chance to see both sides of any religious or moral question.* They know the *Pro*, but not the *Con*.

Even this objection must fall.[63] For when the Church has proven conclusively her divine institution from the life and words of Christ; when she has shown through irrefutable arguments her infallible authority; then any one who may wish to learn the truth in religious and moral matters, is obliged to go to this Church. To turn to the works contrary to the Church's teachings is, to say the least, a waste of time. But unfortunately, because man, by reason of original sin, is strongly prone to evil, and because irreligious and immoral writers hide their poison in such a way that it cannot be easily detected by the average reader, to turn to such works is decidedly dangerous and usually very harmful.

As a matter of fact, when a Catholic is well founded in his religion and needs to see the opposite side so that he may answer its objections, permission is easily obtained from the Church to read such works. Moreover, "Catholic books on any important subject, give both sides of the question with admirable fairness... What a fool any man is who puts his mind in the power of ruthless brigands... who hate the faith and Christian morality so intensely that they stop at nothing if only they can thrust a poisoned dagger home."[64]

Again, in the matter of food and medicines, men do not taste and eat everything indifferently so that they may find for themselves what is good and what is harmful to their health. What a tragic end one would suffer, if, upon being sick, he entered a drug store, and tasted every medicine he found there, until he should discover the one which he needed. Men do not act that way. They take suggestions from others who know what is good or bad; they take medicines scrupul-

---

63. Heymans, n. 216.
64. Lord, *I Can Read Anything*, p. 29.

ously according to the prescriptions of doctors. In like manner, they should take the dictates of the Church when she points out for them what is good and forbids them what is evil.

Finally, if one wishes to learn how to keep in good health he does not go and live in the midst of people with contagious diseases. Similarly, if he wishes to know the truth and be good, he cannot expect to learn this from books infected with unbelief or immorality.

A similar answer must be given to another objection that the Church, by her drastic measures against a certain class of writings has done much *harm* to *literature and science*. The Church has always fostered true literature and true science. However, she has forbidden and tried to destroy any work which, even though regarded by the world as of great literary or scientific value, she considers harmful to the faithful because of its hostility to religion and morality. The literary or scientific value of such a work is often only apparent; but, even if it were genuine, that would not be sufficient to justify the circulation of a book hostile to religion and morality.[65]

There are many, even within the fold, who find objections to the *Index of Prohibited Books* on the grounds that by it an evil work is advertised, its sale increased, its harm multiplied, for, they say, a desire is thus aroused in many to read that which is forbidden. Therefore, according to them, no book should be condemned by name and there should be no *Index of Prohibited Books* in the Church.

Let us grant for the sake of clearing up this objection, though we do not admit as true,[65a] that by means of the Index

---

65. *Index of Prohibited Books* (Engl. ed., 1930), p. IX; Heymans, *De Eccl. Libr... Prohibit.*, p. 87 ff. No conflict can exist between true religion and true science as long as both keep within their bounds. Cf. Leo XIII, const. *Providentissimus Deus*, 18 Nov., 1893, §9 (*Fontes* n. 621); Tanquerey, *Syn. Theol. Dogmat.*, II, n. 329; Windle, *The Church and Science, passim*; and any apologetic treatise.

65a. St. Alphonsus, *De Prohib. Libr.*, Cap. V. n. 9 f.; Arndt, *De Libr. Prohib.*, n. 164; Cavagnis, *Institutiones Juris Publici Ecclesiastici*, II, p. 145; Cocchi, *Commentarium in Cod. J. C.*, VI, n. 57, B; Heymans, *De Eccl. Libr. Prohib.* nn. 77-78; Betten, *The Roman Index*, p. 27 f.

"an evil work is advertised, its sale increased, its harm multiplied." The Index, even then, would be the lesser evil which the Church would have to choose to procure the protection of her faithful children. The Index might advertise a bad book to a mind anxious to find some alluring evil topic, but, on the other hand, the Church would offset this evil by turning away numberless souls from the disaster that such a book would cause if attention were not called to it by its notorious position among the proscribed publications.

The Church has a grave duty to warn her children against all that might taint their faith and morals and thus endanger their eternal salvation.[65b] Therefore, she must be true to her trust. She has no choice. She must be alert as to the kind of books that are current among the people and eliminate those which are harmful. She, the guardian of souls, applies to herself the words of the Lord to Ezechiel:[65c]

> And if the watchman see the sword coming and sound not the trumpet: and the people look not to themselves, and the sword come and cut off a soul from among them: he indeed is taken away in his iniquity, but I will require his blood at the hand of the watchman. So thou, O son of man, I have made thee a watchman to the house of Israel: therefore, thou shalt hear the word from my mouth and shalt tell it them from me.

The devout children of the Church "will hearken with a ready ear to the voice of the Good Shepherd, Jesus, and to His Vicar on earth, the Pope..." "Apart from cases of dire necessity, in which the Holy See is accustomed to grant a dispensation, they will always scrupulously observe the rules of the Index, abstaining from reading, or even from having in their possession, books in any wise condemned by the Church."[65d] Therefore, even though some people misuse the prohibitory decrees of the Church to their own perdition, the true faithful children of the Church abide by them and keep their souls free from the poison contained in the books prohibited. Their obedience and their shunning of the dangers pointed out by the Church are sufficient justification for the individual prohibition of books and for the Index. One good

---

65b. Cf. supra p. 11 ff.

65c. XXXIII, 6-7.

65d. Preface to the *Index of Prohibited Books* (English ed., 1930), p. XII.

Catholic has the right to secure guidance in preserving his faith and morals, even if many others in bad faith discover evil books from the same source of guidance. If an incendiary steal a lighted candle from an altar to commit arson, this does not militate against the use of candles.

We have granted, but not admitted, that by means of the Index "an evil work is advertised, its sale increased, its harm multiplied". Indeed it would be hard, if not impossible, to verify that. Can any one truthfully say that any book has ever gained in market value by its position on the Index? Furthermore, let us not forget that the Church takes extreme measures only when absolute necessity requires. She acts not on the spur of the moment but after long and careful thought based on the law of God and the human wisdom which she has acquired through long experience.

In conclusion God is to be thanked for having given men an all-wise Church to lead them through the dangerous pathways of earth and take them safely to Heaven.

ART. II

BRIEF HISTORICAL REVIEW OF THE ECCLESIASTICAL PROHIBITION OF BOOKS[66]

Sect. 1. *From the Apostles to Sixtus IV*

I — Ante-Nicean Legislation.

While it is certain that the practice of forbidding books in the Church is as old as herself, yet it is not known at what Council or with what Pope formal legislation on this matter began.[67] The first indication of the Church's attitude towards ungodly books, as it has already been pointed out, is found in the burning of books at Ephesus before the Apostle Paul.[68]

66.　Hilgers, *Der Index der verbotenen Bücher; The Roman Index and Its Latest Historian;* "Censorship of Books", *Catholic Encyclopedia,* III, 519; Boulx, *Tract. de Curia Rom.,* p. 394 ff.; Wernz, *Jus Decretal.,* III, n. 100; Heymans, *De Eccl. Libr... Prohibit.,* n. 35 ff.; Gretser, *De Jure et More,* lib. I, cap. V.

67.　St. Alphonsus, *De Prohib. Libr.,* Cap. II, n. 2.

68.　*Acts* XIX, 19. Cf. supra p. 18.

In the first Christian centuries many books were written which were attributed to this or that inspired writer. These at times were not only spurious but also heretical. Therefore, lists were drawn up to point out to the faithful which books were inspired and which were apocryphal. The earliest list of this kind which is known to us is the *Muratorian Canon,* a work of the second half of the second century.[69] This valuable document gives us the canon of the New Testament and after naming some apocryphal books, which are not to be read in public, it continues: "...and there are several others which cannot be received by the Catholic Church, for it is not suitable for gall to be mingled with honey."[70] This canon seems to have been used later by Gelasius.[71] Towards the end of the second century[72] the *Acta Pauli* was condemned, a book falsely attributed to St. Paul. Its author, a priest of Asia, was condemned and deposed for having written this book in the name of the Apostle, even though it was not heretical. What prompted this action of the Church was the desire to allow none but inspired books to be accepted by the faithful as Scripture. This is recorded by Tertullian[73] and by St. Jerome.[74] No explicit mention is made of the proscription of the book itself. But it seems impossible that a book, which alone was the cause of a priest's deposition (a most severe punishment) should have been allowed to circulate freely among the faithful as the work of St. Paul. Besides, St. Jerome puts it among the apocryphal writings and among the old writers "apocryphal" meant forbidden.[75]

---

69. Funk, *Manual of Church History,* I, 108; Gigot, *General Introduction to the Study of the Scriptures,* p. 99.

70. *Ante-Nicene Fathers* (Am. ed.), V, 603.

71. Cf. *infra* p. 31

72. Vouaux, *Les Actes de Paul et Ses Lettres Apocryphes,* p. 2; G. J. Reid, "Apocrypha" *Cath. Encycl.,* I, 612; T. J. Shahan, "Acta Pauli", *Catholic University Bulletin,* X (1904), 486. Zaccaria, *Storia Polemica,* pp. 4-5, has good arguments showing that it dates back to about the year 66.

73. *De Bapt.* cap. 15-*C S E L,* XX, 215.

74. *De Viris Ill.,* cap. 7 - *M P L,* XXIII, 841.

75. Zaccaria, *Storia Polemica delle Proibizioni dei Libri,* lib. I, epoca 1ª n. 4. Cf. also St. Jerome, ep. 107. *Ad Loetam, C S E L,* LV, p. 303.

In the first book, Chapter VII, of the *Apostolic Constitutions* Christians are strictly forbidden to read Gentile books on the authority of the Apostles.[76]

The early Fathers and ecclesiastical writers give us in unmistakable terms the attitude of the early Church on bad books. A few examples will suffice for our purpose. St. Cyprian, in writing about the year 252 to Pope Cornelius of a book which he forbade, says: *"Danda opera est ut talia cum a quibusdam scribuntur per nos respuantur."*[77] Origen, who died in 254, writes in the ninth Homily on *Numbers:* "If the Princes of the Churches were to judge today those who have brought on themselves the vengeance of God for teaching things opposed to the doctrines of the Churches, would they not decide that whatever these have spoken, taught, or written should perish with their ashes?"[78]

II.   From the Council of Nicaea to Leo the Great.

The first formal condemnation of a book of which record has come down to us[79] was issued by the Council of Nicaea in 325. One of the most vital doctrines revealed by Christ, His divinity, was being attacked and, like an epidemic, this pernicious error was rapidly making its way among the people. Arius, its chief exponent, wrote a book, *Thalia,* which contained all his errors. The Church, therefore, at the First Oecumenical Council at Nicaea, solemnly condemned Arius, his doctrines, and his book.[80] The decision of the Fathers of the Council was followed by a decree of the Emperor Constantine which ordered the burning of all the copies of Arius' book under the pain of death for anyone refusing to throw the book

---

76.   This and the other first five books of the Constitutions, a collection of c. 400, date back to the time of the *Didascalia* from which they were taken, i. e., the second half of the third century. Cf. Funk, *Manual of Church History*, I, 113, 222; Gretser, *o. c.*, lib. I, cap. V, C, p. 28; Lugo, *De Virtute Fidei*, disp. 21, sect. 2, n. 24.

77.   Ep. 45 Cypriani Ad Cornelium — *C S E L*, III, 2.

78.   *MPG*, XII, 624.

79.   Wernz, *Jus Decretal.*, III, n. 100.

80.   Socrates, *Hist. Eccl.*, Lib. I, cap. 9; Hefele, *History of the Christian Councils*, p. 295; Baronius, *Ann. Eccl.*, year 325.

to the flames.[81] This is the first time a civil ruler aids the enforcement of an ecclesiastical prohibition of a book, an example imitated by many Catholic rulers of succeeding ages, though not to the same extent.

Towards the end of the fourth century, in the Fourth Council of Carthage, a canon was drawn up which reads thus: *"Episcopus libros gentilium non legat, haereticorum autem pro necessitate aut tempore."*[82] The common interpretation of this canon is that bishops were forbidden to read habitually books of pagans to the exclusion of sacred literature, or to read the most scandalous of their works. But when their pastoral office required it, they could read heretical works, e.g., to refute them. These regulations reflect the mind and practice of the Church of those times. It shows also that the positive prohibition of books does *not* bind equally the flock and the shepherds, a principle which has been followed throughout the centuries except in some rare instances when it was thought necessary to extend the prohibition to bishops, e.g., at the Second Nicene Council in 787,[83] and in Leo X's Constitution *Exsurge Domine* of June 10, 1520.[84]

It was about this time that St. Augustine, commenting on Psalm 61,[85] wrote of a convert: *"Perierat iste. Nunc quaesitus, inventus, adductus est. Portat secum codices incendendos per quos fuerat incendendus, ut illis in ignem missis, ipse in refrigerium transeat."*[86]

In the year 400, Theophilus, the bishop of Alexandria, in a council with the other bishops of Egypt, condemned the books of Origen because of the many errors they contained. The fact that these works were very valuable did not stop the bishops from proscribing them because "the books which the Church has received are more than sufficient. Therefore, the reading (of books) which would be more harmful to the unwise than useful to the wise should be rejected (forbid-

---

81. Socrates, *l. c.*
82. C. 1, D. XXXVII.
83. Can. 9 — Mansi, XIII, 429.
84. §5 (*Fontes* n. 76).
85. *MPL*, XXXVI, 747.
86. Cf. also Suarez, *De Fid.*, disp. 20, sect. 2, n. 5.

den)".[87] This shows that the Church was willing to make any sacrifice for the sake of the truths of Christ. It proves also that a book had to be received by the Church before its reading could be regarded as lawful. This action of the Egyptian bishops was at once made known by them to the Roman Pontiff, St. Anastasius, who called a council in Rome and condemned the books of Origen in the same year.[88] Before long the same was done all throughout the East and the West.[89]

The next Pope, Innocent I, in 405 sent to Exuperius, Bishop of Toulouse, the Canon of the Scriptures. In his letter, he enumerates some of the apocryphal writings which *"non solum repudianda, verum etiam noveris esse damnanda."*[90] Hilgers states that this is the first attempt at a catalogue of forbidden books.[91] The same Pontiff, in 417, condemned a book of Pelagius which the African bishops had sent to him.[92] This book contained the erroneous teachings of Pelagianism which denied the necessity of grace.

A few years later, in 431, the Third General Council met at Ephesus to condemn Nestorianism which taught that in Christ there are two persons and that Mary is the mother of the man Christ and not of the Son of God. Nestorius was the most prominent defender of this heresy so that both he and his works were condemned by the Council,[93] and, at the suggestion of the Fathers of the Council, the emperors enforced their condemnation by issuing a law against all the books of Nestorius.[94] The same Council proscribed the *Asceticon*, the book of a sect called Messalians.[95]

---

87. Sulpicius Severus, *Dialogus,* I, 6, *C S E L,* I, 157; Gretser, *o. c.,* I, cap. XI, p. 41.

88. *Ep. ad Simplicianum* — Mansi, III, 945.

89. Arndt, *De Libris Prohibitis Commentarii,* p. 4; Gretser, *l. c.*

90. VII — Mansi, III, 1040.

91. Hilgers, *Der Index,* p. 405.

92. *Ep. ad Aurelium, Alypium, Augustinum, Evodium, Possidium, Episcopos* — Mansi, III, 1079.

93. *Sacrae Synodi ad religiosissimos imperatores de Nestorii depositione relatio* — Mansi, IV, 1239.

94. *Cod. Theod.* XVI, 5, 66 (435, Aug. 3); *C.* 1, 1, 3. 3; *N.* 42, 1, 1, 2.

95. *Definitio Sanctae et Oecumenicae Synodi Ephesinae contra impios Messalianistas* — Mansi, IV, 1477.

While the Nestorian heresy was being checked in the East, at Rome Manichaeism was secretly infecting the souls of many. The Supreme Pontiff, St. Leo the Great, soon became aware of this and at once struck at the root of this new pestilence by condemning and burning the books of the sect in 443.[96] In 447 the same Pope through a letter to Turibius, Bishop of Asturias, ordered the prohibition of the books of the Priscillianists in Spain, and of the Apocryphal Scriptures, which were to be burned.[97] He writes among other things: *"Quomodo enim decipere simplices possent, nisi venenata pocula quodam melle perlinirent ne usquequaque sentirentur insuavia quae forent futura mortifera?"* Behold here the Supreme Shepherd anxious lest his flock, tempted to eat whatever tastes sweet, might perchance swallow poison!

III.   From the Decree of Gelasius to the II Council of Nicaea.

Many heretical books had been condemned by Popes, Bishops, and Councils, but because a complete list of them did not exist, the prohibition of a good number of them was unknown to the faithful. The ever vigilant Bishop of Rome felt this need and issued a catalogue of books, made up principally of three sections; the first containing the Canon of the Scriptures; the second, good and useful books; and the third apocryphal and heretical works which were all condemned and forbidden even for private reading. It is called the *Decretum Gelasii* because it was promulgated by Gelasius in 496 at a Roman Synod.[98]

---

96.   Prosper of Aquitane, *Chronicum*, a. 443.

97.   Ep. XV *ad Turribium Asturicensem Episcopum*, Capp. XV, XVI — Mansi, V, 1198 ff.

98.   C. 3 D. XV; Arndt, *o. c.*, p. 7; Zaccaria, *Storia Polemica*, p. 33 ff.; St. Alphonsus, *De Prohib. Libr.*, Cap. III, n. 5. In the last two references there is mentioned and discussed the opposite opinion that this decree was issued by St. Damasus in 379. Cf. also Zaccaria, *o. c.*, p. 13, ff.; Ernst Von Dobschütz, *Das Decretum gelasianum De libris recipiendis et non recipiendis in kritischem Text herausgegeben und undersucht* (Leipzig, 1912); Zahn, *Geschichte des Neutestam. Kanons*, 1890, II, 1, 259 f.; Augustine, *A Commentary*, VI, p. 430; Bouix, *Tract. de Curia Rom.*, p. 405; Denzinger, *Enchiridion Symbolorum*, nn. 83 and 162.

The successor of Gelasius, Pope Hormisdas, republished the decree of Gelasius with some additions.[99]

Pope Vigilius in 548 anathematized, because of their many errors and impious statements, the celebrated "Three Chapters", that is, Theodore of Mopsuestia with his works, the writings of Theodoret of Cyrus against Cyril of Alexandria and the Council of Ephesus, and the Epistle of Ibas.[100] In 553 the Fifth General Council at Constantinople repeated the same condemnation with almost identical words.[101]

Memorable is the condemnation which some bishops, gathered in a council at Toledo in 589, issued against a book which they themselves had written before their return from Arianism.[102]

In a letter to Bishop Anastasius of Antioch in 599, St. Gregory the Great makes a statement which shows that, in his time at least, if an author was condemned, his works also were to be regarded as condemned. He writes that a certain book treating of the Council of Ephesus is to be rejected because

> Quaedam in se oblata capitula, adserit adprobata quae sunt Caelestii atque Pelagii praedicamenta. Et quum Caelestius atque Pelagius in ea Synodo sint damnati, quomodo poterant illa capitula recipi quorum damnabantur auctores?[103]

But even though this rule existed and was known to the faithful, the Church ordinarily, in condemning heretics, expressly condemned their writings as well. Thus, Martin I, forbade the writings of the Monothelites in 649 at the Lateran Council[104] and at the Sixth General Council, held at Constantinople in 680, the same heretical works were burned.[105] The Council *in Trullo* in 692 ordered the burning of some fictitious *Acts of Martyrs*, and anathematized anyone who would admit

---

99. Zaccaria, *o. c.*, p. 54; Wernz, *Jus Decretal.*, n. 100; Denzinger, *o. c.*, n. 162 (nota).

100. *Constitutum Vigilii Papae de Tribus Capitulis*—Mansi, IX, 61.

101. Mansi, IX, 375.

102. *Fidei Confessio Episcoporum* etc. — Mansi, IX, 986 (C. 16).

103. Mansi, X, 139.

104. Can. XVIII — Mansi, X, 1158.

105. *Actio* XIII (end) — Mansi, XI, 582.

what they contained.[106] In 745 Pope Zacharias, in a Roman Council, condemned the heretics and impostors Adalbertus and Clement who were spreading superstitious errors throughtout the kingdom of the Franks.[107] Their books were condemned, but, contrary to the ancient custom, the Pope decided not to burn them but to reserve them in the secret archives *"ad reprobationem et ad perpetuam confusionem."* One of these books was a life which Adalbertus had written of himself entitled: *In nomine D. Jesu Christi incipit vita Sancti et Beati Dei famuli et praeclari atque per totum speciose ex electione Dei nati Sancti Adalberti Episcopi.*[108] Who will not thank the Church for such a condemnation?

The eighth century was a period of strife and riots occasioned by attacks on holy images on the part of the emperors and even of some ecclesiastics. The Second Nicene Council in 787 defined the Catholic Doctrine which forbids adoration and allows veneration of images. Furthermore, it commanded that all lampoons, books, and other works written against this doctrine should be given to the Bishop of Constantinople, to be kept in his palace with books of other heretics. If a bishop, a priest, or a deacon, is found to hide such works, he is to be deposed; if a monk or a layman, he is to be excomunicated.[109] This same Council ordered a book called *Itinera Apostolorum*,[110] to be burned. In the prohibition against Iconoclast literature something new and strange is noted, namely, its application under pain of deposition to bishops. This seems to be the first time such an extraordinary measure was taken, for it was always understood, if not

---

106. Can. LXIII — Mansi, XI, 971.

107. *Epistola Gemuli Diaconi E. R. ad Bonifacium Archiepiscopum* — Mansi, XII, 384.

108. Arndt, *De Libris Prohibitis*, p. 13.

107. Omnia puerilia, ludibria, insanasque debacchationes atque conscripta quae falso contra venerabiles imagines facta sunt dari oportet in episcopio Constantinopoleos, ut recondantur cum coeterorum haereticorum libris. Si vero quis inventus fuerit haec occultare, siquidem episcopus aut presbyter vel diaconus fuerit, deponatur; si vero monachus aut laicus anathematizetur.

Can. 9. — Mansi, XIII, 429.

110. *Actio* V — Mansi, XIII, 167-175.

among the people, at least among the hierarchy,[111] that bishops could read forbidden books in order to refute them. This extraordinary measure can be attributed to the fact that even some bishops were suspected of the errors condemned.[112]

IV. Nicholas I — Sixtus IV

Nicholas I, one of the holiest, most learned, and firmest Pontiffs, was reigning in the See of Peter, when the Bulgarians were converted to the Catholic faith in the year 864, or the beginning of the year 865. Their king Bogoris, among other things asked the Pope what to do with the books which the Bulgarians had taken from the Saracens. The Pontiff answered, ordering their destruction, *"corrumpunt enim, sicut scriptum est, mores bonos, colloquia mala."*[113]

In 865 Nicholas also received from Emperor Michael III, a very ardent defender of the Schism of Photius, a letter full of abuse and insults to the Holy See. This staunch custodian of the Faith felt the obligation of defending the authority of the See of Peter, and answered the emperor with prudence and yet with firmness, condemning that letter and commanding that it be burned publicly.[114] In reading this important document one cannot help but notice that, like Christ, His Vicar speaks with authority even to the mighty emperors.

A book of Photius attacking Pope Nicholas and the Holy See was burned by his successor at a synod in Rome,[115] and the Eighth General Council at Constantinople in 869 burned the same book and the other writings of Photius.[116]

From now to the time of Innocent VIII many books were condemned by the Church because in some way or other they endangered the faith and morals of Christians. Thus history records the proscription by Councils and Popes of Scotus

---

111.   C. 1, D. XXXVII.
112.   Arndt, *o. c.*, p. 41.
113.   Resp. CIII — Mansi, XV, 432.
114.   Mansi, XV, 186 ff.
115.   *Vita Epistolae et Decreta Hadriani Papae II* — Mansi, XV, 812.
116.   *Actio VII* — Mansi, XVI, 125; *Actio VIII* — Mansi, XVI, 135 ff.

Erigena's works in 855 and 1050;[117] of Abelard and Arnold of Brescia in 1141;[118] of Gilbert de la Porrée in 1149;[119] of the Abbot Joachim in 1215;[120] of translations of Aristotle's philosophy in 1209 and 1231,[121] of the Talmudic books, of books written by William of Holy Love in 1256,[122] Pierre Jean Olivi in 1325,[123] Marsilius of Padua and John of Jandun in 1327,[124] and Raymond Lull in 1376.[125] The books of Wyclif and Hus were proscribed by several local councils, individual bishops, and finally by the Council of Constance in 1415, and by Pope Martin V in 1418.[126] To complete the list of the principal writings, condemned before Innocent VIII, mention must be made of a book of Aeneas Sylvius de Piccolomini which the author himself, then Pope Pius II, condemned in the bull *In minoribus agentes* which he sent to the University of Cologne on April 26, 1463[127] and one of Pedro Martinez de Osma, professor of Salamanca, proscribed by the archbishop of Toledo by order of Sixtus IV in 1479.[128]

V. Some New Developments in the period between the twelfth and fifteenth centuries

At this point it is well to point out a few important developments, which Church legislation on books underwent in the period between the twelfth and the fifteenth centuries. The condemnation of Gilbert de la Porrée's Commentary

---

117. *Concilium Valentinum III*, Cann. 5-6 — Mansi, XV, 5-6; *Conc. Vercellense* — Mansi, XIX, 773.

118. *Ep. Innocentii Papae II* — Mansi, XXI, 565.

119. *Ep. Gaufredi Monachi ad Episcopum Albunensem* — Mansi, XXI, 732.

120. *Conc. Lateranense IV*, Cap. II — Mansi, XXII, 981 ff.

121. *Conc. Parisiense*, Cap. II — Mansi, 804; Raynaldi, *Ann. Eccl.*, a. 1231, n. 48.

122. Zaccaria, *Storia Polemica*, p. 84. Against the book of William of Holy Love St. Thomas Aquinas wrote a treatise. Cf. D. J. Kennedy "St. Thomas Aquinas", *Cath. Encycl.*, XIV, 665.

123. Zaccaria, *o. c.*, p. 86.

124. *Fontes* n. 38.

125. Eymericus, *Directorium Inquisitorium*, p. 255.

126. *Fontes* n. 43, §4.

127. *B R T*, V. 173.

128. Mansi, XXXII, 378.

on Boethius in 1148, is probably the first case on record in which a book was to be considered condemned until it would be corrected by the Church at Rome.[129] This created a precedent followed afterwards in many prohibitory decrees and expressed with the clause *donec corrigatur.*

It is also at this time that one begins to read of limitations in the use of the Bible, which the Church, as a wise mother, imposed on Christians whenever it became necessary, in much the same way that a doctor forbids food to his patients whenever food is harmful to them.[130] So, Innocent III by a decretal of 1199 forbade the people of Metz to read the French translations of the Bible, because they were made by suspected translators and were productive of abuses among the readers.[131] The Albigensian heresy made it imperative for a Council at Toulouse in 1229 to forbid laymen the reading of the Bible, except the Psalter, the Breviary, and the Office of Our Lady.[132] The reason was that heretics misused the Scriptures for their own ends and to the perdition of themselves and others. To quote from Merry del Val's preface to the *Index of Prohibited Books:*[133]

> It was only in consequence of heretical abuses, introduced
> particularly by the Waldenses, the Albigenses, the followers
> of Wyclif, and by Protestants broadly speaking (who with

---

129. *"Nisi prius eum Romana Ecclesia correxiset"* — Mansi, XXI, 732. Cf. also Reusch, *Der Index de Verbotenen Bücher*, I, 17.

130. Zaccaria, *o. c.,* p. 343.

131. Innocent III, *Regestorum sive Epistolarum*, Lib. II, Ep. 141, 142 — *M P L*, CCXIV, 595 ff.; Raynaldi, *Ann. Eccl.*, year 1199, nn. 26-27. Cf. also Pennacchi, *In Const. Apost. Offic. ac muner.,* p. 75, note a.

132. Mansi, XXIII, 197 (c. 14).

133. Engl. ed., 1930, p.X. These and similar restrictions on the use of the Bible, necessary for the protection of its integrity and for the good of the people, will be found in every succeeding century, and today we have them in the Code of Canon Law, canons 1385, 1, 2; 1391; 1399, n. 1, n. 5; 1400. The Church does not forbid the reading of the Bible as such, rather she wishes her children to read the editions of the Bible produced under her supervision, which, therefore, are free from poison. Cf. Lenhart, *The "Open Bible" in Pre-Reformation Times;* Nicholas Le Maire, *Le Sanctuaire fermé aux profanes ou la Bible defendue au vulgaire;* Malou, J. B., *La lecture de la Sainte Bible en langue vulgaire jugée d'aprés l'Ecriture, la tradition et la saine raison;* Pope, *The Catholic Church and the Bible.*

sacrilegious mutilations of Scripture and arbitrary interpretations vainly sought to justify themselves in the eyes of the
people; twisting the text of the Bible to support erroneous
doctrines condemned by the whole history of the Church) that
the Pontiffs and the Councils were obliged on more than one
occasion to control and sometimes even forbid the use of the
Bible in the vernacular.

From the middle of the thirteenth century, mention is
made now and then of a group of Cardinals or a committee
of theologians, or of both Cardinals and theologians, who are
commissioned to examine suspected books. This was done, e.g.,
in the cases of William of Holy Love in 1252, of Pierre Jean
Olivi in 1325, of Marsilius of Padua in 1327. In this procedure are found the first vestiges of the two congregations
of the Holy Office and of the Index which were formally
established in the sixteenth century.

A new period of censorship of books was beginning. The
duty and right of the Catholic Church to defend the truths
of Christ and to preserve the faithful from doctrinal and
moral errors implies not alone the power to forbid evil books,
but also the right to examine books before they are given out
to the public. This preventive censorship obviates possible
financial and even moral loss to many an author, which
usually follows the condemnation of an already published
work, and it averts the spiritual danger and ruin of many
who might not be affected by a subsequent prohibition.[134] In
the early days of Christianity individual approbation of each
book was not required. The orthodoxy of the author was generally taken as a guarantee for the orthodoxy of his work.
Accordingly the rule was that if a book carried the name of
the author and the author was orthodox, the book was allowed,
otherwise it was forbidden.[135] Nevertheless, history records,
even during the early ages of Christianity, many cases in
which writers sent their works to the Supreme Pontiff for
approval, e.g., St. Augustine[136] Caesar of Arles,[137] Honora-

---

134. Pederzini, *Ragionamento*, p. 17 f.
135. C. 3, D. XV; C. 1, D. XXXV.
136. St Augustine, *Contra duas epistolas Pelagianorum*, lib. I,
Cap. I, n. 3 — *M P L*, XLIV, 551.
137. Gennadius, *De Script. Eccl.*, 86 — *M P L*, LVIII, 1111.

tus,[138] Gennadius of Marseilles,[139] Possessor,[140] Eulogius,[141] and others.[142] Gradually the custom arose of sending every book on dogmatic subjects to the Pope for approbation, as is clear from the words of Nicholas I to Charles the Bald: *"Relatum est Apostolatui nostro, quod opus Beati Dionysii Areopagitae...quidam vir Joannes, genere Scotus, nuper in latinum transtulerit quod juxta morem nobis mitti et nostro debuit judicio adprobari."*[143]

In the fifteenth century with the invention of printing, books, both good and bad, were multiplied by the hundreds. Therefore new methods were devised to cope with the new necessities, as we shall see in the following chapter.

Sect. II.   *From Innocent VIII to The Index of the Council of Trent*

I.   Innocent VIII — Clement VII

The new art of printing placed in the hands of men a powerful instrument for good, because, through it, the doctrines of faith, the moral precepts and the sciences could be spread with unprecedented facility and rapidity. However, history reveals that, shortly after its discovery, some used the press as a means for disseminating far and wide what is most harmful to the truths of religion and to good morals.

As long as the press limited itself to the production of good, wholesome and orthodox works, the Church did not interfere with it in any way, rather she encouraged it and thanked God for this new means of spreading His message. When abuses first began to creep in, the Church did not become alarmed, knowing that some abuse is unavoidable. However, when the evil grew worse, she was obliged to enact strict laws to stop the harm caused by bad publications.

---

138.   Gennadius, *Op. cit.*, 99 — *M P L*, LVIII, 1119.
139.   Gennadius, *Op. cit.* 100 — *M P L*, LVIII, 1120.
140.   *B R T*, App. I, 521.
141.   *Ep. 35 Gregorii ad Eulogium Patriarcham* — Mansi, X, 230.
142.   St. Alphonsus, *De Prohib. Libr.*, Cap. II, n. 8 ff.
143.   *M P L*, CXIX, 1119. Cf. also Baronius, *Ann. Eccl.*, year 496, and Raynaud, *Erotemata de malis ac bonis libris*, p. 275; Arndt, *De Libris Prohib.*, p. 47.

The first printed work against which action was taken
by the Church authorities is an anonymous pamphlet entitled: *Disputatio seu Dialogus inter clericum et militem super
potestate ecclesiastica.* It was printed in Cologne and its author attacked the superiority of the ecclesiastical authorities
over the civil authorities, and the immunities of the clergy.
The Church authorities of Cologne appealed to the magistrate
of the city of Cologne against this work, already in its fourth
edition and on September 21, 1478 they were granted powers
to prosecute the printers of the *Disputatio seu Dialogus.*[144] To
stop the circulation of this revolutionary work the rector and
deans of the University of Cologne appealed to the Pope. Sixtus IV granted them, by a brief of March 17, 1479,[145] the fullest
powers to punish by censures all printers, buyers and readers
of heretical books. This is the first papal decree of prohibition
directed against *printed* books.[146] Beginning with 1474 works
were printed at Cologne with the approbation of that University. Thus, by examining writings previous to their publication, the publication of at least some objectionable works
was avoided.

In 1482 the Bishop of Würzburg prohibited the printing
and circulation of the proclamation of a reopening of the
council of Basle by the ill-famed Archbishop of Granea, Andrea Zuccalmaglio.[147] On that occasion he also enacted a law
of censorship for his diocese. Soon after, namely May 24,

---

144. Otto Zaretzky, *Der erste Koelner Zensurprozess* (Cologne,
1906). Zaretzky has exploded the formerly current opinion that the
printing of Rolewink's *Fasciculus temporum* occasioned the repressive
measures taken by the Church against printed books because in it Rolewink censures the scandalous lives of popes and other ecclesiastics and
laments the decline of the Church. As a matter of fact, the ecclesiastical
authorities let that work pass through many editions under their own
eyes without putting a stop to it. They were severe with the *Disputatio
seu Dialogus,* because of its attack upon the immunities of the clergy.
Such an attack was most harmful to the Church.

145. Hilgers, *Der Index,* p. 479; Ortwin Gratius, *Lamentationes
Obscurorum Virorum,* p. 19.

146. Hilgers, "Censorship of Books", *Cath. Encycl.,* III, 521.

147. Hilgers, "Buechervebote und Buecherzensur des XVI Jahrhunderts in Italien", *Zentralblatt für Bibliothekswesen,* XXVIII
(1911), 114.

1482, the Bishop of Basle prohibited the same libellous writing of Andrea Zuccalmaglio and commanded under pain of excommunication, that all copies be delivered up to the ecclesiastical authorities within three days' time.[148] On March 22, 1485[149] and again January 4, 1486[150] the Archbishop of Mayence issued some regulations regarding the printing or circulation of the German translations of certain works.

In Rome, Pope Innocent VIII condemned by a bull of August 4, 1487, the edition of John Pico della Mirandola's *Theses Nongentae* or *Conclusiones Nongentae* which appeared in print at Rome on December 7, 1486.[151] Moreover, this Pope became aware of the fact that many evil books were being published, with untold harm to the fold of Christ. Therefore, by the Bull *Inter multiplices* of November 17, 1487,[152] he ordered censorship of books for the whole Church.[153] This is the first instance of a general papal legislation on censorship of printed works.[154]

Having pointed out the great harm of which the art of printing had been made the instrument, the Pope orders, under pain of excommunication *latae sententiae* and of a pecuniary fine, that: 1. Henceforth no works shall be printed without the permission, in Rome, of the *Magister Sacri Palatii*, and elsewhere of the Ordinary, which permission is to be granted only after a through examination of the writings

---

148.   Hilgers, *ibidem.*

149.   Pallmann H., "Des Erzbischofs Berthold von Mainz ältestes Censuredict," *Archiv für Geschichte des Deutschen Buchhandels,* IX (1884), 238-241.

150.   Hilgers, *Der Index,* p. 407.

151.   Const. *Etsi ex iniuncto nobis,* Aug. 4, 1487 — *B R T,* V, 327 ff. Cf. also Mansi, XXXV, 1553. This decree was confirmed by Alexander VI through a brief, *Omnium Catholicorum,* June 18, 1493 — Du Plessis d'Argentré, *Collectio Judiciorum de Novis Erroribus,* I, 2, 321. Cf. also Hilgers, *l. c.*

152.   *Statuta Seu Decreta Provincialium et Dioecesanarum Synodorum Sanctae Ecclesiae Coloniensis* (Cologne, 1554), p. 280. Cf. also Hilgers, *Der Index,* p. 408; p. 480.

153.   *Ibidem.*

154.   Hilgers, *o. c.,* p. 408; "Censorship of Books", *Cath. Encycl.,* III, 521; J. Rest, "Die erste allgemeine papstliche Zensurverordnung", *Zentralblatt für Bibliothekswesen,* XXXI (1914), 68 f.

in question. This applies to *all* works on *any* subject, a substantial departure from the custom of the Middle Ages when only doctrinal books came under preventive censorship.[155] 2. All printers shall present complete inventories of the works they have published to the *Magister Sacri Palatii* in Rome, and to the Ordinary elsewhere. Any work or works which will be found by these ecclesiastical authorities to contain *"aliqua fidei catholicae contraria, impia, adversa, scandalosa, aut male sonantia"* shall be brought to them to be burned, and all are forbidden to read such books. Moreover, the authors of these writings are to be sought out and, if necessary, punished with ecclesiastical censure. In carrying out these orders, the Church authorities should seek the aid of civil authorities.

These strong and thoroughgoing regulations, if followed out, would have surely stopped the spread of pernicious books. But, strange to say, apparently this Bull was promulgated only by Archbishop Hermann of Cologne.[156] How it came about that it was ignored elsewhere, even in Italy and in Rome, is not known.[157] Certainly in Cologne the press was being used by the enemies of the Church against her. It was from Cologne that in 1479 an appeal was made to the Pope to stop the circulation of *Disputatio seu Dialogus inter clericum et militem super potestate ecclesiastica.*[158] The Archbishop of Cologne, therefore, was only too happy to execute the wishes of the Holy See with regard to censorship of books, as he himself, like the Pope, was very much concerned for the faith of his people. Probably the bull of Innocent VIII was also carried out in Spain. As a matter of fact, beginning with the year 1487, a few books are found printed there with episcopal approbation, e.g., Diez, *De la sacratissima conceptio* (Valencia: 1487); Raymund Lull, *Janua Artis* (Barcelona: 1488). In Italy censorship was introduced in 1491 into the Republic

---

155. This application of Church preventive censorship to all books, existed until the nineteenth century when, once more, religious and ethical books became the only object of preventive censorship.

156. Hilgers, J., *Der Index*, p. 408.

157. Hilgers, "Buecherverbot und Buecherzensur des XVI Jahrhunderts in Italien", *Zentralblatt für Bibliothekswesen*, XXVIII (1911), 113.

158. Supra p. 39.

of Venice by the Papal legate Nicolo' Franco, who also prohibited Pico della Mirandola's *Conclusiones*.[159]

On June 1, 1501, Pope Alexander VI, issued for the ecclesiastical provinces of Cologne, Mayence, Trèves and Magdeburg, the bull *Inter multiplices*[160] which is almost identical with that of Innocent VIII.[161] All those who oppose or rebel against these measures, of whatever dignity, state, rank, order or condition they may be, including communities, universities, and all other colleges, are to be brought to their senses through sentences of excommunication, suspension, interdict and other ecclesiastical punishments, the civil power being called upon for aid if necessary.

The same censorship of the press, with some slight changes, was extended by Leo X at the V Lateran Council to the entire Christian world through the Constitution *Inter sollicitudines* of May 4, 1515.[162] No writing may be printed without being examined and approved by the Cardinal Vicar and the *Magister S. Palatii* in Rome, and in the rest of the world by the Ordinary and the Inquisitor. He who knowingly and willfully violates this law shall incur the loss of the books printed, which will be burned, shall pay one hundred ducats, shall be suspended from printing for a year, shall be excommunicated, and, if his contumacy becomes more grave, he shall be punished with all penalties of the law so that others may not follow his example and attempt similar things.

This is the first general decree of censorship which was universally accepted.[163]

---

159. Hilgers, "Buechervebot und Buecherzensur", *Zentralblatt für Bibliothekswesen*, XXVIII (1911), 114.

160. Zaccaria, *Storia Polemica*, p. 133; Hilgers, *Der Index*, p. 408; Pastor, *History of the Popes*, VI, 154 ff. The reason for the application of strict censorship regulation to only those provinces must have been that the archbishops of those provinces petitioned for it.

161. Cf. supra p. 40 f.

162. *Fontes*, n. 68. Cf. also Gretser, *De Jure et More*, lib. I, Cap. XVIII.

163 Hilgers, *l. o.* In treating of the Bull of Leo X *Inter sollicitudines*, Putman in his book *The Censorship of the Church of Rome*, I. p. 83, if not through malice, surely out of ignorance of the document, states: "The fatherly care for the true faith and for the preservation of the morality of Christendom are, in the wording of this papal utter-

The fact which strikes one who reads the three mentioned bulls of Innocent VIII, Alexander VI and Leo X is that, while they were very anxious to have all books examined before they went to the press, this scrutiny was not necessarily to be made by the Bishop, for, if he were not well versed in the matter treated in the book, the examination was to be entrusted to one who was an expert in the subject matter of the book. The Church always took extreme care lest a book should be forbidden unjustly through the ignorance of the censor. This passing remark, based on documentary evidence, ought to be enough to answer the objection of the enemies of the Church censorship that ignorant men are asked to judge the works of scholars. This point will become clearer when Benedict XIV's legislation will be discussed.[164]

The laws of the Church contained in the Papal documents just mentioned, and the penalties attached to them, were entirely disregarded by Luther and the printers of his pernicious writings. His errors spread like fire throughout Germany and other countries. In order to stop this evil which like an epidemic, was infesting the souls of many of the Lord's sheep, Pope Leo X issued the bull *Exsurge Domine* on June 15, 1520.[165] In it he condemned Luther's errors and all his writings, whether printed or still to be printed, forbidding them to Catholics under severe penalties,

> Ne scripta etiam praefatos errores non continentia, ab eodem Martino quomodolibet condita vel

---

ance, placed in the background, while the main contention is devoted to the assertion of the authority of the pope and of the special responsibility of the pope..." A glance at the Bull in question would be sufficient to assure Putman that in it there is *nothing but* an expression of the Pope's *"fatherly care for the preservation of the morality of Christendom"* and not even a single statement can be found "devoted to the assertion of the authority of the pope". (See text in *Fontes* n. 68). This is one of the many errors made by Putman throughout his work, due, perhaps, to carelessness, ignorance, slavish copying from prejudiced sources, or even to bias. Cf. Hilgers, *The Roman Index and Its Latest Historian* for a correct appreciation of Mr. Putman's work.

164. *Infra*, p. 55 ff.

165. *Fontes* n. 76. Leo prohibited also the *Epistolae Obscurorum Virorum* by a brief of Mar. 15, 1517, and Reuchlin's *Augenspiegel* on June 23, 1520 — Hilgers, "Censorship of Books", *Cath. Encycl.*, III, 521.

edita, vel condenda vel edenda ... legere, asserere, praedicare, laudare, imprimere, publicare, sive defendere per se vel alium seu alios, directe vel indirecte, tacite vel expresse, publice vel occulte, seu in domibus suis, sive aliis locis publicis, vel privatis, tenere quoquomodo praesumant, quinimmo illa comburant.

On May 8, 1521, Charles V, like Constantine of old, issued at the Diet of Worms an edict whereby to write, print, keep, read or in any way to handle the books proscribed by the Pope was made a civil crime and punishable accordingly.[166]

---

166. Zaccaria, p. 136 ff. Since the time of Emperor Justinian the censorship and suppression of books had been a prerogative of the emperor. This law was incorporated into the Codex of civil law. However, in the fifteenth century the emperor and the civil authorities did not concern themselves with this prerogative. But, when the Church became active regarding censorship of books, they became jealous of the exercise of that power on the part of the Church. The Diet of Worms held in 1495 put forth the demand that censorship should not be left in the hands of the Church authorities, but should be given over to the Emperor and the Princes of the Empire. Apparently this motion was defeated. Nevertheless, about the year 1500, we find in Spain alongside with books approved by the Bishops, other books published with the approval of the Spanish Rulers, thus showing that civil authorities there were exercising the power of censorship which had been denied to the German Rulers in 1495. In the Republic of Florence, in Italy, in 1507, we find what is considered to be the oldest law of censorship enacted by a civil government. (Hilgers, "Buechervebot und Buecherzensur", *Zentralblatt*, XXVIII [1911], p. 108.)

As early as 1515 an Act of Parliament was passed by the Parliament of Scotland at Edinburgh forbidding any one to publish or print any books, ballads, songs, "blasphematious" rhymes or tragedies, in Latin or English, until such had been "seen, viewed and examined by some wise and discreet persons" duly appointed (Roberts, William, *The Earlier History of English Bookselling*, p. 25).

The most important enactment of censorship on the part of civil authorities is the edict of Charles V, of Aug. 8, 1521. The Emperor not only forbade the printing, selling, buying and reading of Luther's books or others attacking the Pope or the clergy, but he also commanded all civil authorities under him to burn all such works whenever found, to imprison the writers, printers and sellers of the same and to confiscate their goods. He also laid down strict regulations of previous censorship with the threat of severe penalties for the violators of his orders.

Up to that time the Pope's and Bishops' efforts had been seconded only by a few states. Henceforth the ecclesiastical and civil authorities

Similar action was taken in France by King Francis I, in 1521, in England by Henry VIII in 1526 and in Milan in 1523.[167] Adrian VI again set forth the prohibition against Luther's writings in 1522.[168]

In 1524 Clement VII put in the *Bulla in Coena Domini*[169] the excommunication against Luther and those who used his books:

> Libros ipsius Martini, aut quorumvis aliorum ejusdem sectae sine auctoritate nostra et Sedis Apostolicae quomodolibet legentes, aut in suis domibus tenentes, imprimentes, aut quomodolibet defendentes...[170]

Provincial Councils met at Bruges (1528), Paris (1528), Canterburg (1529), and Cologne (1536)[171] in order that the Popes' decrees against evil books might be carried out.

II. Paul III — Paul IV

The Lutheran heresy continued to claim victims in great numbers. Practically, every dogma of Christianity was being attacked and its very foundations were being shaken by the heretics. A General Council was being contemplated by the

---

go hand in hand to exercise censorship of books throughout the largest part of the civilized world.

The imperial edict of Aug. 8, 1521 was the beginning of a series of imperial, royal, ducal and magisterial laws of censorship. The prosecutions of civil powers against the dissemination of bad books, which had been only sporadic before 1521, became thereafter more regular in Catholic States. The Protestant States and Protestant Free Cities opposed the enforcement of the imperial laws of censorship and passed laws in their own favor against Catholic books.

167. Hilgers, "Buechervebot und Buecherzensur", *Zentralblatt für Bibliothekswesen*, XXVIII (1911), 109 f.

168. Hilgers, "Censorship of Books", *Cath Encycl.*, III, 521.

169. This was a Bull, containing various excommunications. It was read to the faithful every year on Holy Thursday. In its most ancient form it dates back to Gregory IX in 1228. Cf. Mansi, XXIII, 161 f.; Hilgers, *The Roman Index and its Latest Hist.*, p. 26. Therefore Putnam, *o. c.* (I, 111) and even Vermeersch-Creusen, *Epit. Jur. Can.* (III, n. 509) are not correct in giving Urban V (1364) as the author of the earliest form of this Bull.

170. Zaccaria, *o. c.*, p. 139.

171. Arndt, *De Libris Prohibitis*, p. 71.

Church. Meanwhile, as the Council had to be postponed for some time, Paul III by the Bull *Licet ab initio* of July 21, 1542[172] instituted the Universal Roman Inquisition or the Congregation of the Holy Office.[173]

The purpose of this new institution was to watch most carefully over the purity of the Faith and to judge of the doctrines propounded in any part of the Church either orally or by writing. Therefore, a great part of its duty consisted — at least before the Congregation of the Index was founded — in examining and condemning evil books.

But, as the number of pernicious books had grown beyond measure and had pervaded practically all Europe, more comprehensive and more efficacious remedies were needed. And, first of all, the faithful needed a complete list of the books which were forbidden. Therefore, Paul IV in 1557 entrusted the Sacred Congregation of the Inquisition with the task of drawing up a complete catalogue of forbidden books.

The same year, the general Index was ready, but, as it did not please the Pope, this edition was never published.[174] The Congregation then, by order of Paul, set to work for a larger and really complete Index and, on December 30, 1558, the new Roman Index was approved and appeared in print; it was first distributed early in January 1559.

This Index of Paul IV of 1559 is the first general Roman Index ever published and the first one to carry the name Index.[175] Under each letter of the alphabet a threefold classification is made:

1. Names of heretical authors whose works are *all* forbidden.
2. Forbidden books of known authors.
3. Forbidden anonymous works.

---

172. *B R T*, VI, 344.
173. Bouix, *Tractatus de Curia Romana*, p. 155.
174. Hilgers, *Der Index*, p. 7.
175. Hilgers, *l. c.* This Index was preceded by local Indexes drawn up by the Sorbonne in 1542, the Senate of Milan in 1538 (Hilgers, "Buechervebot und Buecherzensur", *Zentralblatt*, XXVIII [1911], 114 ff.), the University of Louvain in 1546, 1550, 1558, that of Cologne in 1549 and by the Inquisition in 1554, in Spain by the Inquisition in 1550, in Florence in 1552, and in Milan in 1554. Cf. Arndt, *o. c.*, p. 71.

Due to the rigor of this Index, the Grand Inquisitor, Card. Michael Ghislieri, later St. Pius V, by order of the Pope drew up and issued a decree *De libris orthodoxorum patrum* which mitigated its extreme regulations. While Arndt,[176] Pennacchi[177] and Boudinhon[178] following Zaccaria[179] give as the date of this decree June 24, 1561, Hilgers proves conclusively that at the latest it dates to the first few days of January 1559.[180]

By reason of the mitigated decree:

1. Books which had been forbidden *simply* because published by suspected printers are to be taken off the Index.

2. Translations of Catholic works, made by heretics, if cleared of heresy, are also to be taken off the Index.

3. Catholic books placed in the Index because they have the preface, summaries or explanations written by heretics, if purged of them, are to be tolerated.

Besides this decree of mitigation, which many editions of 1559 have, some editions of this Index, e. g., that of Naples, and the Valdes edition, have the Brief of Paul IV, *Quia in futurorum eventibus*, of December 21, 1558, by which he revoked the permission to read heretical books which Bishops, Cardinals and others had, but not those which Inquisitors had.[181]

III.   Index of the Council of Trent

The censorship of the press was one of the many problems which the Council of Trent had to face. In the IV Session (April 8, 1546), the Fathers of the Council drew up a *Decretum de editione et usu sacrorum librorum* in which, besides establishing the Vulgate as the authentic Bible to be used in public discussions, sermons, etc., they prescribed that

---

176.   *De Libris Prohibitis*, p. 72.
177.   *In Const. Apost. Offic. ac muner.*, p. 14.
178   *La Nouvelle Legisl. de l'Index*, p 52.
179.   *Storia Polemica*, p. 145.
180.   Hilgers, *Der Index*, pp. 8, 490.
181.   Hilgers, *o. c.*, p. 496. Cf. the Valdes edition of the Index of 1559 which may be seen at the Library of Congress, Washington, D. C.

no books shall be printed on religious subjects without the previous approbation of the ecclesiastical authorities.[182]

Later the Council selected some of the most learned and prudent Fathers for the study of the question of the censorship of books, and of the Index, the revision of which had been expressly asked and authorized by Pius IV.

In the XVIII Session (February 26, 1562), the formation of this committee was made public so that others might help this important work with suggestions.[183] By December 1563 the committee had finished its arduous task with most satisfactory results.

They presented to the Council, in the XXV and last Session, the legislation they had drawn up concerning dangerous literature. It consisted of a catalogue or Index of forbidden books and of *ten general rules* which henceforth were to regulate the censorship, expurgation and reading of books. These rules may be summarized as follows:

1. All books, condemned before 1515 by Popes or Oecumenical Councils, remain forbidden, though not in the Index.

2. All books of heretical leaders published after 1515, and those on religion by heretics are absolutely forbidden.

3. Latin translations of ecclesiastical writers, edited by condemned authors, if containing no error, are permitted. Latin translations of the Old Testament may be permitted by the Bishop under some conditions, but the translations of the New Testament by authors of the First Class[184] cannot be allowed.

4. The Bible translated into the vernacular by Catholics may be permitted in writing by the Bishop to those who will derive benefit from it. Violators are to be punished.

5. Collections of otherwise good works (e. g., Lexica, Concordances, etc.) compiled by heretics are to be permitted, after any necessary expurgation.

---

182. *Canones et Decreta Sacrosancti Oecumenici Concilii Tridentini,* Sessio IV.

183. *Canones et Decreta,* Sess. XVIII; Pallavicino, *Istoria del Concilio di Trento,* lib. XV, cap. 18, 19.

184. Cf. *Index of the Council of Trent* and supra, p. 46.

6. Works containing in the vernacular controversies between Catholics and heretics are allowed under the same restrictions as the vernacular Bibles. Pious books are permitted and, if expurgated, even books of Catholics condemned in some localities.

7. Obscene books, except the old classics, are forbidden.

8. Books, the principal part of which is good, if cleared of all objectionable portions, can be permitted.

9. All superstitious books, e. g., of magic, are forbidden.

10. Preventive censorship is required for all books. The regulations concerning it are about the same as those laid down by Leo X at the V Lateran Council.[185]

The punishment for reading or keeping heretical books is excommunication *latae sententiae*. To read or keep other forbidden books is a mortal sin, and punishable, like all other offences against the Ten Rules and the Index, according to its gravity.[186]

The triple classification of forbidden writings found in the Index of Paul IV is kept in the *Index of the Council of Trent*.[187]

At its closing session, the Council decided to send this new Index to Pope Pius IV for approval and promulgation. The Supreme Pontiff, after having examined the whole work personally and through a committee of erudite and holy Prelates, approved and promulgated it[188] by the Bull *Dominici gregis* of March 24, 1564.[189] The Shepherd of all Christians thus begins this important document:

Dominici gregis custodias, Domino disponente, praepositi, vigiliis more pastoris non desistimus ipsi gregi ab imminentibus periculis quanta maxima possumus cura, et diligentia praecavere, ne propter negligentiam nostram pereant oves quae pretiosissimo Domini nostri Jesu Christi sanguine sunt redemptae.

---

185. *Fontes* n. 68; supra, p. 42.
186. *Canones et Decreta*, p. 298.
187. Preface of F. Foreiro to the Tridentine *Index*.
188. The title is: *Index Librorum Prohibitorum cum regulis confectis per Patres a Tridentina Synodo delectos auctoritate Sanctiss. D. N. Pii IIII Pont. Max. comprobatus*. Romae. Apud Paulum Manutium.
189. *Fontes* n. 105.

This is an echo of his predecessors from the time of St. Peter. Pius IV, like those who occupied the See of Peter before him, fulfilled his duty of warning the sheep against the dangers of bad literature. His words will be reechoed, and his action imitated by all his successors whenever necessary.

The Tridentine *Index* is the first Index that, besides the catalogue of forbidden books, gave general rules which were to serve as a guide to the reader for books not found in the catalogue.

On the 24th of August of the same year 1564, Pius IV gave the Cardinals of the Holy Office the faculty to read and keep forbidden books, and to give to or revoke from others the same permission.[190]

NOTE: *Protestant Censorship and Prohibition of Books*

The Catholic Church and the Catholic rulers were not the only ones who realized the vast influence of the printed word and, accordingly, controlled literature for the preservation and spread of Catholic faith and morals. The Protestant sects and the Protestant rulers also were convinced of the power of the press and took every possible measure to curb all literature opposed to their creed or to their aims. In fact, history shows that Protestant enactments surpassed in number and rigor all similar Catholic decrees and at times reached a bitter and brutal stage unheard of in Catholic practice.

We may be permitted to quote, in this regard, George N. Putman, a non-Catholic, who cannot be accused of prejudice in favor of the Catholic Church. In his work *The Censorship of the Church of Rome*, in 2 volumes, he writes on page 49 ff. of the first volume:

The responsibility for the policy pursued during the centuries since the advent of printing for a censorship control of literature does not rest alone with the Catholic Church. In all of the Protestant States, attempts were made from time to time to control and to restrict the operations of the printing press. In the Protestant States of Germany, the preparation of the local Indexes or lists of books condemned, and the issue of the decrees for the separate condemnation of any individual work, were in part placed in the hands of the Pro-

---

190. Hilgers, *Der Index*, p. 502.

testant ecclesiastics and in part managed directly by the civil authorities. The authority, however, under which the orders were issued and the penalties were enforced was always that of the State. The edicts were given out in Dresden, or in Berlin, as in Brussels, Madrid, or in Paris, in the name of the ruler. The series of such decrees or censorship actions is long and complex.

There can, of course, be no question that from the outset the leaders of the Protestant Reformation believed as thoroughly in the necessity and in the rightfulness of the censorship of literature as did the ecclesiastics of Rome or of Spain. The duty of protecting the minds of the faithful against the insidious and wrong doctrine was just as clear to Calvin, to Zwingli, and to Luther, as it was to Loyola or to Brasichelli. The Protestant ecclesiastics were, however, not in a position to enforce or even to threaten any such penalties as could be imposed by the authorities of Rome, and as in fact were imposed most consistently and effectively by the Inquisition in Spain. They had under their control no such dread penalty as excommunication. The leaders of the Protestant faith were compelled to rely upon the civil authorities of their several States for carrying out the provisions of such censorship policy as might be decided upon, and concerning the wisdom of which they had been able to convince the civil rulers.

Irrespective of the censorship initiated by the divines, which had for its purpose the maintaining of a specific creed and the preservation from attack of "sound theology," there is record of a long series of attempts (attempts which have in fact continued into the 20th century) to enforce what may be called political censorship, — that is to say, the control of literary production in the interests of the State and in support of the authority of the State, against opinions believed to be inimical to such authority. It may at once be admitted that the series of Protestant prohibitions, whether ecclesiastical or political in their origin, do not compare favourably with the similar prohibitions issued under the authority of the Church of Rome. There is far less consistency of purpose, and, at least as far as the political edicts are concerned, there are more examples of bitter and brutal oppression than can be matched anywhere in the States controlled by the Roman Church outside of Spain.

The list of books which came into condemnation under such Protestant censorship during the centuries in question was very much more considerable than the aggregate of all the lists of the Indexes issued in Rome or issued under the authority of the Roman Church. The censorship policy of the Protestants was more spasmodic, and may be admitted to have been directed on the whole by a less wholesome, dignified, and honourable purpose. It represented very much more largely the spirit of faction or of personal grievance, while the political censorship was, of necessity, influenced by the action of the party which happened for the moment to be in control or of the minister who had for the time the ear of the ruler.[191]

SECTION III

From Pius V to Benedict XIV

I.   Pius V — Alexander VII

While the ecclesiastical authorities of the various parts of the Catholic world were enforcing the regulations of the *Index of the Council of Trent*, Pope Pius V was doing all in his power to render compliance with those regulations comparatively easy, and thus secure their observance everywhere.

With this end in view, by a *motu proprio* of November 19, 1570, he requested the Master of the Sacred Palace to expurgate some forbidden books which, if purged, would be of great utility especially to students. On March 5, 1571, he founded the S. Congregation of the Index[1] and entrusted it with all that concerns the censorship and prohibition of books. Pope Gregory XIII, with the Bull *Ut pestiferarum* of September 13, 1572, confirmed it and gave it exclusive and universal powers to explain, reform, and direct the legislation of the Index.[2] When Sixtus V, by the Bull *Immensa Aeterni Dei* of January 22, 1588,[3] reorganized the Roman Congregations, he made no changes in the Congregation of the Index, but simply

---

191.   Cf. also Gretser, *o. c.*, lib. I, cap. XXI; Zaccaria, *o. c.*, p. 256 ff.

1.   Catalanus, *De Secretario Sacrae Congregationis Indicis*, p. 20; Preface to the *Index of Prohibited Books* (Engl. ed., 1930), p. v; Hilgers, *Der Index*, pp. 10, 513, ff. The contention of others who attribute the institution of this Congregation to Sixtus V cannot stand in view of Hilgers' documentary evidence; nor can Zaccaria's date 1566 be maintained. Cf. also Bouix, *Tract. de Curia Rom.*, p. 449.

2.   "*Omnes et quascumque obscuritates et difficultates in ipso Indice et ejus regulis exortas et imposterum emergentes declarare, aperire et deffinire, libros haereticorum aut suspectorum aut quoquomodo improbatorum scriptorum expurgare, quos libros prohibendos prohibere, quos permittendos esse censebitis permittere, in eo Indice non comprehensos deponere...*" Hilgers, *o. c.*, p. 514 f.

3.   *B R T*, VIII, 985.

defined its rights. With the foundation of this new Congregation, the Holy Office was relieved of much of its work in connection with book legislation. However, it continued to examine and proscribe books, when they were exceptionally destructive of faith or morals.

By order of Sixtus V, a new amended *Index* was prepared by the Congregation of the Index and was printed in 1590. In it the Tridentine Rules had been replaced by twenty-two new ones. But this *Index* was never published because Sixtus died before approving it and his successors did not promulgate it.[4]

Nevertheless, Clement VIII gave orders for the preparation of a new Index which would answer the needs of the day. It was ready by 1596 and Clement VIII promulgated it with the Bull *Sacrosanctum fidei*, which accompanied it. Besides the catalogue of forbidden books, this Index contains the Ten Rules of Trent together with some remarks on the Fourth and Ninth Rules, on the Talmud and other Jewish books, on the Magazor, and finally an Instruction on the prohibition, expurgation and printing of books.

This Instruction reminds the Bishops and Inquisitors of their rights in the matter of the prohibition of books; in particular they are told of the necessity of drawing up local Indexes, copies of which are to be sent to Rome. All translations of a book whose original is condemned are likewise forbidden. The second part of the Instruction states who can expurgate books, how this is to be done and what is to be cancelled. After completing the corrections, an *Index Expurgatorius* is to be published. The third part gives detailed regulations on what is to be done before and during the printing of a book. This is little more than an amplification of some rules of censorship laid down in the V Lateran Council in 1515 and of the Tenth Rule of the Index Tridentinus. Like his predecessors, Clement demands that the censors of books be men of known piety and great learning and absolutely impartial, "seeking only the glory of God and the utility of the Christian people."[5]

---

4. Wernz, *Jus Decretal.*, III, n. 103, note 28.
5. *Fontes*, n. 426, towards the end.

Alexander VII on March 5, 1664, published another edition of the *Roman Index*, prefaced by the Brief of promulgation *Speculatores*. This is the first Papal Index which, having abandoned the three-class division introduced by Paul IV,[6] listed all the books and authors alphabetically. Besides this change of arrangement (suggested by a private edition of the Index in alphabetical order by Capiferri in 1632), the Pope has an observation on the Tenth Rule, in which he insists again on the requirements of censors.

Between 1664 and 1753 there is little of importance for our purpose. Many books, especially Jansenistic, were forbidden by the Congregations of the Inquisition and the Index, and by special decrees of the Popes. At times, whole classes of writings were condemned and placed in the Index under the word "Libri". The Indexes published during this period are only new editions of the Tridentine *Index*, containing, besides the additions made by Clement VIII, Alexander VII and Clement XI (on Chinese Rites), the books condemned since the preceding editions.

II. Benedict XIV

With Benedict XIV, one comes to a very important step in the history of the Church's legislation on forbidden books. In the Constitution *Sollicita ac provida* of July 9, 1753[7] he laid down detailed rules to be followed by the Congregations of the Holy Office and the Index in the censorship and prohibition of books. This document is a most convincing answer to the many objections that even now are made against Roman prohibitions of books. Due to its vast importance, and because it is still the norm followed by the Holy Office,[8] a very brief summary of it is here given. It begins by stating the duty of the Holy See to forbid evil books and by giving a short history of the Church's legislation on books. Then, the Pope shows the scrupulous and extreme care taken by the Church before she prohibits a book. This is based on his

---

6. Supra, p. 46.
7. *Fontes*, n. 426.
8. De Meester, *Jur. Can. et Jur. Can. Civ. Compendium*, III, p. 253, note 1; Wernz-Vidal, *Jus Canonicum*, II, p. 483, note 33.

own long experience with the Congregations of the Holy Office and of the Index. Finally, in order to leave absolutely no ground for the accusations against the procedure of the Church in the examination and prohibition of books, he lays down regulations which are to be followed in every case.

A. *Procedure to be followed by the Congregation of the Holy Office.*

A book is given to one of the *Qualificatores*[9] or censors or to one of the consultors. After a very diligent and thorough examination of the work, he gives in writing a detailed report of his inquiry, pointing out the pages where the objectionable parts are to be found. Then the book with the examiner's remarks is sent to each of the consultors. At their weekly meeting on Monday, the consultors have a discussion and take a vote as to whether the book is to be forbidden, allowed or corrected. Then the book, the censor's report and the consultors' votes are studied by the Cardinals at their regular Wednesday session and the final verdict is given. The verdict together with all the facts of the case is then referred to the Holy Pontiff who gives the final decision.

In case the author of the book in question be a Catholic, and the consultors, after the unfavorable report of the censor, vote against it, another censor is to examine the book and the observations of the first censor, whose identity shall not be revealed to him. If this new examiner judges that the book should be condemned, then the matter is referred to the Cardinals for decision. But if he differs from the first censor, a third one is to be appointed to review the book and the remarks of both censors, whose names shall not be revealed to him; this secures absolute freedom from partiality and prejudice. Should the last censor be of the opinion that the book is to be condemned, then the Cardinals will at once take the matter up. If, however, he be opposed, like the second censor,

---

9. *Qualificatores* are those who, upon appointment by the S. Congregation of the Holy Office, examine a book or proposition and give judgment in writing regarding it, declaring with what theological note ("heretical", "proximate to heresy", etc.) that book or proposition is to be marked. Cf. Badii, C., *Institutiones Juris Canonici*, I, 167; Bouix, *Tract. de Curia Romana*, p. 156.

to the condemnation of the book, then the consultors will discuss the case once more before it goes to the Cardinals.

B.   *Procedure to be followed by the Congregation of the Index.*

The Secretary receives the denunciation of a book and secures exact information from the *delator* (the one who denounces the book) as to the reason why he thinks it should be condemned. Then he is to read the work most carefully and decide, with the help of two consultors, approved by the Pope or the Prefect of the Congregation, whether there is any foundation for the charges. If the charges are well founded, the book is given to a *relator*, an expert in the subject treated, also approved by the Pope or the Prefect. The *relator* shall present in writing a report of his examination, having marked the pages where the objectionable statements are to be found. Then the book with the *relator's* remarks is studied at a preparatory meeting in which there shall take part, besides the Secretary and the Master of the Sacred Palace, six approved consultors, chosen by the Secretary according to the subject matter of the book in which they must be well versed. All these facts, together with the judgment of the consultors, are then considered by the Cardinals in general meeting. Their decision with previous findings is to be brought to the Supreme Pontiff for final sentence.

If the writer be a Catholic of good repute and well known, then, whenever it is possible, the decree of condemnation must have the clause *donec corrigatur* or *donec expurgetur*, and is not to be published without previous communication with the author. The decree is to be suppressed if the author submits and makes the necessary changes, and only few copies have been distributed.[10]

------

10.   When the judgment on a book is expressed by the word *dimittatur* the book is not forbidden. However that judgment does not exclude the possibility of philosophical or theological errors being contained in the work. S. C. of the Index, 21 June, 1880 (*ASS*, XIII, 92) ; 5 Dec., 1881 (*ASS*, XIV, 288). Cf. also Zigliara, T. M., *Il Dimittatur* (Rome. 1881).

In every case, the examiners and the consultors must be men of virtue and of learning, of mature judgment and of absolute impartiality. Moreover those who are called to judge a book must have a very good knowledge of the subject treated in it, acquired through years of labor and study.

These and other wise rules are given by Benedict XIV so that both censors and consultors may, in this serious matter, "bear in mind the dictates of their own conscience, the reputation of the writers, the good of the Church and the welfare of the faithful."[11]

Benedict XIV did not confine himself to laying down rules for the examination of future books. He took up also the task of giving the Church a new revised *Index* of forbidden books, free from the many typographical and other errors which in the course of time had crept into previous editions.

On December 23, 1757, by a Brief *Quae ad Catholicae*, he promulgated the new Index which bore the title *Index Librorum Prohibitorum SSmi D. N. Benedicti XIV Pontificis Maximi jussu recognitus atque editus*. Romae MDCCLVIII. The various classes of writings which from time to time had been forbidden and placed in the Index under the work "Libri", now find place in the Benedictine Index immediately before the Catalogue, under the heading: *Decreta de libris prohibitis nec in Indice nominatim expressis*. Among the works enumerated are found especially writings on certain disputed questions such as the Immaculate Conception and the Chinese Rites. This edition of the Index is the best published previous to the Leonine *Index* of 1900.[12]

SECTION IV

From Benedict XIV to Leo XIII

From 1758 to 1897 there is not much development in the legislation of the Church on literature. All the Indexes edited in Rome during this period[1] are no more than reprints of the

---

11. Benedict XIV, Const. *Sollicita ac provida*, July 9, 1753, §20 — *Fontes*, n. 426.

12. Hilgers, *Der Index*, p. 14.

1. *Index* of Pius VI in 1786, of Pius VII in 1819, of Gregory XVI in 1835, of Pius IX in 1855 and 1877, of Leo XIII in 1880 and 1891. Cf. Boudinhon, *La Nouvelle Legisl. de l'Index*, p. 59.

Benedictine Index with the addition, in each case, of the works prohibited since the publication of the preceding edition. In several of them are found one or two *Monita*, reminding especially the shepherds of souls of their obligations in connection with the censorship and prohibition of books. In the *Index* of Pius IX of 1877 there is an extract from the const. *Apostolicae Sedis*, 12 Oct. 1869,[2] containing the penalties against violators of the ecclesiastical prohibition of books, and a *Declaratio* on books treating of the Immaculate Conception.

During this period, the Popes and the Congregation of the Index, at various times, urged the Bishops to enforce the laws concerning the censorship and prohibition of books, and asked all Christians to observe them faithfully. This was done especially by Clement XIII through the Encyclical *Christianae Reipublicae* of November 25, 1766,[3] by Leo XII through a *Mandatum* of March 25, 1825,[4] by the Congregation of the Index through some *Monita* such as the one of March 4, 1828 and the other of January 7, 1836,[5] by Gregory XVI in the Bull *Mirari Vos* of April 15, 1832[6] by Pius IX through the Encyclicals *Nostis et Nobiscum* of December 8, 1849,[7] and *Cum nuper* of January 20, 1858.[8]

However, notwithstanding the constant vigilance of the Church and the good will of most Catholics, the change of times and circumstances and the enormous increase of literature made it practically impossible to observe some of the old rules of censorship and prohibition of books.[9] Therefore, the

---

2. *Fontes*, n. 552.
3. *Fontes*, n. 461.
4. Boudinhon, *o. c.*, p. 381.
5. Boudinhon, *o. c.*, p. 381.
6. *Fontes*, n. 485.
7. *Fontes*, n. 508.
8. *Fontes*, n. 523.

9. For example, for the ecclesiastical authorities to examine all writing on every subject before publication or frequently to visit all the bookshops and printing establishments of every city to search out forbidden books, or for the proprietors of those concerns to have complete lists of their books signed by the Church authorities; all these things were no longer possible.

Church in time either abrogated some of these regulations by special decrees or approved customs contrary to them.[10]

Thus, the custom grew up to submit for censorship only works of religion and morality. This was made a law by Pius IX for the Papal States in an Encyclical of June 2, 1848.[11] In the rest of the world, the custom gained strength by this law and by the publication in 1869 of the Constitution *Apostolicae Sedis*[12] which restricted the excommunication against writers and printers, who would not submit their books for censorship, to writers and printers of Scriptural works. From the Acts and Decrees of the Plenary Councils of Baltimore[13] and other provincial councils and synods in America such as the Fifth Synod of New York (Nov. 1886, N. 10), it is evident that, long before the Leonine reform, in the United States only writings on religion and morality were to be submitted for censorship.

But this was only a small part of the reform needed in the book legislation of the Church. The documents from which one had to draw information on this matter were so many and at times so obscure that even scholars at times were at a loss in trying to decide some questions. Naturally this caused great confusion with the result that, while some were very uneasy in conscience, others found this an excuse for neglecting or entirely ignoring the laws of the Church on books.

Therefore, Pius IX called upon experts to study the situation and submit to him their opinion whether or not the Rules of the Index should be changed. Their answer was that they should be changed.

Meanwhile, the Vatican Council met and many Bishops requested that the whole Index legislation be revised. Thus, the French Bishops were of the opinion that *"illae regulae et*

---

10. *"Plures Regularum Indicis praescriptiones quae excidisse opportunitate pristina videbantur, vel decreto ipsa (Ecclesia) sustulit, vel more usuque alicubi invalescente antiquari benigne simul ac provide sivit."* — Leo XIII, const. *Officiorum ac munerum*, January 25, 1897 (*Fontes*, n. 632).

11. Pennacchi, *In Const. Apost. Offic. ac muner.*, p. 21 ff.

12. IV, 4 — *Fontes*, n. 552.

13. I, 9 May, 1852, N. 85; II, Oct., 1866, N. 503; III, Nov., 1884, N. 220.

universa res Indicis novo prorsus modo nostrae aetati melius attemperato et observatu faciliori instaurentur."[14] This was echoed by many other Bishops of Germany, Italy and other countries. Unfortunately, however, the Vatican Council had to adjourn *sine die* before this matter could even be discussed.

For a while the question of the reform of the Index remained in suspense. But it was not long before Leo XIII took it upon himself to give the Church what it sorely needed, namely, a new Index legislation capable of application and sufficient to offset the immense evil that a flood of pernicious literature was producing.[15]

Accordingly, he entrusted the study of the situation to the Congregation of the Index. The solution of the problem required the framing of new general rules governing the censorship and the prohibition of books, and a revised and improved *Index of Prohibited Books*. The work was by no means easy or of short duration. Nevertheless the new *Decreta Generalia de Prohibitione et Censura Librorum* were promulgated on January 25, 1897[16] through the Const. *Officiorum ac munerum* and the new *Index Librorum Prohibitorum SSmi D. N. Leonis XIII* was published through the brief *Romani Pontifices*, Sept. 17, 1900.[17]

The General Decrees take the place of, and entirely abolish, all previous legislation in this field, even the Tridentine Rules, but not the Constitution *Sollicita ac provida* of Benedict XIV. There are two titles subdivided into chapters, all made up of forty-nine paragraphs.

The first title deals with the Prohibition of Books and gives a safe guide for the faithful to find out whether a book, not listed in the Index, is forbidden or not. It is made up of ten chapters which, in brief, contain the following rules:

1. All books condemned before 1600, including those not found in the Index, unless permitted by these decrees, are forbidden together with the works written by apostates, heretics

---

14. Leo XIII, Const. *Officiorum ac munerum*, January 25, 1897 (*Fontes*, n. 632).

15. Leo XIII, Const. *Officiorum ac munerum*, January 25, 1897 (*Fontes*, n. 632).

16. *Fontes*, n. 632.

17. At the beginning of that Index.

and schismatics in defense of heresy or schism, and those which undermine the very foundations of religion. Moreover all the books of non-Catholics on religion are forbidden unless it is certain that they contain nothing against the faith.

2. The Scriptures, edited or translated by non-Catholics, are allowed only to students of theology or Scripture.

3. Translations of the Bible in the vernacular are permitted only if approved by the Holy See or edited under the vigilance of the Bishop with annotations taken from the Fathers and from learned Catholic writers.

4. Books *ex professo* obscene are prohibited. The classics are permitted to teachers and others who need them.

5. All the books attacking Catholic doctrines, institutions or practices, the Hierarchy or the Apostolic See are condemned; also books teaching magic or other superstitions, works defending duel, suicide, divorce or forbidden societies. Writings on new apparitions, revelations, miracles etc. are forbidden, if published without the approval of the ecclesiastical superiors.

6. Holy images opposed to the sense of the Church and books containing apocryphal indulgences are condemned. New images and all works on indulgences must be approved by the proper authority before publication.

7. All unapproved liturgical and prayer books and litanies are forbidden.

8. Newspapers and magazines which of set purpose oppose religion or morality, are condemned and Catholics, without a just cause, should not write in them.

9. Only the Holy See, and, in particular and urgent cases, the Ordinaries can grant permission to read forbidden books.

10. It is the duty of all Catholics, and especially of the Papal Legates, the Ordinaries and the Rectors of Universities, to denounce pernicious books. The Ordinary should forbid in his diocese all evil writings, and send those which need closer examination to the Holy See.

The second title lays down the regulations concerning the Censorship of Books. It has five chapters:

1. Bibles cannot be printed without the approbation of the Holy See or the Bishop. Books forbidden by the Holy See

can only be printed with the permission of the Congregation of the Index. Books pertaining in any way to the beatification or canonization of the Servants of God may not be printed without the permission of the Congregation of the Sacred Rites, nor can collections of the decrees of any Congregation be published without the authorization of the Congregation concerned. Vicars and Missionaries Apostolic are to follow the rules laid down by the Congregation of the Propagation of the Faith. All other works subject to previous censorship are to be submitted to the Ordinary, and, if the author be a religious, to the religious Superiors also.

2. The censors must be men of learning and piety, and must set aside all personal feelings and seek only the glory of God and the good of souls. The *Imprimatur* is to be given gratis.

3. All the faithful must submit for previous censorship at least those books which deal with the Sacred Scriptures, theology, Church history, canon law, natural theology, ethics and in general all writings which have a special reference to religion and morality. Secular priests must consult their Orinary before publishing any work or editing newspapers or periodicals.

4. A book subject to previous censorship must bear the name of the author and of the editor. Works condemned by the Holy See are forbidden everywhere and in all languages. New editions of approved works must be examined before their publication. Booksellers, especially Catholics, cannot handle obscene books. They must have permission of the Holy See to keep other prohibited books on sale.

5. The sanction for these decrees is: Any one who knowingly reads, keeps, prints or defends books of apostates or heretics which defend heresy or any other book prohibited by name through an Apostolic letter, incurs *ipso facto* an excommunication reserved in a special way to the Roman Pontiff. Those who print or cause to be printed books of the S. Scriptures or annotations or commentaries on the Bible without the approval of the Ordinary or of the Holy See, incur an excommunication not reserved to any one. All the other

violators of these decrees are to be warned by the Ordinary
and, if necessary, punished with canonical penalties.

Many of these rules have been taken from previous legislation, some even bodily, though now their former severe tone
is softened.

The other part of Leo's reform was a thoroughgoing revision of the Index with the general decrees contained in the
constitution *Officiorum ac munerum* as the chief basis and
guide. The Leonine Index was published in 1900 and surpassed
all expectations in every respect, even in that of typographical
perfection. It is introduced by the Brief of promulgation
Romani Pontifices of September 17, 1900 and a very learned
preface of the Secretary of the Congregation of the Index,
Thomas Esser O. P. Then the book is divided into two unequal
parts: the first small section is made up of the two Constitutions which alone regulate the censorship and prohibition
of books, i. e., the const. *Officiorum ac muncrum* of Leo XIII[18]
and the const. *Sollicita ac provida* of Benedict XIV.[19] The
second larger section is the catalogue of forbidden books.

In his preface to the Index, Father Esser, before setting
forth the method followed therein, makes some remarks worth
mentioning. It is a common mistake of Catholics, he says, (and
the same can be said today) that if a book is not listed in the
catalogue of forbidden books, it is at once considered to be
allowed by the Church. That a book may be considered as
permitted by the Church, two facts must be certain, i. e.,
a) that the book is not found in the Index, and b) that it
is not contained in any of the classes of books forbidden in
the general decrees. This naturally leads to the question:
What is the use of the Index if the general decrees already
include all forbidden books? The answer is that there is
always a particular reason why a book is condemned by
name and placed in the Index. As a rule the reason is af-
forded by the denunciation of the book to the Holy See.
For, when a Bishop sends a book to Rome for examination,
he has some special motive for doing so, e. g., the author has
mixed errors and truths so cleverly that it is difficult for

---

18.   Jan. 25, 1897 (*Fontes*, n. 632).
19.   July 9, 1753 (*Fontes*, n. 426).

the average Catholic to recognize it as a forbidden book; or there is divergence of opinion regarding its orthodoxy; or, again, a sentence of condemnation from the Supreme Authority would be more effective for the common good. Another reason is that sometimes books are circulated which, though not strictly contained in the general decrees, are very harmful to faith and morals. Moreover, incidentally, the Index helps towards a correct understanding of the general rules, by giving examples of what the Church considers evil literature.

The Leonine legislation on books was binding on the whole Christian world, including English-speaking countries, as the S. Congregation of the Index answered on May 23, 1898.[20]

SECTION V

From Leo XIII to the Present Day

The Church legislation on the Index since the Leonine reform has undergone very few and slight changes so that today the faithful are governed practically by the rules and the *Index* of Leo XIII.

Pius X by a motu proprio of April 25, 1904[1] laid down rules to be followed in the censorship of books of Gregorian Chant. Later by a letter to the Bishops and Archbishops of Italy *Pieni l'animo* of July 28, 1906,[2] he reminded them of paragraph 42 of the constitution *Officiorum ac munerum* which forbids priests to direct daily papers or periodicals and to publish writings of any kind without the permission of the Ordinary.

The pernicious doctrines of Modernism were spreading rapidly not only among the people but also among the clergy with deadly effects on the faith of many. Mindful of his duty as the Supreme Shepherd of Christendom, Pius X in the Encyclical *Pascendi*[3] which he sent to all the Patriarchs, Primates, Archbishops and Bishops of the world on the 8th

---

20. Boudinhon, *La Nouv. Legisl. de l'Index*, p. 66, note 1.
1. *Fontes*, n. 660.
2. *Fontes*, n. 676.
3. *Fontes*, n. 680.

of December, 1907, raised a cry of warning against the new and insidious errors, and prescribed efficacious means to check the evil of Modernism. In the 44th paragraph (sect. III and IV) the Pope gives stringent orders in regard to the reading and writing of books and papers. The Bishops have the right and duty to forbid all writings which are tainted with Modernism, even though they should have an *Imprimatur,* and to prevent the publication of similar works. *Censores ex officio* must be established in every diocese:[4] secular and religious priests of mature age, erudition and prudence. Finally, he calls the attention of the Bishops to some of the rules of the constitution *Officiorum ac munerum.*

By the motu proprio *Praestantia Scripturae* of November 18, 1907,[5] Pius X forbids any one to write against the decrees of the Biblical Commission.

Two very important events took place in 1917 under Benedict XV. By the motu proprio *Alloquentes* of March 25, 1917,[6] the Congregation of the Index was abolished and its duties were allotted to the Holy Office. Circumstances had made its foundation necessary in 1571. Different circumstances now made its abolition most advisable. After all, since the province of the Holy Office is to safeguard the doctrines of faith and morals, and the censorship of books exists for just that purpose, it is only right that this Congregation should have charge over it. Besides, many controversies of competency are thus precluded. Pius X had contemplated this change when he systematized the *Roman Curia* with his const. *Sapienti Consilio,* June 29, 1908,[7] but the time was not ripe as yet for it.

The other event of 1917 was the promulgation of the much expected *Codex Juris Canonici* with the Encyclical *Providentissima Mater Ecclesia* of May 27, 1917.[8] However, the Leonine

---

4. This is the first time that diocesan *Censores ex officio* are prescribed. The Pope suggests also a censor for each Catholic paper and magazine.

5. *Fontes,* n. 68.

6. *A A S,* IX (1917), 167.

7. *Fontes,* n. 682.

8. See beginning of *Codex.*

legislation on the censorship and prohibition of books suffered only slight changes, for it was embodied almost *verbatim,* though in a modified order, into the Code. It is to be found in canons 247 §4; 1385 to 1405, and 2318.

Since 1900, the Index of Leo XIII has been reprinted at intervals, each new edition differing from the previous one only in the matter of a few corrections and the addition of the books prohibited in the meantime. Even the first Index after the publication of the Code, i. e., the *Index Librorum Prohibitorum Leonis XIII Summi Pontificis auctoritate recognitus SSmi D. N. Pii PP. XI jussu editus,* Romae 1922, differed very little from the preceding Index. It added a few corrections, additional forbidden books, slight changes due to the new Code, the canons which contain the present law of the Church on books and the motu proprio of Benedict XV which abolished the Congregation of the Index.

The latest edition of the Index is the *Indice dei Libri Proibiti riveduto e publicato per ordine di Sua Santità Pio Papa XI* (Città del Vaticano: Tipografia Poliglotta, 1929). This edition marks a departure from those which immediately preceded it inasmuch as it omits both the constitution of Benedict XIV, *Sollicita ac provida,* and that of Leo XIII, *Officiorum ac munerum,* as well as the long preface of Thomas Esser, O. P. In their place, it contains a brief and scholarly preface of Cardinal Merry del Val, then Secretary of the S. Congregation of the Holy Office; the Declaration of the Sacred Congregation for the Oriental Church on the binding force of the Index decrees on the faithful of the Oriental Rites; the Instruction of the Holy Office with regard to sensual and sensual-mystic literature (May 3, 1927), the decree of condemnation of the works of Charles Murras and of the paper *Action Française* (Dec. 29, 1926) and a few explanatory remarks. Another noteworthy innovation is that, while the works prohibited are referred to in the form and language in which they were published, the title of the new Index, the preface, the canons of the Code, relating to the prohibition of books, the Declaration of the Sacred Congregation for the Oriental Church, the footnotes and the explanatory remarks are all in Italian.[9]

---

9. This Index is now available also in the other principal modern

This concludes our brief summary of the history of the Church's legislation on books. No one will deny the truth of the words of Leo XIII:

> Romani Pontifices, quibus grande illud munus in beato Petro Apostolo principe commissum est, universum pascendi Christi gregem toti in eo constanter fuerunt ut pretiosissimum fidei depositum integrum inviolatumque servarent et Christianas toto orbe gentes salutaris doctrinae pabulo enutrirent.[10]

---

languages, i. e., English, French, German and Spanish. The title of the English edition recently published is *Index of Prohibited Books Revised and Published by Order of His Holiness Pope Pius XI* (new ed., Vatican Polyglot Press, 1930).

10. Brief *Romani Pontifices*, September 17, 1900 (at the beginning of the Index of Leo XIII).

PART II

PRESENT LAW OF THE CHURCH ON
PROHIBITION OF BOOKS

The present legislation of the Church concerning the Prohibition of Books is contained in the canons 247, §4, 1384, 1395 to 1405, 2318 of the *Code of Canon Law,* and in the *Index of Prohibited Books:*

All the general decrees, constitutions and other enactments issued by the Church before the Code, even the constitution *Officiorum ac munerum,* do not hold any more. The reasons are:

a) The very nature of the Code, as expressed in the motu proprio *Arduum sane munus* of Pius X, 19 Mar. 1904,[1] and in the const. *Providentissima Mater Ecclesia* of Benedict XV, 27 May 1927.[2] In the latter document we read: *"Decessor noster (Pius X)... consilium iniit universas Ecclesiae leges, ad haec usque tempora editas, lucido ordine digestas in unum colligendi."*

b) Canon 6. Cf. Chelodi, *Ius de Personis,* n. 58, c, and 59; Neuberger, *Canon 6,* p. 19.

c) Canon 22, according to many authors, such as De Meester *Juris Canonici et Juris Canonico-Civilis Compendium,* III (Pars I), n. 1339; Vermeersch-Creusen, *Epitome Iuris Canonici,* II, n. 720. Strictly speaking, this Canon refers only to laws subsequent to the Code, while Canon 6 refers to laws which preceded the Code. Nevertheless it confirms what is already proven.

d) Omission of all legislation previous to the Code in the latest edition of the *Index of Prohibited Books* (1929).

e) Unanimity of authors. Thus, cf. De Meester, *l. c.;* Vermeersch-Creusen, *l. c.;* Cocchi, *Commentarium in Codicem Juris Canonici,* VI, n. 58; Ayrinhac, *Administrative Legislation,* p. 277.

---

1. *A A S,* IX (1917), 439.
2. At the beginning of the Code.

CHAPTER I

GENERAL PRINCIPLES

Art. I. *Nature and Subject of Prohibition of Books*

Prohibition, as used in this work, may be defined as an act of ecclesiastical jurisdiction by which certain books of bad or dangerous reading are forbidden to the faithful.[1] In forbidding a book the Church considers the book itself and the evil effects it will produce on the average reader. She is not very much concerned with the character or the intention of the author.[2]

Every Christian, i. e., *every baptized person*, whether he practices the Catholic religion or not, is bound to observe the laws of the Church governing the prohibition of books. For Baptism makes one a member of the Church of Christ with all the duties and rights of a Christian. Only on the matter of rights may one be excluded from them by reason of a censure or some other impediment.[3] All general laws of the

---

1. Wernz, *Jus Decretalium*, III, n. 111 (note 53).

2. Therefore, justice does not require that before a work is condemned by name the author be given a hearing. However, since, indirectly, such an action would reflect on the reputation of the author, if he be a Catholic of good repute, and the work is liable to correction, either he is called to defend his work personally or one of the consultors of the S. C. of the Holy Office is appointed *ex officio* for the same purpose. Cf. Benedict XIV, const. *Sollicita ac provida*, 9 Jul. 1753, §10 (*Fontes*, n. 426) ; Lugo, *De Virtude Fid.* disput., 21, sect. 2, nn. 26-27; St. Alphonsus, *De Prohib. Libr.*, Cap. IV, n. 25. In former times books were occasionally forbidden *in odium auctoris*. In such cases, the Church considered an author so dangerous that *all* his writings were forbidden. Cf. the second rule of the C. of Trent; Wernz, *Jus Decretalium*, III, n. 98 (10) ; De Meester, *o. c.*, III, n. 1359, note 2; *infra*, p. 133.

3. Canon 87. Cf. also Vermeersch-Creusen, *o. c.*, I, n. 78; De Meester, *o. c.*, I, n. 310; Chelodi, *Jus De Personis*, n. 37.

Church, then, which make no exception for baptized non-Catholics, bind them.[4] Accordingly, as no express exemption is made for them in these laws, baptized non-Catholics are bound by them.[5]

Are *Orientals* bound by the ecclesiastical prohibition of books? Certainly they are bound by the decrees of the Holy Office condemning books and newspapers, according to a declaration of the Sacred Congregation for the Oriental Church, May 26, 1928.[6] The reason is that these decrees directly concern the doctrine of the Church, and not its discipline. As for the general legislation of the Church on forbidden books, contained in the Code, Orientals certainly are subject to those laws which *declare* the natural or the positive divine law,[6a] e.g., the prohibition to *publish*[6b] works which try to under-

---

4.   Canon 12; Solieri, *Juris Publici Ecclesiastici Elementa*, n. 342.

5.   Vermeersch-Creusen, *o. c.*, I, n. 78; II, n. 721; Lugo, *De Virtute Fidei*, Disput. 21, sect. 2, n. 61; Cocchi, *o. c.*, VI, n. 59, B; 70, a; Noldin, *Summa Theol. Mor.*, I, n. 148; Toso, *Ad Codicem Juris Canonici Commentaria Minora*, I, p. 37; Chelodi, *o. c.*, nn. 37, 65 (and note 2 on page 113). Augustine, *A Commentary on the New Code of Canon Law*, VI, p. 482, n. 46, states that only Catholics are bound by the laws of the Church on prohibition books. Perhaps he bases his view on the last paragraph of the const. *Officiorum ac munerum*, in which Leo XIII mentions only "Catholici homines"; or he may base it on the opinion of some theologians and canonists who think that baptized non-Catholics are bound to observe the Church laws intended for public order but not those meant for the personal sanctification of the subjects, among which is classed the prohibition of books. However, the first reason is without value after the Code, because now the Code must be considered and not any previous legislation which differs from it. (Cf. Canon 6, n. 1 and n. 3). The second argument is also untenable, since the Code makes it clear that it legislates for all who are validly baptized unless it makes express exception of baptized non-Catholics (Cf. Canons 12, 87, 1070 §2, and 1099; Chelodi, *o. c.*, p. 113, note 2). Of course, violation of these laws by non-Catholics who either are ignorant of or cannot see the validity of these laws of the Church, is not a formal sin.

6.   *A A S*, XX (1928), 195 f.

6a.   Can. 1; Cappello, *De Curia Romana*, I, p. 271.

6b.   The other actions mentioned in can. 1398 are not *always* forbidden by the natural law, but only when they place the person who performs them in proximate spiritual danger. The law of the Church, then, goes further than the natural law: it forbids everyone what the natural law forbids the average individual. In those cases, the Church does *not*

mine the very foundations of religion, or openly attack religion and morality or are *ex professo* obscene, or which combat Catholic dogmas, foster superstition, defend duel, suicide, divorce (cann. 1398, §1 and 1399 *passim*) ; the prohibition to *read* books which expose the reader to proximate danger of sinning (can. 1405, §1) ; and finally the prohibition under pain of excommunication reserved in a special way to the Apostolic See, to *publish* or *defend* books of apostates, heretics or schismatics advocating apostasy, heresy or schism (can. 2318, §1).[6c] However, Orientals are not bound by those canons of the Code which *determine and apply*, but do not declare, the natural or the positive divine law. For can. 1 clearly states that the Code does not bind the Oriental Church, except in those matters which of their very nature affect also the Oriental Church, e.g., canons which propose a dogma, *declare a natural or positive divine law*, grant spiritual favors or expressly mention Orientals.[6d]

Those are also bound who see no danger for themselves in reading a forbidden book. For these laws are enacted to ward off the general danger of such writings, and, therefore, bind even in the individual cases in which the danger does not exist, as Canon Law prescribes in can. 21.[7] As a matter of

---

simply declare the law of God (natural or positive), but it *determines and applies* it. Consequently, Orientals are not affected.

6c. Cappello, *De Censuris*, n. 22; Duskie, *The Canonical Status of the Orientals in the United States*, p. 134. Duskie, *o.c.*, considers the Orientals subject also to the excommunication for *reading* and *keeping*, knowingly and without permission, books of apostates, heretics and schismatics advocating apostasy, heresy and schism. However, for the reasons adduced in the preceding note, the prohibition to *read* and *keep* such works is *not simply a declaration* of the natural law. Therefore this part of the law, and the excommunication attached to it, does not affect Orientals. Kelly, *The Jurisdiction of a Simple Confessor*, p. 65, n. 10, doubts that any part of can. 2318 affects Orientals.

6d. Vermeersch-Creusen, *Ep.*, I, n. 49; encyclical of the S. C. for the Propagation of the Faith, Aug. 6, 1885 (*Collect. S.C. P.F.*, II, n. 1640).

7. Cf. De Meester, *o. c.*, III, n. 1336, 3°; St. Alphonsus, *De Libr. Proh.*, Cap. V, n. 1; Lugo, *o. c.*, n. 66; Wernz, *Jus Decretalium*, III, n. 97; Reiffenstuel, *Jus Canonicum Universum*, lib. V, tit. VII, n. 65-66. This clearly differs from the prohibition of books arising from the natural law which binds only those for whom the danger exists and as far as it exists (Cf. above, p. 3).

fact some books are forbidden simply because they carry no
ecclesiastical approbation,[8] and probably in some of them there
is not much danger. Yet the Church forbids them all.

The reasons for this are as follows. First, if it were left
to the individual to judge whether a book is dangerous to him
or not, many would be inclined to think that no danger exists
for them. Secondly, they might be poisoned by the reading of
a book, before becoming aware of its dangerous character.
Finally, the Church, by her laws in this matter, wishes also
to discourage writers and editors from producing evil literature. She aims at removing such harmful reading matter entirely from the faithful. This aim is realized through the
application of the laws to every case, even to that in which
no danger is seen by the reader. Therefore, these laws bind
also learned men and those who would use forbidden books
to answer objections of the Church's enemies.[9]

Cardinals, Bishops and all Ordinaries are exempt from
the Church laws on forbidden books.[10] Students of Scripture
and Theology are allowed to read certain forbidden editions of
the Bible.[11] Moreover, permission is granted to some, for special reasons, to read forbidden books.[12] Finally, authors generally admit the use of epikeia in urgent cases, i. e., when
moral necessity or great utility requires the reading of a forbidden book and there is not sufficient time to secure permission.[13] However, more will be said later[14] about these exemptions from the general law of the Church, and permissions to
read prohibited books.

Art. II.   *Interpretation*

1. *Means of interpretation.* Like all other Church laws,
the laws concerning the prohibition of books must be understood according to the *meaning proper to the words used*, tak-

---

8.   Canon 1399, n. 5.

9.   St. Alphonsus, *Theol. Mor.*, VII, nn. 283 and 291.

10.   Canon 1401.

11.   Canon 1400.

12.   Canon 1402.

13.   Cf. *infra*, p. 214.

14.   *Infra*, p. 193 ff.

ing into consideration their text and context. If the sense of the law still remains doubtful, then recourse must be had to parallel passages in the Code, if there be any, to the end and circumstances of the law and to the mind of the legislator.[15] Moreover, much light is thrown over the present laws by a study of previous legislation on this subject and its interpretation by approved authors, especially the const. *Officiorum ac munerum* of Leo XIII of January 25, 1897.[16] For the Code itself instructs us that the canons which reproduce the old law in its entirety, are to be judged according to the authority of the old law, and therefore, from the received interpretations of approved authors. The canons which agree only in part with the old law, inasfar as they agree they are to be interpreted according to the old law; inasfar as they differ, they are to be interpreted according to their new wording. In doubt as to whether a prescription of the Canons differs from the old law, one must adhere to the old law.[17]

2. *Method of Interpretation.* If the wording of a law should be such that it could be limited to a certain number of cases (*strict* interpretation) or it could be applied to a number of other cases (*wide* interpretation), which interpretation is to be followed?

A) The *faculties*[18] to grant permission to read and keep forbidden books as well as the *permission*[19] itself permit of *wide* interpretation. The reason is that in both cases there is question of a privilege *praeter jus*, a favor, and, according to the general principle, *odia restringi et favores convenit ampliari*,[20] it admits of wide interpretation.[21]

B) All other prescriptions on prohibition of books, i. e., the *prohibitions* themselves and the *penalties* against their violators, are to be interpreted *strictly*. No doubt has ever existed as to the strict interpretation of the penalties sanc-

---

15. Can. 18.
16. *Fontes*, n. 632.
17. Can. 6, n. 2, n. 3, n. 4.
18. Can. 66, 68 compared with can. 50.
19. Cann. 68 and 50.
20. *Reg. Jur.* 15 in VI°; Cann. 19, 68. 50.
21. De Meester, *Compendium*, III, n. 1339, 2, β and n. 1380, 1, a; Vermeersch-Creusen, *Ep.* II, n. 736.

tioning these laws since the principle in law is and has always been that laws inflicting penalties should be interpreted favorably to the offender, as far as their wording allows.[22] Nevertheless, in the past, even after the publication of the constitution *Officiorum ac munerum*, a few authors contended that the prohibitions themselves were to be interpreted widely.[23] Now it is generally[24] held that all the legislation of the Church on forbidden books (excepting faculties to permit reading and keeping forbidden books, and the permission itself), is to be interpreted strictly, i. e., it must be applied only to those cases clearly contained in the words of the law, and must not be extended to any others. For, according to canon 19 of the Code, laws restricting the free exercise of one's rights, must be interpreted strictly.[25]

Art. III. *Terms defined and explained*

Book *(Liber)*, **Booklet** *(Libellus)*, **Daily Newspaper and Periodical Publication** *(Publicatio diaria, periodica)*.

I. In general, these words must be understood according to the every-day meaning which most people attach to them.[26] Accordingly:

1. By a **book** we mean a volume of considerable *size* and having a certain *unity* of subject, or, at least, of tendency.

---

22. Cann. **19, 2219**; cf. also *Reg. Jur.*, **49**, in VI°; *Corpus Juris Civilis*, Dig. L. **17, 155, 2**; Schmalzgrueber, *Jus Ecclesiasticum Un.*, tom. V, pars. I, tit. VII, n. 55.

23. Suarez, *De Fide Divina*, Disp. **20**, sect. **2**, n. **10**; Van Coillie, *Commentarius*, n. 9, c. However, the great majority of canonists stood for the strict interpretation of the prohibitory laws. Cf. Wernz, *Jus Decretal.*, III, n. 110, IV; Vermeersch, *De Prohibitione et Censura Librorum*, p. 34.

24. De Meester, *o. c.*, III, n. 1339, 2, γ; Ciccognani, *Commentarium ad librum I Codicis*, p. 132; Genicot-Salsmans, *Institutiones Theologiae Moralis*, I, n. 457.

25. Prudence recommends that Catholics should not confine themselves to the minimum obligation. They should go a step further and abstain from all literature which is in any degree dangerous to their souls.

26. Lugo, *De Virt. Fid. Div.*, disp. 21, sect. 2, n. 38.

Authors generally accept the figures of Schmalzgrueber[27] as to the *size* of a book, namely, 10 folio pages or 160 pages in *octavo* (the average book-page) or 320 pages in 16mo. This element must not be judged mathematically but morally[28] and together with the second element of unity.

Some *unity* of subject, or, at least, of tendency, is necessary. Thus, a volume of considerable size which is entirely given to theology or to different problems of science is a book. But a Sunday newspaper which may have more pages than an ordinary book is not a book because of the diversity of subjects treated.

For the lack of either size or unity the following publications are excluded[29] from the category of *books:*

1 — Booklets and pamphlets, even though bound together into a large volume, unless, in the latter case, they have the unity required.
2 — Small magazines.
3 — Newspapers.
4 — Leaflets.
5 — Calendars.
6 — Sermons, and letters published separately. When they are bound together into a volume if they have the size and unity required, they are considered books.

Manuscripts, as well as any other non-printed writings,[30] having the size and unity of a book, are, strictly speaking, books. However, they are not commonly called books. Besides, works which are not published do not come under the prohibition of the Church.[31]

2. By a **booklet** is meant a little work which does not reach the size of a book and yet consists of a number of pages. The average pamphlet is a booklet.

---

27. *O. et l. c.*, n. 55. Cf. also Vermeersch-Creusen, *Ep.*, II, n. 723; De Meester, *o. c.*, III, n. 1339, 3, a; Augustine, *A Commentary*, VI, p. 431; Ayrainhac, *Administrative Legisl.*, p. 275.

28. Lugo, *l. c.*

29. De Meester, *l. c.*; Vermeersch-Creusen, *l. c.*

30. Produced by typewriting, polygraph, lithography, mimeograph, photography, or any other process.

31. *Infra*, p. 80 ff.

3. By a **daily newspaper** is meant a publication issued every day or nearly so, containing principally the news of the day, and, often, articles on various topics, including religion. It lacks usually both the size and unity required to make up a book.

4. By a **periodical publication** (review, magazine, etc.) or simply a **periodical** is meant a brochure which is issued weekly, monthly, quarterly, or at other different intervals. Some periodicals have reached the size and have the unity which ordinarily go to make up a book. Yet they are not called books.[32]

II. In the Church legislation on books contained in Cann. 1384-1405, the word *liber* (book) refers to *all* kinds of *writings* which are *published*, whether they are books, strictly so-called, or not, unless the opposite is evident. For Can. 1384, §2, states:

Quae sub hoc titulo de libris praescribuntur, publicationibus diariis, periodicis et aliis editis scriptis quibuslibet applicentur, nisi aliud constet.[33]

Much controversy had existed before the *Officiorum ac munerum* as to how far the laws on prohibition and censorship of books applied to works which were not books.[34] The controversy diminished, to a certain extent, after the Leonine constitution became known, for, in paragraph 21, it explicitly forbade *diaria, folia et libelli periodici, qui religionem aut bonos mores data opera impetunt.* But authors still had reason to differ as to whether all other laws on prohibition of books referred also to minor publications.[35] The Code has taken away all grounds for controversy on this point.

---

32.   De Meester, *Compendium,* III, n. 1339, 3, b, c; Boudinhon, *La Nouvelle Legislation de l'Index,* p. 188. More will be said of this on page 223 f.

33.   De Meester, *o. c.,* III, n. 1339, 2; Vermeersch-Creusen, *Ep.,* II, n. 722; Boudinhon, *o. c.,* p. 184 ff.; Cocchi, *o. c.,* VI, n. 59, b; Ayrinhac, *o. c.,* p. 274 f.

34.   Suarez, *De Fid. Theol.,* disput. XX, sect. II, nn. 9-10; Lugo, *De Virt. Fid. Div.,* disput. XXI, sect. II, n. 35; Reiffestuel, *Jus. Can. Un.,* lib. V, tit. VII, n. 39; Schmalzgrueber, *Jus Eccl. Un.,* tom. V, par. I, tit. VII, n. 30; Arndt, *De Libris Prohibit,* n. 78.

35.   Van Coïllie, *Commentarius,* nn. 13-14; Wernz, *Jus Decretal.,* III, p. 119, note 75; Moureau, *La Nouvelle Legislation de l'Index,* p. 12;

A) By the words *quae sub hoc titulo*, the legislator evidently restricts this wide application of the term *liber* only to title XXIII of Book III of the Code which consists of Cann. 1384-1405. Therefore, in all other parts of the Code, and particularly in Can. 2318, which refers to the punishments inflicted against violators of the ecclesiastical book legislation, *liber* must be taken in its strict sense as explained above.[36]

B) The phrase *editis scriptis quibuslibet* makes it clear that whatever is legislated in Cann. 1384-1405 on *books* applies equally to *all writings whatever*, provided they are *edited*, i. e., published, put on sale for the general public, accessible to all, offered for public circulation.[37] Usually a work is published by means of *printing*.[38] When the typewriter, lithography, polygraph, mimeograph, photography, hand-writing or any other process is used to multiply the copies of a work, the work is usually intended not for the general public, but for a restricted number of persons, for a private group, such

---

Hurley, *A Commentary on the Present Index Legislation*, p. 147 ff.; Pennacchi, *In Constitutionem Apostolicam Officiorum ac Munerum Brevis Commentatio*, p. 45; Gennari, "Circa la nuova disciplina sulla proibizione e sulla censura dei libri", *Il Monitore Ecclesiastico*, X (Part I, 1897), p. 80 f.

36. Page 78 f. Cf. also De Meester, *o. c.*, III, n. 1339, 2.

37. De Meester, *l. c.*; Vermeersch-Creusen, *Ep.*, II, n. 722; Cocchi, *o. c.*, VI, n. 59, b α; Augustine, *o. c.*, VI, 431; Ayrinhac, *o. c.*, p. 275. A motion picture film is not considered as a book. However, if it contains writing, that writing can be said to be published and therefore comes under the scope of the Church's prohibition of books. If the writing, then, offends against any of the laws expressed in can. 1399, it is forbidden by the positive law of the Church. However, a film is not forbidden merely because it presents in pictures and verbal explanations the matter contained in a book forbidden by the Church, e. g., *Les Miserables* of Victor Hugo, *Alphonse de Jocelyn* of Lamartine. Such films do not share the prohibition of the works in question, for they are distinct from the work prohibited. They may be forbidden if the matter for which the original works were forbidden is *written* on the film. In any case, the natural law must be considered which forbids anything in any form which is dangerous to one's soul. Cf. "Indice e Cinematografo", *Perfice Munus!*, II (1927), 420.

38. That *printing* is not identical with *publishing* is clearly brought out by can. 1386, §2, for, there, the "*Ordinarius loci in quo libri vel imagines publici* JURIS FIANT" is distinguished from the "*Ordinarius loci in quo* IMPRIMANTUR."

as the pupils of a professor, the members of a family, etc. In this case the writing is not considered *published* and, therefore, does not come under the present book legislation.[39] The same is true of the original copy or the *manuscript*, strictly so called. Nevertheless, if by any of the above means a work is made accessible to all promiscuously, then that work, even though not printed, is considered published.[40]

For the same reason, the mere remark in the title, *For Private Circulation Only*, or *Privately Printed* or that it is *Printed as Manuscript*, "does not save a publication which actually sells like other books, or is perhaps distributed widely through other channels outside of the regular book trade." [41]

Therefore, in cann. 1384-1405, under the term *liber* or *book*[42] all *publications* of *any size*,[43] with or without unity, are included.

C) *Nisi aliud constet.*

The word *liber* does not admit the wide application just mentioned, whenever there is a clear indication to the contrary. Thus, in can. 1399, n. 5, by mentioning explicitly *libri ac libelli* the legislator clearly excludes forms of publication smaller than *libelli*.[44] But these exceptions to the first part of can. 1384, 2, must be proven, in order to destroy the presumption of law.[45]

---

39. De Meester, *o. c.*, III, n. 1339, 2; Vermeersch-Creusen, *Ep.*, II, n. 722; Cocchi, *o. c.*, VI, n. 59, c, a; Ferreres, *Institutiones Canonicae*, II, p. 149; Genicot-Salsmans, *Inst. Theol. Mor.*, I, n. 454; Ayrinhac, *o. c.*, p. 275; Betten, *The Roman Index*, p. 42, n. 6. Vermeersch rightly remarks that this remains true even though accidentally some others come to have copies.

40. The natural law, however, is concerned with all writings, even though *not published*, and forbids all those which are dangerous. Cf. supra, pag. 3; De Meester, *l. c.*

41. Betten, *l. c.*

42. Cf. Decree of the S. C. of the Holy Office, Nov. 5, 1920 — *A A S*, XII (1920), 595—for an application of this rule in the case of all publications of the Young Men's Christian Association.

43. This includes leaflets of even one small page. Therefore, Ferreres, *Institutiones*, II, p. 149 (n. 381, C), is not accurate, though he is correct on p. 157, 2.

44. De Meester, *Compendium*, III, n. 1339, 2; Vermeersch-Creusen, *Ep.*, II, n. 722.

45. Vermeersch-Creusen, *l. c.*

CHAPTER II

AUTHOR OF THE PROHIBITION OF BOOKS [1]

The Church has always recognized that, while the Supreme Pontiff and the General Council have the power to forbid books for the whole Church and every part of it, the Bishops individually or at particular councils, have the same power for their own dioceses. The Universities and the inquisitors of dioceses exercised similar powers from the fifteenth and the sixteenth centuries respectively. In the sixteenth century the Pope gave power to forbid books for the whole Church to the Universal Roman Inquisition or the Holy Office and for Rome to the Cardinal Vicar and the Master of the Sacred Palace. In 1571 the Congregation of the Index was established with universal power concerning book legislation.

These were the bearers of authority in the matter of prohibition of books almost up to the time of the Code.[2] The Code deals exclusively with the author of book prohibitions in Cann. 1395 and 247 §4. No mention is made of Universities[3] or Inquisitors having power to forbid books. The Congregation of the Index has ceased to exist and its work is entrusted to the Holy Office.[4] The Abbot of an independent

---

1. Arndt, *De Libris Prohibit.*, n. 163; Bouix, *Tract. de Curia Rom.*, p. 442 ff.; Bargilliat, *Praelectiones Juris Canonici*, I, p. 441; Wernz, *Jus Decretal.*, III, n. 105; Heymans, *De Eccl. Libr... Prohib.*, p. 107 ff.; Pennacchi, *In Const. Apost. Offic. ac muner.*, p. 185 ff.; Gennari, "Circa la nuova disciplina sulla proibizione e sulla censura dei libri", *Il Mon. Eccl.*, X (PartI - 1897), 85.

2. For a more detailed history on this point, see supra, pag. 26 ff.

3. In Can. 1397, §1 the Rectors of Catholic Universities are mentioned among those who have a special duty to *denounce* evil books to the Apostolic See.

4. Benedict XV, motu proprio *Alloquentes*, Mar. 25, 1927 (*A A S*, IX [1917], 167).

monastery, the Superior General and, in some cases, other major superiors of a clerical exempt religious organization now have power to forbid books to their subjects. This was not so before the Code. But, aside from these few changes, the main principle of old has remained true, — that the right and the duty of forbidding books for a just cause rests upon the Supreme Ecclesiastical Authority for the entire Church and upon the particular Councils and the local Ordinaries for their subjects only.

Can. 1395, §1. **Ius et officium libros ex iusta causa prohibendi competit non solum supremae auctoritati ecclesiasticae pro universa Ecclesia, sed pro suis subditis Conciliis quoque particularibus et locorum Ordinariis.**[5]

§2. **Ab hac prohibitione datur ad Sanctam Sedem recursus, non tamen in suspensivo.**[6]

§3. **Etiam Abbas monasterii sui iuris et supremus religionis clericalis exemptae Moderator, cum suo Capitulo vel Consilio, potest libros ex iusta causa suis subditis prohibere; idemque, si periculum sit in mora, possunt alii Superiores maiores cum proprio Consilio, ea tamen lege ut rem quantocius deferant ad supremum Moderatorem.**

I. *The right and the duty of forbidding books for a just cause for the entire Church belongs to the Supreme Ecclesiastical Authority.*[7]

Supreme Ecclesiastical Authority is found in the Roman

---

5. Clement XII, apost. letter *Compertum*, Aug. 24, 1734, dub. XVI (*Fontes*, n. 296); apost. letter *Concredita nobis*, May 13, 1739 (*Fontes*, n. 300); Benedict XIV, const. *Omnium sollicitudinum*, Sept. 12, 1744, §14, dub. XVI, §40 (*Fontes*, n. 348); Gregory XVI, encycl. *Mirari vos*, Aug. 15, 1832 (*Fontes*, n. 485); Leo XIII, const. *Officiorum ac munerum*, Jan. 25, 1897, n. 29 (*Fontes*, n. 632); Pius X, alloc. *Accogliamo*, Apr. 15, 1907 (*Fontes*, n. 678); encycl. *Pascendi*, Sept. 8, 1907 (*Fontes*, n. 680); motu proprio *Sacrorum Antistitum*, Sept. 1, 1910, n. III (*Fontes*, n. 689); encycl. of the S. C. of the Index, Aug. 24, 1864 (*ASS*, XXVII [1895], 702 f.)

6. Encycl. of the S. C. of the Index, Aug. 24, 1864 (*ASS*, XXVII [1895], 702 f.)

7. Can. 1395, §1. The existence of this right and duty of the Church was shown in Chapter II of Part I of this Dissertation.

Pontiff[8] and in the Oecumenical or General Council[9] presided over by the Pope or his representative. The Roman Pontiff, as a rule, exercises this supreme authority through the various departments of the Roman Curia. In everything that concerns the Church's control of literature he has given supreme authority to the Congregation of the Holy Office.[10] Moreover, general laws have been set down in the Code of Canon Law. Finally, on rare occasions and for very serious reasons the Pope proscribes books personally. In such cases he acts either by means of an Apostolic Letter in the form of a Bull, a Brief, an ·Encyclical, etc.[11] or even by means of a decree of the Holy Office as was done in the case of the daily paper *Action Française.*[12]

---

8.   Can. 218.

9.   Can 228, §1.

10.   Can. 247, §4. No other Congregation has universal power to forbid books, not even the Congregation for the Propagation of the Faith, as appears from can. 252 §4, the allocution *Amplissimum Collegium* of Benedict XV, Mar. 22, 1917 and the motu proprio, *Alloquentes,* of Mar. 25, 1917 (*Fontes,* nn. 709 and 710). However, it is still possible, and occasionally it does happen, that other Congregations take action against books dealing with questions which belong to their province. Thus the Congregation of Sacred Rites has power to watch over the liturgical books of the Latin Church, to examine them, to correct them and, whenever there is no question of dogmas or morals, to forbid them. This seems true in view of the fact that the competence of the Congregation of Sacred Rites (can. 253) now is identical with that which it had before the Code, in accordance with the Constitution *Sapienti Consilio* of Pius X, 29 Jun. 1908, I, n. 8 (*Fontes,* n. 682). The official interpretation of that competence, as given in *Normae Peculiares,* Cap. VII, Art. VIII, n. 4, was that the Cong. of S. Rites could even forbid liturgical books. Cf. Vermeersch-Creusen, *Ep.,* II, n. 734, 1; Vermeersch, *De Proh. et Cens. Libr.,* p. 49-50; De Meester, *Compendium,* II, p. 10 and 87, n. 3; Ayrinhac, *o. c.,* p. 288.

11.   De Meester, *o. c.,* III, n. 1385, 2, a.

12.   Decree of the S. C. of the Holy Office, Dec. 29, 1926 (*A A S,* XVIII [1926], 529) ; letter of Pius XI to Card. Andrieu, Archbishop of Bourdeaux (*A A S,* XIX [1927], 5). The daily paper *Action Française* is not condemned there by the Holy Office with the approval of the Supreme Pontiff, but by the Pope himself. This is clear from the words of the decree: "SS*mus* D. N. *damnationem... extendit ad praedictum diarium L'Action Française prout in praesens editur";* from the words of the letter to Card. Andrieu: *ce sont ces révélations qui... Nous font*

The Supreme Ecclesiastical Authority can legislate not only for the Church as a whole but for any part of it.[13]

II. *Local Ordinaries and Particular Councils have the right and duty to forbid books for a just cause to their subjects.*[14]

1. Under the term "Local Ordinaries" come, each one for his own territory: Residential Bishops, Abbots and Prelates *nullius* and their Vicars General, Administrators of vacant dioceses, Vicars and Prefects Apostolic, and those who, in the absence of the aforesaid, take the government in the *interim* according to the prescription of law or approved constitutions, such as the Chapter of canons or, as in the United States, the Diocesan Consultors, the Vicar Capitular, the Pro-vicar and Pro-prefect Apostolic.[15] The Vicar General as a rule should leave this matter to the Bishop.[16] With the exception of Vicars General, the local Ordinaries can attach punishment to their regulations prohibiting books.[17]

2. They may act individually in this matter without consulting any person or at a Council, national, provincial or diocesan.[18]

3. What can local Ordinaries or particular Councils forbid? They can forbid[19] not only *books*, in the strict sense, but

---

proscrire le journal l'Action Française, as well as from the declaration of Pope Pius XI himself contained in *A A S,* XIX (1927), 185: "*Cum Summus ipse Pontifex memoratum Commentarium Indici librorum prohibitorum inseruerit... tam solemni documento ab ipsa Sanctitate Sua proscriptum.*" Cf. also *Il Mon. Eccl.,* XXXIX (1927), 129; Vermeersch-Creusen, *Ep.,* II (ed. 1930), n. 736.

13. Can. 218, § 2.

14. Can. 1395, §1. Cf. also Gregory XVI, Constitution *Mirari vos,* Aug. 15, 1832 (*Fontes,* n. 485); Pius X, allocution *Accogliamo,* Apr. 15, 1907 (*Fontes,* n. 678); encycl. *Pascendi,* Sept. 8, 1907 (*Fontes,* n. 680), and motu proprio *Sacrorum Antistitum,* Sept. 1, 1910 (*Fontes,* n. 689).

15. Can. 198. Cf. also Cann. 427, 429, 431; *A A S,* XII (1920), 120; Vermeersch-Creusen, *Ep.,* I, n. 279.

16. Boudinhon, *La Nouvelle Legislation de l'Index,* p. 79.

17. Can. 2220, §§ 1 and 2.

18. Can. 1395, § 1.

19. By law or decree. Cf. Blat, *Commentarium Textus Codicis Juris Canonici,* III, n. 284.

all kinds of publications[20] which they judge harmful[21] to their subjects among whom they are spread, regardless of the place of publication or the diocese or the standing of the author. A Bishop can forbid even a book which has been approved in another place and carries the *Imprimatur* of some other Ordinary.[22] Pius X, in his great encyclical *Pascendi*[23] gives as reasons for the possible occurrence of such a case that the *Imprimatur* might be spurious, or that it might have been given through carelessness or excessive generosity or because of too much trust in the author. Moreover, a book considered harmless in one place because of its indifferent character, might be dangerous in another place under different circumstances. If great care is taken in the examination of books before the granting of the *Imprimatur*, the occurrence of such a strange and unpleasant case will be generally avoided. On the other hand, a Bishop will be justified in taking this extreme measure only when he has grave and compelling reasons.[24]

A work already forbidden by the Holy See cannot be proscribed by the Bishop.[25] However, he can and, in some cases, must urge his people to heed the condemnation made by the Holy See.

4. The Ordinaries must always have a *just reason* for prohibiting a work. According to Blat,[26] a just reason exists when directly or indirectly the reading of the work might produce harm. They cannot forbid a book merely for the reason that it contains a proposition which they consider dubious but which neither has been condemned by the Church nor approaches a condemned proposition.[27] However, if, due

---

20. Can. 1382, §2. This includes, therefore, an individual newspaper. Cf. Moureau, *La Nouvelle Legisl. de l'Index*, p. 71, n. 3.

21. Blat, *l. c.*

22. De Meester, *o. c.*, III, n. 1354, 2, a; Ferreres, *Casus Conscientiae*, I, n. 613 ff. Cf. also *Regula Ind.*, X; Arndt, *De Libr. Prohibit.*, n. 163, 3, b.

23. Sept. 8, 1907, §44, III (*Fontes*, n. 680).

24. De Meester, *l. c.*; Arndt, *l. c.*

25. Wernz, *Jus Decretal.*, III, n. 111 (29), note 82.

26. *O. c.*, III, n. 284.

27. Benedict XIV, Const. *Sollicita ac provida*, July 9, 1753, §17 (*Fontes*, n. 426). Here Benedict XIV reminds those who are to pass

to peculiar circumstances, the spread of this proposition or doctrine were to constitute a danger for that particular locality, then the Ordinary would be justified in forbidding such a work[28] even with penalties.[29] In doubtful cases the book should be sent to the Holy Office.[30]

5. The decree of a Bishop or Council prohibiting certain works binds *only the subjects* of that Bishop or Council, i.e., those who have domicile or quasi domicile in their territory as long as they actually reside there.[31] If a book is forbidden through a *personal decree or precept*, the person or persons affected are bound by it even outside of their place of domicile or quasi-domicile.[31a] *Peregrini* are not bound by local decrees prohibiting books.[32] *Vagi* are bound by all laws of the place where they happen to be.[33]

Regulars are not bound by particular prohibitions of books issued by the Ordinary of the place wherein they are located. The reason is that, according to the general principle on exemption laid down in the Code of Canon Law, *regulars are exempt from the jurisdiction of the local Ordinary in all things, except those expressly stated by law.*[34] Exemption therefore is the rule. Exception to this rule is not presumed but must be proved.[35] But, nowhere does the Code state that regulars are not exempt in the matter of prohibition of books.

---

judgment on a book that their mind must be free from every prejudice. They must be guided not by their attachment to and the interests of their country, their race, the school wherein they were trained, and the institute to which they belong, but by the dogmas of the Church, and by the common teaching of Catholics, as contained in the decrees of the general councils, the Constitutions of the Roman Pontiffs, and the traditions of the Fathers.

28. De Meester, *o. c.*, III, n. 1355, 4 and note 8; Pennacchi, *In Const. Apost. Offic. ac muner.*, p. 190; Arndt, *De Libr. Prohibit.*, p. 213.

29. Can. 2222.

30. Can. 1397, §5.

31. Can. 13, §2.

31a. Cann. 14, §1, 24; A Coronata, *Inst. Jur. Can.*, II, p. 332.

32. Cann. 91, 14, 24. Cf. also De Meester, *Compendium*, III, n. 1354, 2, d.

33. Cann. 91, 14, §2.

34. Can. 615.

35. Vermeersch-Creusen, *Ep.*, I, n. 717; II, n. 731.

Moreover their exemption is a privilege[36] and, in doubt, it must be interpreted widely.[37] Therefore the particular enactments of local Ordinaries on the matter of prohibition of books do not bind the regulars residing in their territory, as long as there is no danger of scandal.[38]

6. Bishops should make use of this power. When the occasion presents itself and the Ordinary prudently judges

---

36. Can. 615 is one of many canons grouped under the title: Caput II. *De Privilegiis*.

37. Cann. 68, 50.

38. This is *now* the common opinion of canonists and theologians. It is held by Vermeersch-Creusen, *Ep.*, I, n. 717 and II, n. 731; De Meester, *o. c.*, III, n. 1354, 2, c; Noldin, *Summa Theol. Moralis*, II, n. 704, 2, b; Boudinhon, *La Nouvelle Legisl. de l'Index*, p. 222 f.; Genicot-Salsmans, *Institutiones Theol. Moralis*, I, n. 451; Blat, *Commentarium Textus C. J. C.*, III, n. 284; Ayrinhac, *Administrative Legisl.*, p. 289; Woywod, *A Practical Commentary on the Code of Canon Law*, II, 128; Melo, *De Exemptione Regularium*, p. 70 ff. Father Augustine, *o. c.*, VI, 455, differs somewhat. He holds that exempt religious are bound by particular or local enactments on prohibition of books, if these are issued by a provincial or plenary council. His reasons are insufficient. Canon 291, §2, which legislates about the force of the decrees of provincial and plenary councils in the diocese of each Bishop, says nothing about regulars, who are given exemption in Can. 615. Before the publication of the Code authors were divided almost evenly on this matter. A group asserted that exempt regulars were bound by the episcopal prohibitions of books. Among these were: Pennacchi, *In Const. Apost. Officiorum ac numerum Commentarium*, p. 191 ff.; Wernz, *Jus Decretal.*, III, n. 108 (note 38) and n. 111 (note 82); Hurley, *Index Legislation*, p. 187 ff.; and others. The other group stated that the exemption of regulars applied also to the book legislation of Bishops. Among these we find Reiffenstuel, *Jus Canonicum Universum*, lib. I, tit. 31, n. 143 f. (by implication); Vermeersch, *De Prohibitione et Censura Librorum*, p. 50 ff.; Moureau, *o. c*, pp. 15-16; Van Coillie, *Commentarium*, p. 11 ff. and 27; and others. The strongest argument of the first group (Pennacchi, Wernz, etc.) was the wording of n. 29 of Leo XIII's *Officiorum ac munerum*. Therein the Ordinaries are empowered to act against harmful books, also "*tamquam Delegati Sedis Apostolicae*". According to what Wernz (III, n. 111, note 82) calls "melior interpretatio" such delegated papal jurisdiction extended also to exempt regulars. The present law has taken away that phrase "*etiam tamquam Delegati Sedis Apostolicae*". Thus the opinion based on it is no more justified. However, it is still held by Pejska, *Jus Canonicum Religiosorum*, p. 174.

that a book, which has a large circulation[39] among his people, is doing much harm, he should take action at once.[40] It is not necessary that he inform the press of his condemnation. If the object intended can be attained just as well or better by sending out a confidential notice to his clergy,[41] this course should be followed. Then his clergy will communicate the matter to his people at the time and in the manner best suited for the purpose.

7. Pastors or faculties of Colleges or universities have no jurisdiction to forbid books, because they lack jurisdiction in the external forum. They may however, and at times, they ought to point out to those under them the kind of literature which is to be shunned. A great service would be rendered to the Church if Catholic professors wrote articles to show the harmful character of evil writings, to encourage the reading and give lists of good books.[42]

NOTE

The prohibitions of local Ordinaries and Councils admit of recourse to the Holy See but without suspensive effects.[43] Therefore, the prohibitory enactment binds, even though recourse has been made to the Holy See. The proper department to send this recourse is the Holy Office, to which, according to canon 247, §4, is entrusted all matter concerning the examination and prohibition of books.

It is peculiar that the second paragraph of Canon 1395 is placed immediately after the paragraph dealing with episcopal or conciliar decrees and just before the one dealing with

---

39. A work which is not widespread in the diocese cannot be forbidden by the Bishop. He may denounce it to the Holy See. Cf. Bucceroni, *Institutiones Theologiae Moralis*, II, n. 1301.

40. S. C. of the Index., Aug. 24, 1864. (*Collect.* I, n. 1261); Instruction of the S. C. of the Holy Office, May 3, 1927, (*A A S*, XIX [1927], 186); Woywod, *o. c.*, II, 128.

41. Pius X, Const. *Pascendi*, September 8, 1907, §44, III (*Fontes*, n. 680).

42. Wernz, *o. c.*, III, n. 107; Bouix, *Tract. de Curia Rom.*, p. 441.

43. Can. 1395 §2. Cf. also De Meester, *o. c.*, III, n. 1354, 2, e (note 4); Blat, *o. c.*, III, n. 284; Boudinhon, *La Nouv. Legisl. de l'Index*, p. 80; Cocchi, *o. c.*, n. 65.

similar decrees on the part of religious Superiors. Does this mean that recourse to the Holy See is allowed against the decrees of local Ordinaries and Councils and not against the decrees of religious Superiors? That conclusion would seem evident from the place which the paragraph on recourse holds. However, most canonists rightly extend the possibility of recourse to the paragraph dealing with the powers of religious Superiors.[44] For recourse to the Holy See is very large and open practically to everybody, as Canon 1569 would seem to indicate. It would appear unfair, therefore, to refuse this privilege to an author, religious or lay, whose book is forbidden by a religious Ordinary. As a rule, there is little likelihood that the author of a book prohibited by a religious Superior will be a religious of his order, because the Superior would not have authorized the publication by his subject of an objectionable book. A possible case, then, is that the religious Ordinary should forbid a work written by a religious of another order or congregation, or by a secular priest, or by a layman. Now there seems to be no special reason why these people should be deprived of the power of taking recourse to the Holy See. Moreover, Canon 20 states that where nothing is expressly said about a certain thing in law, if there is no question of applying punishments, one should take his norm from laws enacted for similar circumstances; from the general principles of law; from the practice of the Roman Court; from the constant and common opinion of doctors. In this case, then, one may take for the norm §2 of Canon 1395 which, though apparently meant only for §1 of the same canon, may be applied also to §3, due to the similarity of the powers of religious Superiors in §3 with those of local Ordinaries and Councils in §1. Therefore, recourse to the Holy See against prohibitory decrees of religious Superiors is permissible. The Holy Office is the proper Congregation to which this recourse must be had, and not the S. Congregation of Religious since this does not handle matters which are of the province of the Holy Office.[45]

---

44. Cocchi, *l. c.*; Vermeersch-Creusen, *Ep.*, II, n. 731; Boudinhon, *o. c.*, p. 80 f.

45. Boudinhon, *l. c.*

III. *The Abbots of independent monasteries and the Superiors General of exempt clerical religious orders or congregations may, with the aid of their chapter or of their consultors and for a just cause, forbid books to their subjects. If delay should be dangerous, other major Superiors (e. g., Provincials) may, with their counsellors, exercise the same power, but under condition that they refer the matter as soon as possible to the Superior General.*[46]

Before the publication of the Code, it was generally admitted that no religious Superior, not even the General of an exempt clerical religious order, had any jurisdiction to make laws or decrees prohibiting books to his subjects. It was granted that they could forbid books to this or that religious through the dominative power they have over them. But it was denied that any religious Superior had any power to issue a juridical and authentic prohibition such as could be issued by the Pope or the Bishops.[47]   Now, as Vermeersch expresses it,[48] "by an entirely new disposition, since the *causae fidei* are reserved to the local Ordinaries, the Superiors of an exempt clerical religious organization are called to share ecclesiastical jurisdiction even in the matter of prohibition of books. Before, these same could, by reason of their dominative power forbid, not a book but harmful reading to certain individuals."

There still remains a difference between the prohibitions of local Ordinaries and those of religious Superiors. For, while the former are not obliged to any formality, the latter, in order to act validly, must consult the chapter or their consultors.[49]

---

46.   Can. 1395, §3.

47.   Wernz, *Jus Decretal.*, III, n. 108; Pennacchi, *In Const. Apost. Offic. ac muner.*, p. 196.

48.   Vermeersch-Creusen, *Ep.*, II, n. 731, 3. Cf. also Woywod, *A Practical Commentary*, II, p. 128; Augustine, *A Commentary*, VI, p. 456 f.; Ayrinhac, *Administr. Legisl.*, p. 289.

49.   Can. 1395, §3; can. 105. Cf. Cappello, *Summa Juris Canonici*, II, p. 373; Vermeersch-Creusen, *Ep.*, I, n. 197 bis, 2. The consent of the chapter or of the consultors does not seem necessary for validity. Cf., however, Boudinhon, *o. c.*, p. 80; A Coronata, *Inst. Jur. Can.*, II, p. 333; Augustine, *o. c.* VI, p. 456 f.

It goes without saying that "all Superiors, even in a female institution, may in a particular case forbid the reading of a certain book to one of the religious; such an act does not require ecclesiastical jurisdiction but only domestic authority".[50]

---

50. Ayrinhac, *l. c.*

CHAPTER III

DENUNCIATION OF BAD BOOKS[1]

In the preceding chapter, the power to prohibit books proper to the Supreme Pontiff, the local Ordinaries, Councils and religious Superiors was explained in the terms of the Code of Canon Law. However, it is not expected that these persons keep personally in touch with all current literature. Many writings which are well known among the people may escape their attention.[2] Therefore, the Church in Can. 1397 asks all the faithful, particularly clerics, persons constituted in authority or distinguished for their learning, to denounce to the local Ordinary or to the Holy See books which they consider dangerous. After all, bad literature constitutes a grave danger to the individual as well as to society. Therefore, the law of charity and self preservation demands that every man should strive to prevent its spread as far as he can.[3]

This general obligation of denouncing books was never embodied into written law until the time of Leo XIII[4] who placed it in his constitution *Officiorum ac munerum* of Jan. 25, 1897.[5] Paragraphs 27, 28 and part of 29 are almost identical with the present law as found in the Code. The question as to who is to make the denunciation and how it is to be made will be answered in this chapter by presenting and explaining in order the five paragraphs of Canon 1397.

---

1. De Meester, III, *Compendium*, n. 1355; Boudinhon, *La Nouv. Legisl. de l'Index*, p. 212 ff.; Hurley, *Index Legisl.*, p. 175 ff.; Cocchi, *Commentarium C. J. C.*, VI, n. 66; Pennacchi, *In Const. Apost. Offic. ac muner.*, p. 180 ff.; Augustine, *A Commentary*, VI, p. 460 ff.; Blat, *Commentar. Textus C. J. C.*, III, n. 286; Ayrinhac, *Administr. Legisl.*, p. 289.

2. Pennacchi, *l. c.*

3. Ayrinhac, p. 289.

4. Boudinhon, *o. c.*, p. 212 ff.

5. *Fontes*, n. 632.

Persons who are obliged to denounce bad books.

Can. 1397, §1.   **Omnium fidelium est, maxime clericorum et in dignitate ecclesiastica constitutorum eorumque qui doctrina praecellant, libros quos perniciosos judicaverint, ad locorum Ordinarios aut ad Apostolicam Sedem deferre; id autem peculiari titulo pertinet ad Legatos Sanctae Sedis, locorum Ordinarios atque Rectores Universitatum catholicarum.**[6]

Here the legislator distinguishes between two classes of people who should denounce bad books, the faithful who are bound by the general law of charity and those others who are bound by reason of their office. Among the faithful, particular mention is made of clerics, especially of those constituted in ecclesiastical authority, and those who excel in learning. All these are bound to denounce to their local Ordinaries or to the Holy See those books which they judge dangerous. Their obligation is only one of charity.[7] The Legates of the Holy See, local Ordinaries and Rectors of Catholic Universities have a special obligation to denounce bad books by reason of their office. For the Legates are sent to a certain locality that they may watch over the conditions of the Church there and inform the Supreme Pontiff about them.[8] Local Ordinaries are placed in their respective territory to watch over their flock and defend and guard sound doctrine.[9] The Rectors of Catholic Universities are entrusted with the duty of providing for their students the best educational training the Church offers. They should, therefore, be

---

6.   Leo XIII, Const. *Officiorum ac munerum,* Jan. 25, 1897, n. 27 (*Fontes,* n. 632); Pius X, Allocut. *Accogliamo,* Apr. 15, 1907 (*Fontes,* n. 678); Encycl. *Pascendi,* Sept. 8, 1907 (*Fontes,* n. 680); motu proprio *Sacrorum Antistitum,* Sept. 1, 1910, III (*Fontes,* n. 689).

7.   Gennari, "Circa la nuova disciplina", *Il. Mon. Eccl.,* X (1897), p. 84; De Meester, *l. c.;* Boudinhon, *o. c.,* p. 214 f.; Pennacchi, *o. o.,* p. 183; Moureau, *La Nouv. Legisl.,* p. 81; Bucceroni, *Inst. Theol. Mor.,* II, n. 1303. For the principles which govern an obligation in charity, cf. authors of *Moral Theology.* Hurley, *o. c.,* p. 176, writes that, except in very exceptional circumstances, it binds only sub levi.

8.   Can. 267, §1, n. 2.

9.   Pius X, Allocut. *Accogliamo,* Apr. 15, 1907, §8 (*Fontes,* n. 678); Pennacchi, *o. c.,* p. 185 f.

watchful as to the type of literature which is current among their students. The obligation, therefore, of Legates, local Ordinaries and Rectors of Catholic Universities to denounce bad books to the Holy See is one of justice, and generally grave.[10]

When the denunciation is sent to Rome, it is addressed to the Secretary of the Holy Office, as such matters are the province of that Congregation.[11] The faithful in general should send the denunciation of dangerous books to the Bishop.[12]

What books are to be denounced? Those which are regarded as penicious, i. e., either entirely bad or at least dangerous to faith or morals;[13] not, however, the books already placed on the Index.

Manner of denouncing bad books

Can. 1397, §2. **Expedit ut in pravorum librorum denuntiatione non solum libri inscriptio indicetur, sed etiam, quantum fieri potest, causae exponantur cur liber prohibendus existimetur.**[14]

§3. **Iis ad quos denuntiatio defertur, sanctum esto denuntiantium nomina secreta servare.**[15]

No special formality is prescribed for denouncing evil

---

10. De Meester, *o. c.*, III, n. 1355, 1; Cocchi, *o. c.*, VI, n. 66, a; Boudinhon, *o. c.*, p. 215; Pennacchi, *o. c.*, p. 182 f.; Wernz, *o. c.*, III, n. 111 (27); Bucceroni, *o. c.*, II, n. 1303; Hurley, *o. c.*, p. 176.

11. Can. 247, §4. De Meester, *o. c.*, III, n. 1355, 2, adds that, if there is question of persons or places subject to the Congregation for the Propagation of Faith, the denunciation may be sent to that Congregation which, however, will have to transmit it to the Holy Office. If the case calls for it, the denunciation may be made to the Roman Pontiff himself. Cf. also Boudinhon, *o. c.*, p. 215.

12. De Meester, *o. c.*, III, n. 1355, 1; Vermeersch, *De Probit. et Cens. Libr.*, p. 105.

13. Boudinhon, *o. c.*, p. 215.

14. Boudinhon, *o. c.*, p. 216; Hurley, *o. c.*, p. 177 f.; Pennacchi, *o. c.*, p. 183 ff.

15. Benedict XIV, Const. *Sollicita ac provida*, July 9, 1753, §12 (*Fontes*, n. 426); Leo XIII, const. *Officiorum ac munerum*, Jan. 25, 1897, n. 28 (*Fontes*, n. 632); Cocchi, *o. c.*, VI, n. 66, d; Boudinhon, *o. c.*, p. 216; Pennacchi, *o. c.*, p. 185; Moureau, *o. c.*, p. 82; Gennari, *o. c.*, p. 85.

books. Therefore, it may be done orally or in writing. If denunciation is made to Rome, it will always be in writing. However, it is asked that the person denouncing give the exact title of the book in question together with a brief summary of the reasons on account of which he considers the book objectionable. It will be helpful to send a copy of the book, with the objectionable parts marked.[16] In the words of Hurley:[17]

> In denouncing a book it will be useful both to the denouncer himself, and to the *consultores* of the Congregation, to state the reasons why it is deemed worthy of proscription. It will be useful to the denouncer because he will thus show the members of the Congregation that he has been led to make the denunciation neither from personal motives nor from flimsy reasons. It would, indeed, be a strange thing for anyone to denounce a book unless he were able to show he was committing no calumny against the author in doing so. It will also be useful to the *consultores* of the Congregation; for it will make known to them the general tone of the book, and, perhaps, unfold to them the character and history of the author, which will be of the greatest assistance to them in passing a just criticism on the work.

The denunciation of a book does not necessitate the condemnation of it on the part of the Bishop or the Holy Office. For no work is proscribed until a long painstaking examination by a number of skilled *consultors* has proved its objectionable character.[18]

Finally, the person who denounces a book should give his name.[19] He need not be afraid to do so, for his name is kept secret, according to the prescriptions of Can. 1397, §3.

---

16. Pennacchi, *o. c.*, p. 185.

17. *O. c.*, p. 177 f.

18. Details of the process which precedes the condemnation of a book may be read in Benedict XIV, Const. *Sollicita ac provida*, July 9, 1753, *passim* (*Fontes*, n. 426). Cf. also supra p. 55 ff.

19. Wernz, *o. c.*, III, n. 111 (28), writes that anonymous denunciations are not considered. However, since the name is not expressly required in the Code, if the denunciation contains the name of the book and the reason why it should be condemned, it seems likely that it will be considered.

Thus, it is easy for anyone to do his duty in this regard without any danger to himself.

Special Vigilance and Care of Ordinaries

Can. 1397, §4. Locorum Ordinarii per se aut, ubi opus fuerit, per sacerdotes idoneos vigilent in libros qui in proprio territorio edantur aut venales prostent.[20]

§5. Libros qui subtilius examen exigant, vel de quibus ad salutarem effectum consequendum supremae auctoritatis sententia requiri videatur, ad Apostolicae Sedis judicium Ordinarii deferant.[21]

The Bishop of each diocese has received a most precious trust, the flock of Christ living in that territory. He is to care for it most diligently so that none of these souls, redeemed by the precious blood of our Lord, may perish. He has undertaken the duty of fighting error and defending the truth, even though this should cost him his life.[22] He must, therefore, forbid his people literature which is dangerous to their faith or morals, as a good shepherd keeps his sheep away from poisonous weeds.[23] This has been the mind of the Church from the time of the Apostles. The Popes throughout the centuries have reminded the Bishops of this power and duty to prohibit bad writings. This is particularly true since the invention of the printing press. The Popes have constantly urged the Bishops

---

20. Clement XIII, Encycl. *Christianae reipublicae*, Nov. 25, 1766, §2 (*Fontes*, n. 461); Pius IX, Encycl. *Cum nuper*, Jan. 20, 1858 (*Fontes*, n. 523); Leo XIII, Const. *Officiorum ac munerum*, Jan. 25, 1897, n. 29 (*Fontes*, n. 632); Pius X, Encycl. *Pascendi*, Sept. 8, 1907 (*Fontes*, n. 680); motu proprio *Praestantia Scripturae*, Nov. 18, 1907 (*Fontes*, n. 681); motu proprio *Sacrorum antistitum*, Sept. 1, 1910, n. III, VI (*Fontes*, n. 689); S. C. Consist., declar. Sept. 25, 1910, ad II, III (*A A S*, II [1910], 74 f.); S. C. of Holy Office, Mar. 22, 1918 (*A A S*, X [1918], 136); May 3, 1927 (*A A S*, XIX [1927], 186 ff.). Cf. also Boudinhon, *o. c.*, pp. 217-223; Pennacchi, *o. c.*, p. 185 ff.; Cocchi, *o. c.*, VI, n. 66, e.

21. S. C. of the Index, encycl. Aug. 24, 1864 (*A S S* XXVIII [1895], 702 f.).

22. Pius X, Allocut. *Accogliamo*, Apr. 15, 1907, n. 8 (*Fontes*, n. 678).

23. Clement XIII, Encycl. *Christianae reipublicae*, Nov. 25, 1766, §2 (*Fontes*, n. 461).

to be watchful as to the kind of books or other writings which are current among their people.

Pius X, in his great encyclical *Pascendi*, of Sept 8, 1907[24] ordered the establishment in every diocese of a Vigilance Committee (*Consilium Vigilantiae*) made up of secular and religious priests whose duty it was to find out the indications and vestiges of Modernism and the means whereby it was propagated, and to take action against it. Books and literature in general were to be investigated by them and every effort was to be made to stop the spread of writings containing those errors so that the faith of the people and especially of the clergy and the youth might be safeguarded. The obligation of Bishops to have a Vigilance Committee did not cease after the promulgation of the Code, according to an answer of the S. C. of the Holy Office, May 22, 1918.[25]

Now, in Canon 1397, §4, of the Code, the Church once more reminds Bishops of their duty to watch over the writings which are published in their territory or are on sale there. They may do this personally or by means of the Vigilance Committee or of another committee of capable priests.[26]

Upon discovery of pernicious publications some practical and effective steps must be taken to stop entirely or at least to minimize their evil effects. Wherever possible the publishers and booksellers should be approached. The faithful should have explained to them the general laws of the Church on prohibition of books. If the condemnation of the objectionable publication by name be deemed to be a speedier and more effective way of stopping the evil, then the Ordinary should take this measure.[27] However, this is to be done only in extreme cases according to the example of the Holy See.[28] Finally, when a work requires a more thorough and almost an extraordinary examination, and when the judgment of the supreme authority seems to be required in order that salutary

---

24.   §44 (VI) — *Fontes*, n. 680.

25.   *AAS*, *X* (1918), 136.

26.   The Archdiocese of New York has a Diocesan Committe on Literature. Cf. *infra*, p. 217 f.

27.   Can. 1395, §1.

28.   Decree of the Holy Office, May 3, 1927 — *A A S*, XIX (1927). Cf. also supra p. v.

effects may be obtained, then the Ordinaries[29] should send such a writing to the Holy See.[30]

Sometimes, it will be very difficult for a bishop to decide whether a book really deserves condemnation or not. At other times, while there is no doubt as to the objectionable and dangerous character of the work, it is not certain that good results will follow from the condemnation of the work by name.[31] In most cases a book or other publication is not spread simply in one diocese but in many. If one bishop condemns it and the others do not, that prohibition may not have a good effect.[32] Therefore, in these as well as in other doubtful cases, the matter should be referred to the Holy Office.

---

29. Not *local Ordinaries* but just *Ordinaries*. Therefore, the same course of action is to be followed also by religious Ordinaries.
30. Can. 1397, §5. By the Holy See here is meant the Holy Office. Cf. Canon 247, §4.
31. Hurley, *o. c.*, p. 188.
32. Boudinhon, *o. c.*, p. 221.

CHAPTER IV

EXTENSION OF THE PROHIBITION OF BOOKS

In order that there may be little doubt how far the prohibition of a book extends, separate articles will deal with
the extension of the prohibition of a book as regards *place,
language, time of publication, edition* and *parts of the book.*

Art. I. *Extension of Prohibition of Books*
as regards place

**Can. 1396. — Libri ab Apostolica Sede damnati ubique lo-
corum. . . prohibiti censeantur.**[1]

Books condemned by the Holy See are forbidden in every
part of the world. This applies to books which come under
any of the proscribed classes of books described in Canon
1399 and to those condemned by special decrees of the Pope
or of the Holy Office.[2]

There were times when disputes arose in some countries
as to whether the Index legislation applied to those places or

---

1. Leo XIII, const. *Officiorum ac munerum,* Jan. 25, 1897, n. 45
(*Fontes,* n. 632) ; S. C. of the Index, encycl. Aug. 24, 1864 (*ASS,* XXVII
[1895], 702 f.) ; Boudinhon, *La Nouv. Legisl. de l'Index,* pp. 288-289; De
Meester, *Compendium,* III, n. 1356, 1, a; Arndt, *De Libris Prohib.,* p.
101 ff.; Hurley, *Index Legislation,* p. 236; Pennacchi, *In Const. Apost.
Offic. ac muner.,* p. 242 ff.; Blat, *Comment. Textus C. J. C.,* III, n. 285;
Gennari, "Circa la nuova disciplina", *Il Monit. Eccl.,* X (1897), 135;
Bouix, *Tract. de Curia Romana,* p. 464 ff.; Moureau, *La Nouv. Legislat.,*
p. 97 (n. 45) ; Lugo, *De Virt. Fid.,* disp. 21, sect. 2, nn. 68-69; Wernz,
Jus Decretal., III, n. 109; Reiffenstuel, *Jus Can. Un.,* lib. V, tit. VII,
n. 79 ff.

2. De Meester, *o. c.,* III, n. 1356, 1, a; Wernz, *o. c.,* III, n. 109.
Hurley, *o. c.,* p. 236, thinks differently. He writes that "*ab Apostolica
Sede damnati*" refers only to books condemned *nominatim* and placed
on the Index. However he does not prove his statement.

not. Such questions arose, e. g., in Germany,[3] Belgium,[4] Ireland,[5] England and other English-speaking countries.[6]

However, the Holy See always insisted on the universal character of its laws prohibiting books.[7] The wording of Canon 1396 leaves no doubt that prohibitions of books coming from the Holy See bind the whole world, unless the opposite is explicitly stated. If some of these general laws or decrees cannot be observed without serious difficulty in a certain locality for some special circumstances, then the ecclesiastical authorities of that locality should apply to the Apostolic See for instructions. This was done after the promulgation of the const. *Officiorum ac munerum* of Leo XIII, Jan. 25, 1897,[8] by the Bishops of England. The Holy See replied by giving them "ample faculties for dispensation, so that owing to the special circumstances of the country, they might be fully empowered to modify the rigor of the law by their prudence and counsel according to the demands of the case".[9]

One of the principal reasons which gave cause to doubt the application of the general law of the Church on prohibition of books to certain countries, such as Belgium, Ireland, England, North America, etc., was the supposed existence, in these countries, of a custom exempting them from that legislation. Authors freely admit that *some* changes were legitimately brought about upon the Church laws on forbidden books by contrary customs. Pope Leo XIII himself attests this in his Constitution *Officiorum ac munerum.*[10] However, they deny that any nation or community could claim *total exemption* from the legislation of the Church on prohibition of books, on the basis of contrary *custom.*[11] For no custom has any

---

3.   Reiffenstuel, *l. c.*

4.   Heymans, *De Eccl. Libr. . . Prohibit.*, p. 221 ff.

5.   Arndt, *o. c.*, p. 104.

6.   Boudinhon, *o. c.*, p. 66.

7.   Bouix, *o. c.*, p. 460 ff.

8.   *Fontes*, n. 632.

9.   *The Tablet* (London), XC (1897), 961. Cf. also De Meester, *o. c.*, III, n. 1339, 1; Boudinhon, *o. c.*, p. 66; Vermeersch, *De Proh. et Cens. Libr.*, p. 38 f.

10.   Jan. 25, 1897 (*Fontes*, n. 632).

11.   Wernz, *o. c.*, III, n. 109; Vermeersch, *o. c.*, p. 33.

force which lacks the consent, at least implicit or tacit, of the competent ecclesiastical Superior.[12] But nowhere do we find that the Church ever consented to a change in the universal application of her Index legislation. Rather, she has constantly insisted on the observance of her laws throughout the world.[13] This is particularly true after the Leonine Constitution *Officiorum ac munerum* which was meant for "all catholics throughout the entire world".[14]

It is useless, in view of what has been said, to take up the question as to whether or not the Index legislation binds in the United States of America. The answer was affirmative even before the publication of Leo's *Officiorum ac munerum* Jan. 25, 1897[16] and most certainly it is affirmative now.

Art. II. *Extension of Prohibition of Books as regards language*

Can. 1396. — Libri ab Apostolica Sede damnati. . . in quodcumque vertantur idioma prohibiti censeantur.[17]

Once a book is forbidden by the Holy See, it will always remain forbidden, even though translated into another language, and reasonably so, because the evil it contains does not cease to be evil when presented in a different language. The question may be asked here: is a book, condemned by the Ordinary, still forbidden when translated into another language? No author deals with this question and apparently there is little need of it. But, should the case happen, the

---

12.   Can. 25.

13.   See examples of this reiterated insistence of the Church in Arndt, *o. c.*, p. 101 ff. Cf. also Wernz, *o. c.*, III, n. 109, n. 110 (note 44); Reiffenstuel, *o. c.*, n. 90 ff.; Bouix, *o. c.*, p. 487 f.

14.   Pennachi, *o. c.*, p. 25 (n. 33) f.; Van Coillie, *Commentarius*, pp. 19-20; Vermeersch, *l. c.* It is still allowed to make use of some secondary mitigations which were generally admitted before the Code. They are not contrary to the law but rather explain it. For example, Can. 1399, n. 4, forbids religious writings of non-Catholics which contain something against the Catholic faith. Authors generally exclude very old heretics like Tertullian. Cf. De Meester, *o. c.*, III, n. 1339, 1, note 3.

16.   Sabetti, *Compendium Theologiae Moralis*, (7 ed. New York, 1892), p. 772; Arndt, *o. c.*, p. 105.

17.   Pennacchi, *o. c.*, p. 242; Boudinhon, *o. c.*, p. 289.

work translated into another language is not forbidden, unless the opposite be stated in the decree of the Ordinary. For while the Code forbids the translating of any condemned work,[18] in dealing with works thus translated, it expressly forbids only those originally condemned by the Hole See. No mention is made of those condemned by the Ordinary.[19]

Art. III. *Extension of Prohibition of Books as regards time of publication.*

A book which is condemned by the Church in the general law, contained in can. 1399 of the Code of Canon Law, is to be regarded as forbidden, whether it was published before or after the promulgation of the Code.[20] It is true that a *new* law does not affect the lawfulness of *past* acts.[21] Thus, if a man *once* read a book which is *now* condemned by the Church, he did not act unlawfully then because there was no prohibition.[22] Subsequent condemnation of that book did not make his *past* reading of it unlawful. On the other hand, present condemnation of that book which previously could be read with impunity makes the reading of it *now* a violation of the law. The present prohibition, therefore, can very well and does refer not only to books published after its promulgation but also to books published in the past and to the use of them now and in the future.

This is evident and undisputed[23] when the prohibition of a book is based on some cause *intrinsic* to the book, i. e., its contents are opposed to faith or morals. Here, it is the *present* danger of the book that is considered, and not the past intention or sin of the author. Canonists, before the Code,

---

18. Can. 1398.

19. However, the natural law binds even when the positive ecclesiastical law does not apply.

20. De Meester, *Compendium*, III, n. 1358; Wernz, *Jus Decretal.*, III, n. 110 (V).

21. Can. 10.

22. It is supposed here that the work was not clearly forbidden by the natural or positive divine law.

23. De Meester, *o. c.*, III, n. 1358; Wernz, *o. c.*, III, n. 110 (V); Vermeersch, *De Proh. et Cens. Libr.*, p. 44.

however, differed in interpreting that part of the Leonine law[24] in which some books were prohibited because of the *lack of ecclesiastical approbation.* Some[25] held that works which at the time of publication were not subject to ecclesiastical approbation were not included in that prohibition. Wernz,[26] however, rightly contended that the Church's laws prohibiting books affect all works described in those laws regardless of the time of their publication, and irrespective of the reason for their prohibition.[27] For, he explains, the Church in forbidding non-approved works does not consider the *act* of the author or of the publisher, but the *book itself* which she regards as dangerous as long as it is not examined and approved by the Church. Secondly, the Church does not forbid any book entirely and simply because it lacks approbation; there is always a possible danger in works which she has not examined. Finally, if the laws of the Church prohibiting books did not apply to non-approved works published before the promulgation of the present laws, many dangerous books would escape the condemnation of the Church.

No author, after the Code, as far as the writer has been able to ascertain, differs from Wernz. Therefore, there is now little doubt that the prohibition of the Church contained in can. 1399 extends to all the books condemned therein, regardless of the date of publication.[28]

When the Holy See forbids a book by special decree it is always understood that all the editions of that work pre-

----

24. In this matter very much the same as the present law. Cf. Leo XIII, *Officiorum ac munerum,* Jan. 25, 1897, nn. 13 and 20 (*Fontes,* n. 632).

25. Vermeersch, *De Proh. et Cens. Libr.,* p. 44; Van Coillie, *Commentarius,* p. 63.

26. *O. c.,* III, n. 110 (V).

27. Cf. De Meester, *o. c.,* III, n. 1358.

28. It is very difficult to find any time, at least from 1487 (see supra p. 40 f.), when books mentioned in can. 1399, n. 5 (forbidden for lack of approbation) were not subject to ecclesiastical examination and approval, with the exception of vernacular Catholic translations with notes from the Fathers, which needed no approbation before the Code. (Pennacchi, *o. c.,* p. 64 f.) Therefore, there is little practical value in the above controversy.

vious to the condemnation are forbidden,[29] unless the opposite be stated.[30]

Art. IV. *Extension of Prohibition of a book to its parts.*

The principle generally accepted by theologians and canonists is that, when a work is forbidden, the prohibition affects it in its entirety and in all its parts.[31] This was already the general opinion in the time of Suarez, so that he could write: *Notandum est autem, non solum integrum librum, sed etiam quamcumque eius partem prohiberi, ut omnes docent.*[32] Reiffenstuel also calls it the general opinion of his time.[33] However, in the application of this principle to practical cases, authors disagree. In proposing a solution to problems of this type, the common or the more probable opinion is here followed.

Some works are forbidden because they lack the ecclesiastical approbation (Can. 1399, n. 5). Even though every objectionable part should be removed, they cannot be read, kept, etc. For the cause of their prohibition (the lack of approbation on the part of the Church) still remains.[34] Such would be the case if a book of supposed *revelations*, forbidden because not approved, is purged of some statement it may contain contrary to the truths of the Church. The book still remains forbidden until it be approved by the ecclesiastical Superiors.[35]

Other works are condemned for some intrinsic reason, e. g., immorality, heresy. The parts of such books, containing

---

29. Preface to *Index Librorum Prohibitorum.* (ed. 1925); De Meester, *o. c.*, III, n. 1356, 1, a.

30. E. g. When the *Manuel Biblique* was forbidden, the prohibition applied *only* to certain editions specifiied in the decree. *AAS*, XV (1923), 615.

31. De Meester, *Compendium*, III, n. 1357; Arndt, *De Libris Prohib.*, n. 156, 2, a; Van Coillie, *Commentarius*, p. 34.

32. *De Fid. Div.*, disp. 20, sect. 2, n. 9. Cf. also Lugo, *De Virtute Fidei*, disp. 21, sect. 2, n. 36 f.

33. *Jus Can. Un.*, lib. V, tit. VII, n. 42.

34. De Meester, *o. c.*, III, n. 1357, b.

35. S. C. Holy Office, July 26, 1848 (*Fontes*, n. 905).

the errors or attacks for which they are condemned, are always forbidden, even though torn or separated from the rest. The remaining harmless parts may be read and used if they are separated from the condemned matter.[36] Accordingly, if *all*[37] the bad parts of a forbidden book, are taken out of it, the book ceases to be forbidden. This is the more common opinion.[38] Therefore, such a purged book may be freely read and kept. The reason is that that book was considered forbidden *only*[39] because it contained something objectionable, which is now taken out. Once the cause for the condemnation is taken out, there is no more danger for faith and morals, and, therefore, the prohibition of the whole book ceases. This seems to be confirmed in can 1398, §2, where the Church contemplates the case of a forbidden book which has been corrected, and absolutely forbids a new publication of it, without the permission of the Superior who first condemned it. No prohibition is expressed there against the reading or keeping of such a book but only against republishing it. Therefore, it would seem to confirm what has been said, namely, that when all the parts of a forbidden book which are bad and which, therefore, caused the book to be proscribed, are expunged,

---

36. De Meester, *o. c.*, III, n. 1357, b. The same is true of clippings from a forbidden newspaper or magazine. Betten, *The Roman Index*, p. 43.

37. However, in many cases the moral and religious errors are spread over the entire book, e. g., when the whole book propounds heresy or immorality. To take the evil parts out of such a book without destroying it, is practically impossible.

38. De Meester, *Compendium*, III, n. 1357; Betten, *o. c.*, p. 42 (n. 4); Moureau, *La Nouv. Legisl.*, p. 14; Van Coillie, *o. c.*, p. 35, c; Vermeersch, *De Prohib. et Cens. Librorum*, p. 42; St. Alphonsus, *De Prohib. Librorum*, V, n. 5; *Theol. Mor.*, VII, n. 283; Arndt, *o. c.*, p. 193.

39. The Church does not forbid books any more *in odium auctoris*. De Meester, *o. c.*, *III*, n. 1357, C β, note 5; Wernz, *o. c.*, III, n. 98, note 10. Nor are religious books of non-Catholics forbidden *ut sic*, but only when they contain something against the Catholic faith (Can. 1399, n. 4). It was books of this sort — forbidden only because written by heretics and treating *ex professo* of religion — which led old authors like Schmalzgrueber (*Jus Eccl. Un.*, tom. V, pars I, tit. VII, n. 51), De Lugo (*De Virt. Fid.*, disp. 21, sect. 2, n. 60), Reiffenstuel (*Jus Can. Un.*, lib. V, tit. VII, n. 73), and others to deny that corrected or purged works could be used, as is commonly believed now.

torn out, erased or, in some other way, taken out of the work,
the book ceases to be forbidden and may be used. This is true
of books forbidden by the general laws found in Can. 1399.
It is also true of books forbidden by special decree, especially
when the prohibition is accompanied with the clause *donec
corrigatur*. However, in order that a work of that kind may
be lawfully used, one must be *sure* that *all* the parts which
caused its condemnation have been taken out.[40]

The final judgment, in this as well as in all other cases
of expurgated works, must be sought from one who is an
intelligent, learned and devoted son of the Church. The ex-
purgating itself cannot be done by one who lacks the permission to read forbidden books.

When a forbidden work is made up of several volumes,
and it is *certainly* known that only one volume contains the
dangerous part which caused the condemnation, is the prohibition limited to this one volume or does it extend to all
the other volumes? The opinion, which is now commonly held,
is that, if all the volumes are *formally* united, i. e., they all
treat of the *same* argument in an indivisible way, e. g., a
novel,[41] they are all similarly forbidden; but if each volume
treats of a *different* subject, e. g., one deals with religion,
the others with philosophy, history, etc., or they all treat of
the same subject in a divisible way, e. g., dogmatic theology
in several volumes, each one containing some distinct treatise,[42] then, each volume is to be judged by itself.[43]

However, according to the opinion presented above,[44] if
the part which is objectionable is taken out or the entire volume that contains it is removed, the basis of the prohibition
is withdrawn and therefore the condemnation of the rest of

----

40.   Genicot-Salsmans, *Institutiones Theol. Mor.*, I, n. 455, II.

41.   Betten, *o. c.*, p. 41, note 3.

42.   De Meester, *o. c.*, III, p. 275, note 1.

43.   Lugo, *De Virt. Fid.*, disp. 21, sect. 2, nn. 55-59; Suarez, *De
Fid. Div.*, disp. 20, sect. 2, n. 9; Vermeersch, *De Prohib. et Cens. Libr.*,
p. 43; Van Coillie, *o. c.*, p. 35; De Meester, *o. c.*, III, n. 1357, b, γ;
Betten, *l. c.*

44.   Supra, p. 109.

the work vanishes and it may be used.[45] *Anthologies, readers, historical source books* or other similar kinds of publications which contain, among their many selections, parts of condemned books are not, on that account, forbidden. They are to be considered as entirely new works with their compiler as the author and judged on their own merits, according to the prescriptions of can. 1399.[46] The same holds true for *encyclopedias.*[47]

If a forbidden book is bound together with others, the whole bound volume is forbidden.[48] For, while the good books remain good even though they happen to be bound together with bad ones, yet the man who *keeps* and *reads* the good books must of necessity *keep* the bad book. But keeping a bad book is forbidden in Canon 1398, §1. Besides, there is the danger arising from the temptation of reading the forbidden work. Therefore, it is not allowed to keep a bound volume containing good and bad books.

At times a forbidden work is published bit by bit in successive numbers of newspapers or magazines, which are otherwise reputable. Must the numbers of those papers containing the condemned work be considered forbidden? The work, itself, even when reprinted in those papers, is still forbidden and, unless it has been corrected and the objectionable parts removed, it may not be read. However, the newspaper

---

45. De Meester, *o. c.*, III, n. 1857, c. γ; Vermeersch, *De Prohib. et Cens. Librorum*, p. 43. When, by special decree, the existing volumes of a certain work are forbidden, the volumes which may be published after the decree are not *per se* forbidden, but must be regarded as suspicious and even bad, unless it be clear that the author has shown signs of amendment. Cf. *Index Librorum Prohib.*, Preface (ed. 1925); De Meester, *l. c.*; Vermeersch-Creusen, *Ep.*, II, n. 734, 4.

46 Clement VIII, *Instructio Regulis Indicis adjecta*, pars III, §1 (*Fontes*, n. 426); De Meester, *o. c.*, III, n. 1357, b, δ; Betten, *o. c.*, p. 42, n. 7; Vermeersch, *De Proh. et Cens.*, p. 43; Cocchi, *o. c.*, VI, n. 67; Genicot-Salsmans, *o. c.*, I, n. 455, I.

47. Koch-Preuss, *Handbook of Moral Theology*, IV, 407; Ferreres, *Institutiones Canonicae*, II, 157; *Il Mon. Eccl.*, XXIII (1911), 413 f.; Betten, *o. c.*, p. 42, n. 7.

48. Betten, *o. c.*, p. 42, n. 4.

or magazine *as such* does not become forbidden, so that it is not necessary to mutilate the collection or series of such a paper or magazine, by removing those fascicles which contain the forbidden book.[49]

---

49. De Meester, *o. c.*, III, n. 1356, b.

CHAPTER V

Force of the Prohibition of Books

Can. 1398, §1. Prohibitio librorum id efficit ut liber sine debita licentia nec edi, nec legi, nec retineri, nec vendi, nec in aliam linguam verti, nec ullo modo cum aliis communicari possit.[1]

Art. I. *Publication of Forbidden Books.*

To *publish* (*edere*) a book, means to cause a book to be multiplied and disseminated, either at one's own expense or at the expense of someone else.[2] This includes those who are

---

1. Conc. Trid., Sess. IV, *De editione et usu sacrorum librorum;* John XXII, Const. *Super illius*, 1326, §3 (*Fontes*, n. 37); Martin V, (in Council of Constance), Const. *Inter cunctas*, Feb. 22, 1418, art. 9 (*Fontes*, n. 43); Leo X, Const. *Exsurge Domine*, June 15, 1520 (*Fontes*, n. 76); Pius IV, Const. *Dominici gregis*, Mar. 24, 1564 (*Fontes*, n. 105); Sixtus V, Const. *Coeli et terrae*, Jan. 5, 1586, §4 (*Fontes*, n. 157); Urban VIII, Const. *Inscrutabilis*, Mar. 31, 1631, §2 (*Fontes*, n. 210); Clement XII, Ap. Letter *Compertum*, Aug. 24, 1734, dub. XVI (*Fontes*, n. 296); Ap. Letter *Concredita Nobis*, May 13, 1739 (*Fontes*, n. 300); Benedict XIV, Const. *Omnium sollicitudinum*, Sept. 12, 1744, §14, dub. XVI and §40 (*Fontes*, n. 348); Pius VI, Const. *Auctorem fidei*, Aug. 28, 1794, prop. 68 Synodi Pistor. damn. (*Fontes*, n. 475); Pius VII, Const. *Ecclesiam*, Sept. 13, 1821, §11 (*Fontes*, n. 479); Pius IX, Const. *Apostolicae Sedis*, Oct. 12, 1869, §1, n. 2 (*Fontes*, n. 552); Leo XIII, Const. *Officiorum ac munerum*, Jan. 25, 1897, nn. 12, 23, 24 (*Fontes*, n. 632); Pius X, Encycl. *Pascendi*, Sept. 8, 1907 (*Fontes*, n. 680); motu proprio *Sacrorum Antistitum*, Sept. 1, 1910, III (*Fontes*, n. 689); S. C. Holy Office, Decree of Mar. 18, 1666, condemned prop. 45 (*Fontes*, n. 735); Jan. 29, 1817 (*Fontes*, n. 853); (*Malacen.*), July 26, 1848 (*Fontes*, n. 905); Instruction (*ad vic. ap. Myssurien.*), Feb. 1, 1871, n. 2 (*Fontes*, n. 1014); Jan. 13, 1892, ad 1 (*Fontes*, n. 1147); S. C. de Prop. Fide, decree Apr. 13, 1807, n. 1 (*Coll.*, n. 692); (*C. G.-Ceylan*), Aug. 23, 1852, ad 7 (*Coll.*, n. 1080).

2. Koch-Preuss, *Handbook of Moral Theology*, IV, p. 409; Noldin, *Summa Theol. Mor.*, II, n. 706, 1, a; Cappello, *De Curia Romana*, I, p. 272.

the primary and principal cause of the publication among whom are certainly the *editor* and the *author* (if the latter submitted the book with the express intention of having it published). While canonists are unanimous in holding those two persons responsible for the publication of a book, they differ with regard to the *printer*, i. e., the one who owns or superintends the printing establishment.[3] More probably, the *printer* as such is not included, because what the law here forbids is the *publication* and not the printing of a work.[4] Moreover, in Can. 1385, §2, a clear distinction is made between the place where a book is published *(in quo libri vel imagines publici juris fiant)* and the place where the same book is printed *(in quo imprimantur)*. If *locus edendi* may differ from *locus imprimendi*, then the printer as such is not a publisher. Therefore, he is not included under the term *edi* of Can. 1398, §1. Undoubtedly it is always unlawful for a printer to give *formal* cooperation towards the production of an evil book; it is also wrong to give proximate *material* cooperation, except when this is done to avoid an extremely serious evil. Through his cooperation he sins and may even incur the penalties of Can. 2318, by virtue of Canons 2209 §1-3, and 2231. The workers in his shop may share in the guilt by cooperating in a lesser or greater degree towards the production of an evil book.[5] But neither the owner of the printing shop nor his workers, unless they also be publishers or editors, are included under the word *edi* of Can. 1398, §1.[6]

---

3. He is considered as one of the publishers by Noldin, *l. o.*; Pennacchi, *In Const. Apost. Offic. ac muner.*, p. 45; Bouuaert-Simenon, *Manuale Juris Canonici*, p. 551 ff.; Cocchi, *Commentarium C. J. C.*, VI, n. 67; Van Coillie, *Commentarius*, p. 30; Moureau, *La Nouv. Legisl.*, p. 74; Augustine, *A Commentary*, VI, p. 463; Vermeersch, *De Prohib. et Cens. Librorum*, p. 44; *Conference Bulletin of the Archdiocese of New York*, V (1927), 24; Ayrinhac, *Admin. Legisl.*, p. 291.

4. De Meester, *Compendium*, III, n. 1360, 1; Cappello, *De Curia Romana*, I, p. 272; *De Censuris*, p. 214; Chelodi, *Jus Poenale*, p. 75; and most authors who have written after the Code on Can. 2318, in commenting on the word *editores*.

5. Vermeersch, *De Prohib. et Cens. Librorum*, p .44 f.

6. De Meester, *o. c.*, III, n. 1360, 1.

Art. II. *Reading Forbidden Books.*

To *read* a forbidden book is prohibited. According to De Lugo,[7] followed in this by canonists and theologians generally,[8] one is said to read a book *who, going over the book with his own eyes* (or *hands*, if he is blind)[8a] *understands what he reads.* These two elements are essential for the definition of *reading.* It is not necessary to articulate or pronounce out loud what is read. Therefore, it is *not reading*, a) to listen to another person reading,[9] b) to recite from memory,[10] c) to look over a book without knowing the language in which it is written.[11] If, however, one knows the language of the book but does not fully understand it because of the difficulty of the subject treated, or the dullness of his mind, or for lack of concentration, then certainly he is *reading* in the sense just explained.

What of the man who advises, begs or even commands another to read for him some prohibited literature so that he may listen to it? He does not really *read* according to the more common opinion.[12] Nevertheless he commits sin by co-operating so intimately in the reading of a forbidden work, and if he succeeds by his command in getting someone to read

---

7. *De Virt. Fidei*, disp. 21, sect. 2, n. 71 ff.

8. St. Alphonsus, *Theol. Mor.*, lib. VII, n. 292; Noldin, *Summa Theol. Moralis*, II, n. 706, 1, b; Cocchi, *o. c.*, VI, n. 67, b; De Meester, *o. c.*, III, n. 1360, 2; Hurley, *Index Legisl.*, p. 170; Pennacchi, *o. c.*, p. 44; Bucceroni, *Instit. Theol. Mor.*, n. 1165; Gennari, *o. c.*, *Il Mon. eccl.*, X (1897), 154; Suarez, *De Fide Div.*, disp. 20, sect. 2, n. 18 f.; Schmalzgrueber, *Jus Eccl. Un.*, tom. V, pars I, tit. VII, n. 47 ff.

8a. A Coronata, *Inst. Jur. Can.*, II, p. 336; Marc-Gestermann-Raus, *Inst. Mor. Alph.*, I, n. 1317.

9. Bucceroni, *Institutiones Theol. Moralis*, II, n. 1165. *A fortiori* to assist at the presentation in drama of a forbidden work is *not reading.* Cf. also Betten, *The Roman Index*, p. 43, n. 8.

10. Lugo, *De Virtute Fidei*, disp. 21, sect. 2, n. 73.

11. Lugo, *o. et l. c.*, n. 74. However, in doing so one would violate the law by *keeping* a prohibited book (Can. 1398, §2:*nec retineri*).

12. St. Alphonsus, *De Proh. Libr.*, Cap. V, n. 9; Lugo, *o. et l. c.*, n. 75; Vermeersch, *De Proh. et Cens. Libr.*, p. 45 (note 6); Noldin, *o. c.*, II, n. 706, 1, b; Pennacchi, *o. c.*, p. 44; Bouuaert-Simenon, *o. c.*, p. 552; De Meester, *o. c.*, III, n. 1360, 2; Bourdinhon, *La Nouv. Legisl. de l'Index*, p. 308; A Coronata *l. c.*; Marc-Gestermann-Raus, *l. c.*; D'Annibale, *In Const. Ap. Scd.*, n. 36. Augustine, *A Commentary*, VI, p. 463, disagrees.

for him, without permission, books written by heretics, apostates or schismatics defending heresy, apostasy or schism or other books forbidden under pain of excommunication (Can. 2318) he incurs the same penalty which *readers* of such books incur, if otherwise the other person would not have read the book (Canon 2231). A man who subscribes to a forbidden newspaper or magazine usually violates the positive law in more than one way. He *cooperates* towards the support of evil literature (Can. 2209),[13] he *keeps* and *reads* forbidden matter (Can. 1398, §1).

Without permission, no one[14] may read a forbidden work. This applies also to the author himself[15] and the proof-reader.[16] Priests, teachers, professors are not excepted. A professor who has permission to read forbidden works may read parts of such work to his students, whenever it be deemed necessary.[17]

Art. III. Keeping Forbidden Books[18]

It is forbidden to *keep* or *retain* a prohibited book without permission for any purpose whatsoever.[19] A man is said

---

13.   Noldin, *o. c.*, II, n. 124, a. Cf. also allocution of Pius XI, *Misericordia Domini*, Dec. 20, 1926 (*Il Mon. Eccl.*, XXXVIII [1927], 21). For cooperators who incur the censure of can. 2318, cf. *infra*, p. 231.

14.   Supra: Subject of Prohibition, p. 73 ff.

15.   Suarez, *o. et l. c.*, n. 26.

16.   Lugo, *o. et l. c.*, n. 92.

17.   Noldin, *o. c.*, II, n. 106, d; Cocchi, *o. c.*, VI, n. 67, f. As to the question, what constitutes "grave matter" in *reading* a prohibited book without permission, cf. *infra*, p. 233 ff.

18.   De Meester, *Compendium*, III, n. 1360, 3; Cocchi, *Commentarium in C. J. C.*, VI, n. 67, c; Noldin, *Summa Theol. Mor.*, II, n. 706, c; Vermeersch, *De Proh. et Cens. Libr.*, p. 45; Lehmkuhl, *Theol. Mor.*, II, n. 1185; Moureau, *La Nouv. Legisl.*, p. 74; Boudinhon, *La Nouv. Legisl. de l'Index*, p. 310, f.; Gennari, "Circa la nuova disciplina", *Il Mon. Eccl.*, X (1897), 154; Reiffenstuel, *Jus Can. Un.*, lib. V, tit. VII, n. 72; Koch-Preuss, *Handbook of Mor. Theol.*, IV, 409; Bouuaert-Simenon, *Man. Jur. Can.*, p. 552; Genicot-Salsmans, *Inst. Theol. Mor.*, I, n. 456; Hurley, *Index Legisl.*, p. 170; St. Alphonsus, *De Proh. Libr.*, V, n. 11.

19.   Can. 1398, §1. The following proposition was condemned by the S. C. of the Holy Office, Mar. 18, 1666 (*Fontes*, n. 735): "Libri prohibiti donec expurgentur, possunt retineri, usquedum adhibita diligentia corrigantur". Prop. 45. However, c. *infra*: Chapter VIII — *Exemptions and Exceptions.*

to keep or retain a book when he keeps it in his possession permanently or temporarily as his property, or as a deposit or a loan.[20] Even though he places it temporarily in some one else's care, while retaining the ownership of it, he is still *keeping* that book.[21] If, however, he entrusts a forbidden book to one, who has the permission to read it, to keep it until he himself secures the necessary permission, while strictly he still *keeps* the book, yet he acts lawfully.[22] In such a case he can even keep the book himself, while he waits for the requested permission.[22a]

Not only are individual persons forbidden to keep prohibited works, but also collective units. Thus, it is not lawful for any literary guild, club or other group of people to keep such books without permission, because the members of these associations are actually the co-owners and possessors of the books, and therefore, the *keepers* of them.[23]

A *librarian* does not *keep* the books committed to his care in the sense explained, provided he does not take them home or into his own room.[24] *Bookbinders*, according to many commentators, are not considered to keep or retain those books which are given them to bind.[25] These workers, after all, hold such books only for a short period of time; they do not *keep* them but *bind* them. Others,[26] however, claim that a *book-*

---

20. Ayrinhac, *Admin. Legisl.*, p. 291. It makes no difference here whether he knows the language of the book or not.

21. Lugo, *De Virt. Fid. Div.*, disp. 21, sect. 2, n. 84.

22. St. Alphonsus, *Theol. Moralis*, VII, n. 298; Lehmkuhl, *l. c.*; Vermeersch, *l. c.*; De Meester, *l. c.*

22a. Cappello *De Censuris*, n. 234, 3; Noldin, *o. c.*, n. 706 δ; Cocchi, *l. c.*

23. Cappello, *De Censuris*, n. 234, 6.

24. De Meester, *l. c.*; Cocchi, *l. c.*; Ayrinhac, *l. c.*; Noldin, *o. o.*, II, n. 706, c; Boudinhon, *o. c.*, p. 311; Vermeersch, *De Prohib. et Cens. Librorum*, p. 45; Cappello, *De Censuris*, n. 234, 5.

25. De Meester, *l. c.*; Cocchi, *l. c.* (*probabilius*); Boudinhon, *o. c.*, p. 311; Moureau, *o. c.*, p. 74; Koch-Preuss, *o. c.*, p. 400; Bouuaert-Simeon, *o. c.*, p. 552; Genicot-Salsmans, *o. c.*, I, n. 456.

26. Schmalzgrueber, *Jus Eccl. Un.*, tom. V, pars I, tit. VII, n. 33; Gennari, "Circa la nuova disciplina", *Il Mon. Eccl.*, X (1897), 154; Arndt, *De Libris Prohibitis*, p. 235 (n. 173); Vermeersch, *De Prohib. et Cens. Librorum*, p. 45 f.; Noldin, *l. c.*

binder, strictly speaking, *keeps* books in the sense of the law in question. However, if he binds forbidden books for people who have permission to read them, he does not commit sin; neither does he usually commit sin when he binds those books for people who lack the necessary permission, because of the loss he would otherwise incur. Authors also excuse *servants* from sin, if they keep forbidden books for their masters who have permission to keep and read such works,[27] since they do not keep them in their own name.

May one keep forbidden books without permission, not for the purpose of reading them, but for their great artistic or ornamental value, as specimens of typography, binding, water-mark, etc? *Per se*, such works cannot be kept.[28] For, here there is question of *keeping* a forbidden book in the sense of can. 1398, §1. Moreover, the danger of reading it always exists. Permission can be easily obtained. However, some authors would allow the keeping of such books when they have practically ceased to be considered as books and have come to be regarded as ornaments, while, on the other hand, the holder of such works, considers it a hardship to ask for permission. In practice, therefore, the obligation of obtaining permission is not to be insisted upon.[29] The prohibition of keeping forbidden literature applies also to keepers of restaurants, hotels, boarding houses, barber shops and other such places where books, magazines and newspapers are placed at the disposal of customers. They may keep papers and magazines which contain something opposed to faith or morals; but they cannot keep those which *ex professo* attack religion or morality[30] or in some other way clearly come under one of the classes forbidden in Can. 1399.

---

27.   De Meester, *l. c.;* Lehmkuhl, *o. c.*, II, n. 1185; Boudinhon, *l. c.*

28.   Reiffenstuel, *Jus Can. Un.*, lib. V, tit. VII, n. 72; Ferraris, *Bibliotheca*, V (word: "Libri Prohibiti"), 144 (48); *Conference Bulletin of the Archdiocese of New York*, V (1927), 25.

29.   De Meester, *o. c.*, III, n. 1360, 3; Bouuaert-Simenon, *o. c.*, p. 553; Cappello, *De Censuris*, n. 234, 7.

30.   Arndt, *o. c.*, p. 235 (n. 175); Augustine, *A Commentary*, VI, p. 464, n. 19; Vermeersch, *o. c.*, p. 46 f.; Van Coillie, *o. c.*, p. 94 f.; De Meester, *o. c.*, III, n. 1381, 4.

A person who has a forbidden book may not dispose of it by sale or exchange[31] unless the person receiving it has the required permission. He must either *destroy* it, or obtain *permission* to keep it.[32] He cannot keep it without permission, no matter how good his intention is, e. g., to be able to refute the errors contained in it, or to use it for wrapping paper.[33] The same action should be taken also in case the book belongs to another, unless the owner has permission, or grave troubles might arise through failure to return the book, e. g., serious quarrel, blasphemies, hatreds, etc.[34]

Art. IV. *Selling, Translating, Communicating*
Forbidden Books.

1. *Selling.* It is forbidden to sell condemned books.

Booksellers should not keep forbidden books for sale, except with permission from the Holy See. Even then they cannot sell them except to those whom they can reasonably presume to have the necessary permission. They need not ask every customer whether he has permission to read such a work or not. They can usually form a prudent opinion from the nature of the book and the character of the buyer.[35] The Holy See does not grant permission to keep obscene books on sale. This matter will be treated more fully later in commenting on Canon 1404.

2. *Translating* a forbidden work is not permitted, because the danger of a book consists not in the language in which it is written but in the matter which it contains. Therefore, the danger generally exists no matter in what language the book is written. However, if one has permission to read

---

31. "... *nec vendi... nec ullo modo cum aliis communicari possit.*" Can. 1398, §1.

32. Ayrinhac, *o. c.*, p. 291; De Meester, *l. c.*; Cocchi, *l. c.*; Noldin, *l. c.*; Boudinhon, *o. c.*, p. 311. There is no obligation now to give it to the Bishop.

33. De Meester, *l. c.*; Gennari, *o. c., Il Mon. Eccl.*, X (1897), p. 155.

34. De Meester, *l. c.*; Arndt, *o. c.*, n. 176, 2; Genicot-Salsmans, *Inst. Theol. Mor.*, I, n. 456. As to the question, what constitutes "grave matter" in *keeping* a forbidden book, cf. *infra*, p. 234 f.

35. Ayrinhac, *o. c.*, p. 300; De Meester, *o. c.*, III, n. 1360, 4.

prohibited books, he may translate such a book for his own use. Moreover, if the book is not forbidden by special decree but in virtue of Canon 1399, and, in the translation, he omits all objectionable parts, he may even publish it.[36]

3. *Communicating* a book to others includes *lending, donating, exchanging, showing* it to others, *reading* or *transcribing* it for others. All these and other ways of communicating a forbidden book to others who have no permission are prohibited.[37] However, it is permitted to present to others the matter of the book or read or write excerpts for a just cause, e. g., to refute an author.[38]

Art. V. *Republishing Forbidden Books.*

Can. 1398, §2. Liber quoquo modo prohibitus rursus in lucem edi nequit nisi, factis correctionibus, licentiam is dederit qui librum prohibuerat eiusve Superior vel successor.[39]

A book, no matter in what manner it is forbidden, by general law, or by special decree of the Holy See or of the Ordinary, must be corrected before it may be published again. Moreover, if forbidden by special decree of the Holy See or by the Ordinary, the corrected book may not be published without the permission of the person who prohibited it, his Superior or his successor. It is different with works which

---

36. Can. 1398, §2, as interpreted below. Cf. however, Augustine, *o. c.*, VI, p. 464. Also see Can. 1396.

37. De Meester, *Compendium*, III, n. 1360, 6; Ayrinhac, *Administrat. Legisl.*, p. 291; Cocchi, *Commentarium in C. J. C.*, VI, n. 67 f.; Bouuaert-Simenon, *Man Jur. Can.*, p. 553; Noldin, *Summa Theol. Mor.*, II, n. 706, d.

38. Cocchi, *l. c.* Teachers or professors who have the necessary permission to read prohibited books may read short excerpts of such works to their pupils for good reasons. See supra, p. 116.

39. Benedict XIV, Const. *Sollicita ac provida*, July 9, 1753, §9 (*Fontes*, n. 426); Leo XIII, Const. *Officiorum ac munerum*, Jan. 25, 1897, n. 31, 45 (*Fontes*, n. 632). Cf. also Boudinhon, *La Nouv. Legisl. de l'Index*, p. 226; Hurley, *Index Legisl.*, p. 191; Pennacchi, *In Const. Ap. Offic. ac mun.*, p. 187 ff.; Gennari, "Circa la nuova disciplina", *Il Mon. Eccl.*, X (1897), 106; Bouix, *Tract. de Curia Romana*, p. 549 (Prop. XVI); De Meester, *Compendium*, III, n. 1356, b; Augustine, *A Commentary*, VI, 465; Genicot-Salsmans, *Inst. Theol. Mor.*, I, n. 455, 1.

.are forbidden by virtue of Can. 1399. Once they have been corrected, they may be published again without any permission,[40] unless approbation be required because of the subject treated according to the prescriptions of can. 1385. For the words of the Code in question *(nisi... licentiam is dederit qui librum prohibuerat eiusve Superior vel successor)* would seem to indicate that the book, which is to be republished in a corrected form, was previously condemned by name through a *special* decree. Some authors,[41] however, disagree and require permission even when a book is condemned only by general law, provided its prohibition be certain. In practice, there is no necessity of asking for permission to republish a corrected work, unless it was first condemned by *special* decree.

This obligation binds only the publishers[42] of the work. It does not concern those who wish to use the corrected book; for, once the work is purged of all objectionable parts, it may be used (read, kept, etc.).[43] The books particularly considered here are those forbidden with the clause *donec corrigatur.* The correction is usually entrusted to the author himself.[44]

A compendium or summary of a forbidden work is not a new edition of the same, but must be considered as a new work, distinct from the condemned one, and to be estimated on its own merits.[45]

---

40. De Meester, *l. c.*; Pennacchi, *o. c.*, p. 198; Gennari, *l. c.*; Genicot-Salsmans, *l. c.*

41. Van Coillie, *o. c.*, p. 79; Augustine, *o. c.*, VI, 465; Boudinhon, *o. c.*, p. 227 (in theory only).

42. In the sense explained supra, p. 113 f.

43. See supra, p. 109.

44. Benedict XIV, Const. *Sollicita ac provida*, July 9, 1753, §9 (*Fontes*, n. 426); De Meester, *o. c.*, III, n. 1356, b.

45. Noldin, *o. c.*, II, n. 706, d.

CHAPTER VI

Books forbidden by General Law

From time to time the Church has forbidden and does
forbid certain harmful publications by name, either by a decree of the Holy Office or by an Apostolic letter. All the
works thus condemned by a special decree of the Holy See
are placed on the *Index of Prohibited Books*. But the number
of dangerous and evil works coming daily from the printing
presses of the world is so vast that it is practically impossible to condemn each evil book or publication by name. Therefore, the Church, like a provident mother, has laid down general rules to declare which books or works she[1] forbids. These
general rules are found now in Canon 1399. A book, therefore, which is not listed by name in the *Index of Prohibited*

---

1. What is stated in can. 1399 is *ecclesiastical law*, applying and
determining, generally, the natural prohibition of books. While the natural law forbids certain books only to certain persons for whom they
are dangerous, the ecclesiastical law determines the books which are
dangerous to the average reader and applies the prohibition to all. That
can. 1399 deals with the ecclesiastical and not with the natural prohibition of books, is clearly shown by can. 1401, which treats of exemption
from the ecclesiastical prohibition of books. The canons dealing with
the permission to read forbidden books prove the same thing, since no
permission can be given to any one to read a book which the natural
law forbids him. (can. 1405). Finally, the very first canon (1384) of
Title XXIII of Book III of the Code, which contains can. 1399, indicates
that that title treats of the exercise of the power of the Church to
examine and forbid books, and, therefore, of ecclesiastical legislation.
Cf. Leo XIII, const. *Officiorum ac munerum*, Jan. 25, 1897, n. 21 (*Fontes*,
n. 632); De Meester, *Compendium*, III, pp. 245, 281; Cocchi, *Commentarium in C. J. C.*, VI, n. 68; Ayrinhac, *Administrat. Legisl.*, p. 292;
Wernz, *Jus Decretal.*, III, p. 110, n. 53.

Books[2] nor in a general way in Canon 1399, is not to be considered as forbidden by the positive law of the Church.[3] It may, however, be forbidden by the local Ordinary or by the natural law. This division of book legislation into general laws and an Index of books prohibited by name goes back to the Council of Trent. In fact the Index published by that Council and approved by Pius IV through his Constitution *Dominici gregis*, of March 24, 1564,[4] consisted of two parts: ten general rules regulating the censorship, expurgation and reading of books, and a catalogue of books prohibited by name.[5] This division has been followed ever since, even in the latest edition of the *Index of Prohibited Books.*[6]

In this chapter a brief explanation of each one of those rules will be given in the order found in Canon 1399. It is well to remind the reader that, whenever the word "book" or *"liber"* is mentioned, reference is made not only to a book strictly so called, but also to every kind of publication unless the opposite is evident.[7]

Art. I. *Non-Catholic Editions and Translations of Holy Scripture.*

Can. 1399. — **Ipso iure prohibentur:**

1° Editiones textus originalis et antiquarum versionum catholicarum sacrae Scripturae, etiam Ecclesiae Orientalis, ab acatholicis quibuslibet publicatae; itemque eiusdem versiones in quamvis linguam, ab eisdem confectae vel editae.[8]

---

2. Books forbidden by special decree of the Holy Office after each edition of the Index are also considered as being in the Index. They will be inserted in the following edition of the same.

3. Preface to the *Index Librorum Prohibitorum Leonis XIII Summi Pontificis Auctoritate recognitus, SSmi D. N. Pii P. P. XI iussu editus* (Rome: 1925), p. XIV.

4. *Fontes*, n. 105.

5. Supra p. 48 f.

6. Vatican: Polyglott Press, 1929.

7. Can. 1384, §2. Cf. also supra, p. 80 ff.

8. Leo XIII, Const. *Officiorum ac munerum*, Jan. 25, 1897, §5 (*Fontes*, n. 632); Cocchi, *Commentarium in C. J. C.*, VI, n. 69; Augustine, *A Commentary*, VI, p. 467 ff.; Blat, *Commentar. Textus C. J. C.*, III, n. 288; Hurley, *Index Legisl.*, p. 67 ff.; Pennacchi, *In Const. Apost. Offic. ac muner.*, p. 60 ff.

The Church considers the Scriptures as the word of God. She takes every possible measure to protect this sacred treasure from all unscrupulous attacks made against it. She is fully aware that the enemies of God and of His Church have distorted, abused and mishandled the Written Word of God in the effort to justify their erroneous tenets and practices. The Church, therefore, is justified in suspecting all Biblical works of non-Catholics. For this reason she forbids *all editions of the original text of the Sacred Scriptures, and of old Catholic versions of the same — of the Eastern as well as of the Western Church — published by non-Catholics; also all translations of the same Scriptures into any language made or published by non-Catholics.*

1. By the *original text* here is meant the text in that language and form in which the Sacred Scriptures were first written.[9] The original language of the Old Testament is Hebrew, with the exception of Wisdom, the second book of the Machabees which were written in Greek, and Jeremias X, 11; Esdras IV, 8-VI, 18; VII, 12-26; Daniel II, 4-VII, which were written in Aramaic.[10] The original language of the New Testament is Greek[11] except for the Gospel of St. Matthew which was first written in the language of the Hebrews.[12]

A *version* is the same as a translation, and the ancient Catholic versions are the various Catholic translations of the Sacred Scriptures of the first six or seven centuries.[13]

Now, all non-Catholic editions of the original text of Holy Scripture or of any ancient Catholic version of the same of the Western or Eastern Church are forbidden. This is true also of those editions which render the original text or the original version with integrity and faithfully and do not attack any dogma of Catholic faith in the introduction or in

---

9. Pennacchi, *o. c.*, p. 60; Hurley, *o. c.*, p. 68.

10. Gigot, *General Introduction to the Study of the Holy Scriptures*, p. 176 f.

11. Gigot, *o. c.*, p. 221 ff.

12. Eusebius, *Hist. Eccl.*, III, 39.

13. Hurley, *o. c.*, p. 68; Pennacchi, *o. c.*, p. 61. Cf. also Gigot, *o. c.*, p. 307 ff.; 260 ff.; 287 ff. These authors may be consulted for examples of old Catholic versions.

the footnotes.[14] This is clear from canon 1400 which allows the use of those works prohibited in can. 1399, n. 1 (and those edited against the prescription of Can. 1391) to biblical and theological students, provided the same books are edited with integrity and faithfully, and in the introduction and in the annotations contain nothing against the dogmas of Catholic faith. If this special permission is granted to a certain class of people, the rest of the faithful are not free to use such works.

2. All translations of the Sacred Scriptures into any language, vernacular or otherwise, *made* or *published by non-Catholics* are forbidden, no matter how good or faithful the translation.[15] This rule is quite comprehensive. It forbids all non-Catholic translations of the Scriptures in any of the dead or literary (non-vernacular) languages, whether non-Catholics made them and published them or merely published them.[16]

This rule also forbids all vernacular translations of the Scriptures made or published by non-Catholics. The Church is absolutely uncompromising in this matter.[17] The reason is that she is *certain* that many errors have been fraudulently[18] or ignorantly incorporated in some such translations and she is *rightly* suspicious of all non-Catholic translations of the

---

14.   Can. 1400. Cf. De Meester, *o. c.,* n. 1362; Hurley, *o. c.,* p. 71.

15.   Leo XIII, Const. *Officiorum ac munerum,* Jan. 25, 1897, §§ 6, 7, 8 (*Fontes,* n. 632) ; *Monitum* of S. C. of the Holy Office, *A A S,* XVII (1925), 137; De Meester, *o. c.,* n. 1362, b; Hurley, *o. c.,* pp. 72-77; Pennacchi, *o. c.,* pp. 62-84; Gennari, *o. c., Il Mon. Eccl.,* X (1897), 35; Boudinhon, *o. c.,* p. 110.

16.   It does not include, if such there be, translations made by non-Catholics but published by Catholics with the Church's approval. Pennacchi, *o. c.,* p. 62, and Hurley, *o. c.,* p. 72, give the following examples of non-Catholic Latin translations: *Versio Munsteri,* (1534 A. D.); *Oecolampadii,* (1534, A. D.) ; *Figurina* of Leo the Jew, (1543) ; *Sebastiani Castalionis,* (Basle, 1551) ; *Junii et Tremelii,* (Geneva, 1590) ; *Genevensis.*

17.   S. C. of the Holy Office, July 26, 1848 (*Fontes,* n. 905) ; and *A A S,* XVII (1925), 137.

18.   E. g., Luther deliberately perverted the Epistle of St. Paul to the Romans, by adding the words "only" (*nur*) in III, 20 and IV, 15, and "alone" (*allein*) in III, 28. Cf. Janssen, *History of the German People,* XIV, 419-425.

Scriptures. She has witnessed in her long experience what
havoc has been caused by the reading of such vernacular
translations as those made by some Frenchmen in the 13th
century,[19] by Wycliff[20] in the 14th century, by Luther in the
16th,[21] and in particular by the so-called Biblical Societies so
often condemned by the Holy See.[22] She loves the Sacred
Scripture. She considers it the word of God. She, as the
Church of God, cannot allow God's children to be poisoned
by adulterated or suspicious Bibles, for then, "the faithful
might drink deadly poison at that fountain from which they
should draw the waters of salutary wisdom".[23] The Church
not only allows[24] but encourages[25] and rewards[26] with indulgences the reading of Catholic editions and translations of
the Bible, when properly approved according to Canons 1385,
§1, n. 1 and 1891. This shows how false is the statement of
many non-Catholics that the Church forbids the reading of
the Bible. For, as has been said, she does not forbid the Bible
itself but only non-approved and non-Catholic editions and
translations of the Bible; her aim is the protection of both
the Word of God and the faithful.[27]

----

19.   Counc. of Toulouse year 1229, Can. 14 (Mansi, XXIII, 197);
Gregory XVI, Encycl. *Inter praecipuas*, May 5, 1844, §4 (*Fontes*, n. 502).

20.   Counc. of Oxford, year 1408 under Archbishop Arundel (Mansi,
XXVI, 1038).

21.   Gregory XVI, encycl. *Inter praecipuas*, May 5, 1844, §4 (*Fontes*, n. 502).

22.   Gregory XVI, *Ibidem*; Leo XIII, const. *Officiorum ac munerum*, Jan. 25, 1897, §8 (*Fontes*, n. 632).

23.   Pius VII in a letter to Stanislaus the Archbishop of Mohilew,
4 Sept. 1817 (Cf. Pennacchi, *o. c.*, p. 69).

24.   Can. 1399, §5.

25.   Letter of Pius VI to Anthony Martini, Apr. 1, 1778 (before
preface of Douay Version). Cf. also Leo XIII, encycl. *Providentissimus
Deus*, Nov. 18, 1893, §2 (*Fontes*, n. 621), wherein he writes: "The
solicitude of the Apostolic office naturally urges, and even compels us,
not only to desire that this great source of Catholic revelation should
be made safely and abundantly accessible to the flock of Jesus Christ,
but also not to suffer any attempt to defile or corrupt it."

26.   Leo XIII, Dec. 13, 1898 (Also before preface of Douay Version).

27.   Pope, *The Catholic Church and the Bible*; Lenhart, *The "Open
Bible" in Pre-Reformation Times*; Malou, *De la lecture de la Bible en*

Editions of the original text of Holy Scripture or of any old Catholic versions as well as translations of the Scriptures into the vernacular or other languages, published by Catholics, in accordance with the prescriptions of the Church (cann. 1385, 1391), are allowed. Cf. *infra*, pp. 145, 150.

Art. II. *Books Opposing or Undermining Religion.*

Can. 1399. — **Ipso iure prohibentur:**
2° **Libri quorumvis scriptorum, haeresim vel schisma propugnantes, aut ipsa religionis fundamenta quoquo modo evertere nitentes.**[28]

Faith is the greatest gift of God to men. The Church has always been and still is conscious of the infinite value of Faith. She remembers the words of St. Paul.[29] "Keep that which is committed to thy trust, avoiding the profane novelties of words, and oppositions of knowledge falsely so called." She, therefore, warns her children against all that is opposed to their Faith and, in the words of St. Jude,[30] pleads with them that they "contend earnestly for the faith once delivered to the saints." The history of the Church's legislation on books[31] shows that she was always concerned in a special way about books which were destructive of religion. Today she is still severe and firm in condemning such works, as is seen in can. 1399, n. 2. The Church here forbids all

---

langue vulgaire; Gibbons, *The Faith of Our Fathers,* chapter VIII: "The Church and the Bible"; Conway, *The Question Box,* pp. 83-84, and other apologetic works.

28. Leo XIII, const. *Officiorum ac munerum,* Jan. 25, 1897, n. 2 (*Fontes,* n. 632); De Meester, *Compendium,* III, n. 1363; Cocchi, *Commentarium in C. J. C.,* VI, n. 69, b; Vermeersch-Creusen, *Ep.,* II, n. 733, 2; Pennacchi, *In Const. Apost. Offic. ac muner.,* p. 53 ff.; *Conference Bulletin of the Archdiocese of New York,* V (1927), 25 ff.; Ayrinhac, *Administr. Legisl.,* p. 293; Boudinhon, *La Nouv. Legisl. de l'Index,* p. 85 ff.; Wernz, *Jus Decretalium,* III, n. 111 (2, nota 55); Hurley, *Index Legisl.,* p. 56 ff.; Van Coillie, *Commentarius,* p. 37 f.; Gennari, "Circa la nuova disciplina", *Il Mon. Eccl.,* X (1897), 16; Moureau, *La Nouv. Legisl.,* p. 41 ff.; Noldin, *Summa Theol. Mor.,* II, n. 708, 2.
29. I *Tim.,* VI, 20.
30. V, 3.
31. Cf. *supra,* p. 26 ff.

*works of any writer, defending heresy or schism, or tending
in any way to undermine the very foundations of religion.*

By the words *quorumvis scriptorum*, can. 1399, n. 2,
rules out any distinction between Catholic and non-Catholic
authors.[32] This canon forbids two classes of works: (1) those
which defend heresy or schism and (2) those which tend to
undermine in any way the very foundations of religion.

1. Libri... *haeresim vel schisma propugnantes.*

Heresy consists in a stubborn denial or doubt of any of
the truths of divine Catholic faith, i. e., those truths which
are contained in the Word of God, as written or handed down
to us, and which are, either by solemn pronouncement or by
the ordinary and universal teaching of the Church, proposed
for belief as divinely revealed truths.[33] An author defending
in his writing what is opposed to truths of divine Catholic
faith can be called a heretic only if he is baptized,[34] but his
writings are said to defend heresy whether he is baptized
or not.

Schism is the voluntary separation from the unity of the
Church. The unity of the Church consists in the union of
its members among themselves and of all the members with
its visible head. Therefore, schism is the refusal of a baptized
person to be subject to the Supreme Pontiff or to have communication with the members of the Church subject to the
Pope.[35] Rebellion against the Ordinary or contempt of some
particular precept of the Supreme Pontiff is not schism.[36]

---

32. De Meester, *o. c.*, n. 1363, a. A book written by a Catholic
containing heretical, schismatical or irreligious *statements* of other men
for the purpose of refuting them *is not* forbidden. On the other hand, a
book originally written by a Catholic, if it be published by another man,
with notes defending heresy, schism or other errors subversive of Faith,
is forbidden. Cf. St. Alphonsus, *De Prohib. Librorum*, V, n. 10; Moureau,
o. c., p. 42, 3.

33. Can. 1325, §2, and 1323, §1.

34. Can. 1325, §2.

35. Can. 1325, §2. Cf. also St. Thomas Aquinas, *Summa Theol.*,
II - II, Quaest. 39, art. 1; Pennacchi, *o. c.*, p. 54.

36. De Meester, *o. c.*, n. 1363, a. However, as Vermeersch-Creusen
remark in their *Epit.* II, n. 660, if one rebels against the Bishop because
and insofar as the Bishop is in union with the Pope, then he is really
schismatic. Cf. also Schmalzgrueber, *Jus Eccl. Un.*, tom. V, tit. VIII, n. 12.

"Haeresim vel schisma *propugnare"* means to defend and maintain heresy or schism by means of arguments. Hence, if a work merely contains some heretical or schismatical statements without proofs or arguments for them, it cannot be said to fall under the rule. St. Alphonsus thus puts this matter in his *Theol. Mor.*, VII, 287:

> Propugnat haeresim liber qui accitis rationibus haeresim stabilire et pro viribus defendere intendit. Eccontra non propugnat haeresim liber in quo obiter et paucis verbis ac quasi aliud agendo haeresis aliqua proponitur. Attamen ut liber haeresim propugnare dicatur, opus non est ut materia libri per se sit religiosa, sed sufficit, ut ad evincendam haeresim aliquam dirigatur, quam data opera et ex instituto probare et defendere conetur.[37]

Authors generally allow the use of heretical writings of such ancient authors as Tertullian, Origen, Eusebius and others.[38]

2. Libri... *Ipsa religionis fundamenta quoquo modo evertere nitentes.*

Books in which the very foundations of religion are undermined are all forbidden. But what is meant by *ipsa religionis fundamenta?* Certainly it applies to all those general *truths of the natural order* which are essential to religion, e. g., the existence of God, the existence and immortality of the soul, freedom of the will, the possibility of miracles, their proving force, the existence of revelation, etc. Some authors[39] restrict the meaning of the *religionis fundamenta* to these and other truths of the natural order. Most authors,[40] however,

---

37. Cf. De Meester, *o. c.*, n. 1363, a; Vermeersch-Creusen, *Ep.*, II, n. 733, 2; and other authors referred to above (page 128, n. 28). An excommunication, reserved in a special manner to the Apostolic See, is incurred *ipso facto* by those who publish, read, keep or defend books written by apostates, heretics and schismatics to foment apostasy, heresy or schism. Can. 2318, §1, and *infra*, p. 219 ff.

38. Cf. *infra*, p. 139 f.

39. Vermeersch-Creusen, *Ep.*, II, n. 733, 2; Noldin, *o. c.*, n. 708, 2 b; Moureau, *o. c.*, p. 42; Genicot-Salsmans, *Inst. Theol. Mor.*, I, n. 452, 1.

40. De Meester, *o. c.*, n. 1363, b; Cocchi, *o. c.*, VI, n. 69, b; Pennacchi, *o. c.*, p. 55; Hurley, *o. c.*, pp. 60-61; Wernz, *o. c.*, III, n. 111

extend the meaning of that phrase also to fundamental *truths of the supernatural order*, i. e., of Christian revelation, such as the divinity of Jesus Christ and the inspiration of the Holy Scriptures. This disagreement of authors has little practical importance, because, if the fundamental truths of the supernatural order are not included in the phrase *religionis fundamenta*, they are certainly included under the general term *heresy* of the same Canon 1399, n. 2.

The attack against the foundations of religion need not be made directly. An author may try to undermine religion directly or indirectly, by argumentation or by pseudo-learned phrases, by calumny or by ridicule, or in other ways.[41] But, whatever be the form in which the attack is made, the book is forbidden.

Therefore, works defending atheism, materialism,[42] skepticism, theosophy,[43] works denying the freedom of the will, the existence of Christian revelation, the divinity of Jesus Christ, the inspiration of the Scriptures, are forbidden.

Art. III. *Books attacking Religion and Good Morals.*

Can. 1399. — **Ipso iure prohibentur:**

3° **Libri qui religionem aut bonos mores, data opera, impetunt.**[44]

(note 55) ; Augustine, *A Commentary*, VI, p. 468 f.; Bouuaert-Simenon, *Man. Jur. Can.*, p. 553; Ferreres, *Institutiones Can.*, II, p. 156; Bucceroni, *Institutiones Theol. Mor.*, II, n. 1305; Cappello, *De Curia*, I, p. 274.

41. Bucceroni, *o. c., II*, n. 1305; De Meester, *o. c.*, III, n. 1363, b; Boudinhon, *o. c.*, p. 88; Wernz, *o. c.*, III, n. 111 (note 55); Pennacchi, *o. c.*, p. 55.

42. "Do historical works, textbooks, etc., which advance materialistic views of human society and its development fall under prohibition? Not unless they propound and defend materialistic philosophy, alleging arguments in its favor and making it clear that they aim to destroy the foundations of religion. Ordinarily, this is not apparent in historical works, scientific textbooks, etc., but the generality of works of this kind by materialistic authors are exceedingly harmful to the young."; *Conference Bulletin of the Archdiocese of New York*, V (1927), 27. Cf. also Genicot-Salsmans, *Casus Conscientiae*, n. 241.

43. Holy Office, June 16, 1919 — *A A S*, XI (1919), 317.

44. De Meester, *Compendium*, n. 1364; Noldin, *Summa Theol. Mor.*,

A very large number of dangerous publications, especially daily and periodicals ones, attack not only single doctrines
of religion, but all religion and all morality. In such writings religion is made to appear as superstition and morals as
obsolete customs. Against such the Church legislates in Can.
1399, n. 3, which forbids books and all other forms of publications (Can. 1384, §2) which of set purpose attack religion
and good morals.

1. Canonists differ here, as in the preceding number of
Can. 1399, in giving the meaning of *religio*. Some authors[44]
claim that it refers to religion in the abstract, to divine
worship, to religious truths wherever found. Accordingly,
this law would proscribe books which attack all religion or
worship of God such as atheistic or materialistic works, as
well as those works which attack the Catholic faith. Others,[46]
however, would restrict the meaning of *religio*, as used here,
to apply to the Catholic religion which alone is true. Therefore, according to these, Can. 1399, n. 3 prohibits works attacking the Catholic religion. For, they say, the Code takes
religion as it is in reality and not in the abstract, and in
reality there is only one true religion, namely the Catholic
religion. On the other hand those who understand *religio* to
mean not alone the Catholic religion, but all religion, prove
their contention by the fact that in the same can. 1399 and
in Can. 1400 the legislator uses the two expressions *religio*
and *fides catholica* not indiscriminately but with a purpose.

II, n. 708, 3; Vermeersch-Creusen, *Ep.*, II, n. 733, 3; Cocchi, *Commenta-
rium in C. J. C.*, VI, n. 69, c; Boudinhon, *La Nouv. Legisl. de l'Ind.*, p.
184 ff.; Hurley, *Index Legisl.*, p. 147 ff.; Pennacchi, *In Const. Apost.
Offic. ac muner.*, p. 162 ff.; Gennari, "Circa la nuova disciplina", *Il Mon.
Ecc.*, X (1897), 81; *Il Mon. Eccl.*, XXXVIII (1927), 21; Van Coillie,
Commentarius, p. 64 ff.; Wernz, *Jus Decretal.*, III, n. 111, note 76;
Lehmkuhl, *Theol. Mor.*, II, n. 1333.

45. Vermeersch-Creusen, *Ep.*, II, n. 733, 3; Pennacchi, *o. c.*, p.
162; Noldin, *l. c.*; Hurley, *o. c.*, p. 90 f.; Augustine, *A Commentary*, VI,
p. 469; Bouuaert-Simenon, *Man. Jur. Can.*, p. 554; Ferreres, *Inst. Can.*,
II, p. 157, n. 2; Boudinhon, *o. c.*, p. 188; Bucceroni, *o. c.*, II, n. 1308;
Putzer, *Commentarium in facultates apostolicas*, (1893), n. 157, II;
Lehmkuhl, *o. c.*, II, n. 1333; Ayrinhac, *Administr. Legisl.*, pag. 293.

46. De Meester, *o. c.*, n. 1364, b; Cappello, *De Curia*, I, p. 287;
Wernz, *o. c.*, III, n. 111 (note 76).

Thus in canons 1399, n. 4, and 1400, the legislator uses the phrase *fides catholica* when he wishes to refer to dogmas of the Catholic faith. In can. 1399, n. 3 he uses *religio* and not *fides catholica,* leading one to understand by it all religion and not simply the Catholic religion. This is the better opinion. Therefore, whether a work attacks religion or divine worship in general or the Catholic religion in particular, it is forbidden by this canon.[47]

2. By *boni mores* is meant *morality,* or all that pertains to right living, particularly chastity.[48] Any work, therefore, which attacks a moral law made known to us either by nature or by revelation, is forbidden. Thus, books against some or all of the Ten Commandments, books defending and promoting divorce, abortion, contraception, suicide and the like are all proscribed by the Church. Pornographic literature also falls under this rule if in it the author not only describes obscene things but also sets out to attack and destroy the precepts of morality. Otherwise it comes under n. 9 of this same canon 1399.

3. *Data opera*[49] *impetunt.* A book or a daily or periodical publication which contains an incidental remark now and then against religion or morality is not forbidden.[50] A publication falls under this law if it attacks religion or morality systematically, of set purpose, deliberately. By the frequency of the irreligious or wicked statements and remarks contained in a paper or magazine or by the line of thought running like a thesis throughout a book the intention of the author or pub-

---

47. Pennacchi, *o. c.,* p. 163; Ayrinhac, *o. c.,* p. 293.

48. Ayrinhac, *o. c.,* p. 293; Vermeersch-Creusen, *Ep.,* II, n. 733, 3; Pennacchi, *o. c.,* p. 84; Augustine, *o. c.,* VI, p. 469; Genicot-Salsmans, *Inst. Theol. Mor.,* I, n. 452, 2; Cappello, *De Curia,* I, p. 287.

49. De Meester, *o. c.,* n. 1364, c; Noldin, *o. c.,* II, n. 708, 3, b; Pennacchi, *o. c.,* p. 164; Augustine, *o. c.,* VI, p. 469; Bouuaert-Simenon, *o. c.,* p. 554; Lehmkuhl, *o. c.,* II, n. 1333; Genicot-Salsmans, *o. c.,* I, n. 452, 2; Hurley, *o. c.,* p. 151 ff.

50. De Meester, *o. c.,* n. 1364, c, d; Ayrinhac, *o. c.,* p. 293. For a newspaper or magazine *as such* to be forbidden it is necessary that it attack religion or morality habitually and systematically. Otherwise, if only a particular number or issue contains such objectionable articles, that number and not the periodical as such, is forbidden. Cf. also Wernz, *o. c.,* III, n. 111 (note 76).

lisher to attack religion or morality becomes clear. The work
is then said to attack religion or morality *data opera*, and is
therefore forbidden.

In the case of a periodical which is forbidden because
it attacks systematically and habitually religion or morality,
all its issues and parts are forbidden, even those which are
harmless in themselves.[51]

Art. IV. *Books of Non-Catholics on Religion.*

Can. 1399. — **Ipso iure prohibentur:**
4° **Libri quorumvis acatholicorum, qui ex professo de religione tractant, nisi constet nihil in eis contra fidem catholicam
contineri.[52]**

The Church suspects religious works written and published by non-Catholics. There are so many errors in the
minds of non-Catholics generally, that they are liable to express their errors in their writings. The Church therefore
wishes her children to learn their religion from safe and approved Catholic sources and not from doubtful non-Catholic
sources.[53] The second of the Tridentine Rules of the Index[54]
proscribed all religious books of heretics. From that time on
until recent times the prohibition against such works was
absolute, that is, it held even when they contained nothing
opposed to Catholic faith. However, in the Leonine constitution[55] and in the Code, the prohibition against non-Catholic

---

51. De Meester, *o. c.*, n. 1364, d. However, cf. supra, p. 109 f.
52. Leo XIII, Const. *Officiorum ac munerum*, Jan. 25, 1897, n. 3
(*Fontes*, n. 632); De Meester, *Compendium*, n. 1365; Cocchi, *Commenta-
rium in C. J. C.*, VI, n. 69, d; Vermeersch-Creusen, *Ep.*, II, n. 733, 4;
Boudinhon, *La Nouv. Legisl. de l'Index*, pp. 89-94; Noldin, *Summa Theol.
Mor.*, II, n. 708, 4; Ayrinhac, *Administr. Legisl.*, p. 293; Pennacchi, *In
Const. Apost. Offic. ac muner.*, p. 55; Moureau, *La Nouv. Legisl.*, p. 43;
Van Coillie, *Commentarius*, p. 39; Gennari, "Circa la nuova disciplina",
Il Mon. Eccl., X (1897), 17; Lugo, *De Virt. Fid.*, disp. 21, sect. 2, n.
48; Hurley, *Index Legisl.*, p. 62 f.; Arndt, *De Libris Prohib.*, p. 115 ff.
53. Lugo, *l. c.*
54. *Fontes*, n. 426.
55. *Officiorum ac munerum*, Jan. 25, 1897, n. 3 (*Fontes*, n. 632).
Cf. proemium of that constitution and supra, p. 58 f., for the reasons
which led to this and other changes in the Church laws on books.

works on religion does not hold if it can be proved that they
contain nothing against the Catholic faith.

In Can. 1399, n. 4, the Church forbids *books of any non-
Catholic treating of religion ex professo, unless it is certain
that they contain nothing contrary to the Catholic faith.*

1. *Quorumvis acatholicorum,* just like *acatholicis quibuslibet* of Can. 1399, n. 1, refers to *all non-Catholics,* baptized
and not baptized. Protestants or other heretics, schismatics,
Jews or infidels and all those who are not in union with the
Catholic Church.[56] This is certainly true, not only because
the word *acatholicus* is used throughout the Code of Canon
Law with that general meaning (e. g., Can. 1099, §1, n. 2;
1964, etc.), but also because the legislator, by adding the word
quorumvis (not found in the corresponding decree of *Officiorum ac munerum,* n. 3), intended to prevent any possible
doubt. However, neither works written by persons suspected
of heresy (as long as they were not heretics)[57] nor those
written by non-Catholics, while they still were in the Catholic
Church come under the class of "libri acatholicorum".[58] On
the contrary, this class includes works written by a committee of Catholics and non-Catholics;[59] also works consisting

---

56.   De Meester, *o. c.,* n. 1365; Boudinhon, *o. c.,* p. 90; Vermeersch-
Creusen, *Ep.,* II, n. 733, 4; Cocchi, *o. c.,* VI, n. 69, d; Noldin, *o. c.,* II, n.
708, 4; Van Coillie, *o. c.,* p. 39; Gennari, *o. et l. c.;* Wernz, *Jus Decretal.,*
III, n. 111 (note 56); Sabetti-Barrett, *Compendium Theologiae Moralis,*
n. 345, quest. 4; Augustine, *o. c.,* VI, p. 469 f.; Bouuaert-Simenon, *o. c.,*
p. 554; Bucceroni, *o. c.,* II, n. 1305; Cappello, *De Curia,* I, p. 274; Genicot-Salsmans, *o. c.,* I, n. 452, 3. However, Genicot, *l. c.,* adds: "non
autem increduli seu apostatae in Ecclesia Catholica baptizati." The
exception seems wrong in view of the general meaning of the word
"acatholici" as recognized by all the authors mentioned. The opinion
of Pennacchi (*o. c.,* p. 55 f.) and Hurley (*o. c.,* p. 62), according to
which only baptized non-Catholics were referred to in the word "acatholicorum" is ruled out by the Code. No author, since the Code, holds it,
as far as the writer has been able to find out.

57.   Can. 2515.

58.   Lugo, *De Virtute Fid. Div.,* disp. 21, sect. 2, nn. 41 and 44.

59.   Suarez, *De Fid.,* disp. 20, sect. 2, n. 13; De Meester, *o. c.,* n.
1385, b. The work must be *ex professo* on religion. Otherwise there is
no prohibition on this score. Thus "encyclopedias and similar works
compiled by Catholics and non-Catholics in collaboration, even though
the articles contributed by the latter may contain heresies or champion

of a text and a commentary when the larger part (text or commentary) was written by a non-Catholic.[60] This is not the case when a Catholic quotes in his work some heretical or perverse passages for the purpose of refuting them, provided these passages are not so copious that they form the larger part of the work.[61]

2. *"De religione* tractant."* Religion here is taken in its widest sense. Any book which treats of the relations between God and man treats of religion. Under this class, therefore, come books on the Holy Scriptures, theology, canon law, Church history, morals, liturgy, asceticism, books of devotion, and even books on philosophy insofar as they deal with the duties of men towards God and the religious society.[62] It makes little or no difference whether the work of a non-Catholic treats of the Catholic religion, or of his own religion or any other religion or of religion in general. In all cases, as long as the topic is religion, the book is forbidden, unless it contains nothing contrary to the Catholic faith.[63] However, books of magic and other superstitions usually do not belong to the class of religious works, unless they claim to have reference to God and divine power.[64]

3. *"Ex professo* de religione tractant."* Books of non-Catholics which refer to religion only here and there and in

---

materialism and other grievous errors" are not forbidden, Koch-Preuss, *Handbook of Moral Theology,* IV, p. 407. However, even such works may be forbidden in their totality or in the individual volumes if they come under any of the classes of books described in can. 1399. See supra, p. 110 f.

60.   De Meester, *l. c.;* Suarez, *o.* et *l. c.,* nn. 46-47; Lugo, *l. c.;* Schmalzgrueber, *Jus Eccl. Un.,* tom. V, pars 1, tit. VII, n. 36; Wernz, *o. c.,* III, n. 111 (note 56); Arndt, *o. c.,* n. 103, 2.

61.   Suarez, *o.* et *l. c.*

62.   Noldin, *o. c.,* II, n. 708, 4, b; De Meester, *o. c.,* n. 1365, b, α; Ayrinhac, *l. c.,*; Boudinhon, *o. c.,* p. 90; Van Coillie, *o. c.,* p. 39; Arndt, *o. c.,* n. 102, a, n. 104; Reiffenstuel, *Jus Can. Un.,* lib. V, t. VII, n. 46; Wernz, *o. c.,* III, n. 111 (note 56).

63.   Augustine, *A Commentary,* VI, p. 470; Bouuaert-Simenon, *Man. Jur. Can.,* p. 554; Genicot-Salsmans, *Inst. Theol. Mor.,* I, n. 452, 2. Cf. list of non-Catholic works on religion given by Benedict XIV in the decrees attached to his Index of 1758. This may be seen in the Index itself or in Arndt, *o. c.,* n. 104 ff.; Boudinhon, *o. c.,* p. 92.

64.   Lugo, *o.* et *l. c.,* n. 54. They are forbidden in can. 1399, n. 7.

passing, are not included in this class.[65] In order that the book of a non-Catholic fall under this canon, it must treat of religion *ex professo*. This means that religion is a principal subject matter of the book, that the author, throughout the whole book, or in notable parts of it (e. g., a chapter) states his tenets on a religious question, then brings forward arguments and reasons to establish them and finally endeavors to answer and explain away opposing doctrines. It is not necessary that the title or the matter of the whole book be about religion.[66] This description applies to some sermon books, Bible commentaries, Bible stories, doctrinal treatises, etc., written by non-Catholics but not, generally, to non-Catholic Rituals or prayer books[67] since these usually do not treat of religion *ex professo* in the sense just explained.[68]

4. *"Nisi constet nihil in eis contra fidem catholicam contineri."* Books of non-Catholics dealing *ex professo* with religion cannot be read, unless it is *certain* that they *contain nothing* against the Catholic faith. The presumption is that

---

65. Leo XIII, const. *Officiorum ac munerum*, Jan. 25, 1897, n. 4 (*Fontes*, n. 632).

66. De Meester, *o. c.*, n. 1365, a, b; Boudinhon, *o. c.*, p. 90; Arndt, *o. c.*, n. 102, b; Hurley, *o. c.*, p. 62; Pennacchi, *o. c.*, p. 56; Wernz, *o. c.*, III, n. 111 (note 56); Bouuaert-Simenon, *o. c.*, p. 554; Reiffenstuel, *o. et l. c.*, n. 46. The two phrases *ex professo* and *data opera* are commonly used with the same meaning, to denote, namely, a systematic treatment of a subject at least in a notable part of a work with the intention of convincing the reader. Theoretically, however, to treat something *ex professo* means to do so in the whole book or a notable part of it; to treat something *data opera* refers not so much to the quantity of space used nor to the system followed as to the intention and thesis running throughout a treatise. See on this point, besides the authors just mentioned, Cocchi, *o. c.*, VI, n. 68, b; De Meester, *o. c.*, n. 1359, c; Hurley, *o. c.*, p. 151 ff.; Gennari, *o. c.*, p. 17; Augustine, *o. c.*, VI, p. 469; Cappello, *De Curia*, I, p. 275; Lehmkuhl, *o. c.*, II, n. 1330.

67. Cf. Sanchez, *Opus Morale in Praecepta Decalogi*, lib. II, Cap. X, n. 27. However, cf. Lugo, *o. c.*, n. 42; Suarez, *De Fid. Div.*, disp. 20, sect. 2, n. 12.

68. Therefore, the *Book of Common Prayer*, even though it contains stantements against the Catholic Church, does not treat of religion *ex professo* and, accordingly, is not forbidden in virtue of can. 1399, n. 4. However, it is forbidden because it contains a non-Catholic translation of the book of Psalms. Cf. supra, p. 126 f.

such works contain errors and that the faithful cannot safely use them until the contrary be proven. If, therefore, it becomes morally certain from an official declaration of the Church, or from a statement of theologians, or from the testimony of some learned and reliable person or of some Catholic paper or magazine reviewing it, that a book does not contain anything against the Catholic faith, such a work ceases to be regarded as forbidden.[69] But, what of the person who is unable to find out from others whether a certain non-Catholic work on religion contains anything contrary to the Catholic faith? According to some authors,[70] he may lawfully begin to read the book, but, should he discover that it contains something contrary to the Faith, then he must stop reading it at once. However, this opinion is not justified by the words of the law: "*nisi constet*".

It is not necessary that such a book contain absolutely nothing against the Faith. For non-Catholic books on religion usually contain some errors. Moreover, in those books in which religion is treated *ex professo*, with theses, proofs, answers to objections, etc., to *contain* something erroneous is almost equivalent to *attacking* some article of faith. Therefore, books which contain nothing of importance against the Catholic faith, are not forbidden.[71] By Catholic faith here is meant the complexus of all those truths which are contained in the Word of God as written or handed down to us, and which are, either by solemn pronouncement or by the ordinary and universal teaching of the Church, proposed for belief as divinely revealed truths.[72] There is not much danger

---

69. De Meester, *Compendium*, n. 1365, c; Vermeersch-Creusen; *Ep.*, II, n. 733, 4; Cocchi, *Commentarium in C. J. C.*, VI, n. 69, d; Pennacchi, *In Const. Apost. Offic. ac muner.*, p. 56; Boudinhon, *La Nouv. Legisl. de l'Index*, p. 91; Van Coillie, *Commentarius*, p. 40; Augustine, *A Commentary*, VI, p. 470 f.; Bouuaert-Simenon, *Man. Jur. Can.*, p. 554; Genicot-Salsmans, *Inst. Theol. Mor.*, I, n. 452, 3; Hurley, *Index Legisl.*, p. 63.

70. Boudinhon, *l. c.*; Hurley, *l. c.*

71. Bouuaert-Simenon, *o. c.*, p. 554; De Meester, *o. c.*, n. 1365, b, γ; Augustine, *o. c.*, VI, p. 470; Wernz, *o. c.*, III, n. 111 (note 65). Cf. also Reiffenstuel, *Jus Can. Un.*, lib. V, tit. VII, nn. 51-54.

72. Can. 1323. §1.

that errors against the Catholic faith be found in books of pagan mythology or of Assyrian, Egyptian, Greek or Roman antiquities.

In the first rule of the Leonine Constitution *Officiorum ac munerum,*[73] it was prescribed that all books that had been condemned before the year 1600, either by supreme Pontiffs or by Oecumenical Councils, even though not found listed in the new Index, were to be considered as still forbidden in the same manner as when first condemned, except those which were permitted by the same Constitution. This applied to books of Arians, Macedonians, Nestorians, Eutychians, Berengarius, Abelard, Arnold of Brescia, Marsilius of Padua, Wicliff, Hus, Jerome of Praga, Luther, Calvin, Jansenius and many others. Neither the Code nor the latest edition of the Index (1929) refers to this matter. Such ancient works, therefore, are to be judged according to the rules laid down for all forbidden books in the Code.[74] However, canonists generally allow now, as they have allowed in the past, at least to ecclesiastics, the books of very ancient heretics such as Tertullian, Origen, Eusebius, Pelagius, Novatian, Theodore of Mopsuestia, even though such works, condemned originally, would *strictly* come under the ban of the Church even now, because of the errors contained in them. The reason they adduce in confidently allowing such old works is that their errors are already known and they offer little or no danger of perversion now. The errors are now practically extinct, while the knowledge of those works is very useful for the study of Church history and theology.[75] Therefore, they add, one need

---

73. Jan. 25, 1897 (*Fontes,* n. 632).

74. Can. 1399. For censures issued against those works originally, cf. Pennacchi, *o. c.,* p. 47, and *infra,* p. 220.

75. Lugo, *De Virt. Fid.,* disp. 21, sect. 2, n. 29; Arndt, *De Libris Prohib.,* n. 97; De Meester, *Compendium,* III, n. 1363; Boudinhon, *La Nouv. Legisl. de l'Index,* pp. 83-85 and 303; Pennacchi, *In Const. Apost. Offic. ac muner.,* p. 49 ff.; Moureau, *La Nouv. Legisl.,* p. 41; Van Coillie, *Commentarius,* p. 37; Schmalzgrueber, *Jus Eccl. Un.,* tom. V, pars I, tit. VII, n. 31; Suarez, *De Fid. Div.,* disp. 20, sect. 2, n. 12; Bouuaert-Simenon, *Man. Jur. Can.,* p. 553; Bucceroni, *Inst. Theol. Mor.,* II, n. 1305; D'Annibale, *In Constitutionem Apostolicae Sedis,* n. 35, nota 4; Lehmkuhl, *Theol. Mor.,* II, n. 1183, Nota; Genicot-Salsmans,

not have any fears of conscience for having in his possession
any of Labbe's collections or Migne's Patrologies which contain works of such ancient heretics as Tertullian, Eusebius,
Origen and others for the purpose of keeping in their entirety
the monuments of ecclesiastical tradition.[76] The same thing
cannot be said about heretics of later date such as Luther,
Calvin, Jansenius whose writings are still dangerous.[77]

Art. V. *Books forbidden because of lack
of approbation.*[78]

Books having a bearing on religion or morality may not
be published, even by laymen, without previous ecclesiastical
approval. However, not all such works published without approval are, for that reason, forbidden. Can. 1399, n. 5, gives
an exhaustive list of books which are forbidden when published without the previous approbation of the Church. Outside of those works mentioned in Can. 1399, n. 5, no others
are forbidden for the *sole* reason that they carry no *Imprimatur*, or ecclesiastical approval.[79] This article will be divided
into three sections so that the three parts of Can. 1399, n. 5,
may be properly classified and clearly explained.

I

Can. 1399. — **Ipso iure prohibentur:**
5°   **Libri de quibus in can. 1385, §1, n. 1 (i. e., Libri Sacrarum Scripturarum vel eorumdem adnotationes et commentaria)
si editi fuerint non servatis canonum praescriptionibus.**

Inst. Theol. Mor., I, n. 452, 1; Bouix, *Tract. de Curia Rom.,* p. 530
(Prop. 3); Vermeersch, *De Proh. et Cens. Libr.,* p. 54.

76.   De Meester, *o. c.,* n. 1363.

77.   De Meester, *o. c.,* III, page 283, note 5.

78.   De Meester, *o. c.,* III, nn. 1366-67-68; Cocchi, *o. c.,* VI, n. 69, e;
Wernz, *Jus Decretal.,* III, n. 111 (note 53); Betten, *The Roman Index,* p. 39.

79.   Therefore, books of Catholics on canon law, church history,
theology, theodicy, ethics, ascetics are allowed even if published without an *Imprimatur.* Cf. Noldin, *Summa Theol. Mor.,* II, n. 708, 5, c, γ.
However, there is reason to suspect such works. Cf. Betten, *The Roman
Index,* p. 39.

The Church law prescribes now as it has consistently done from the sixteenth century, particularly from the Council of Trent[80] that all Scriptural works should be examined by her before their publication.[81] This law can be seen working through the centuries. It is repeated at various intervals by different popes, and recently by Pius IX,[82] and Leo XIII.[83] The Leonine constitution, while restating the obligation of previous ecclesiastical approbation for these works, did not make the lack of such approbation a reason, in all cases, for the prohibition of them.

There is no question here of scriptural works of non-Catholics because these have already been attended to in nn. 1-4 of the same canon; nor is there question of vernacular translations of the Bible published by Catholics, as these come under the second part of n. 5. The works therefore contemplated by the words of n. 5 *libri de quibus in can. 1385, §1, n. 1* are: (1) Catholic editions of the original text of the Sacred Scriptures; (2) Catholic editions of the old Catholic versions of Sacred Scriptures, both of the Oriental and of the Latin Churches; (3) annotations and commentaries of the Sacred Scriptures.[84]

All these works are forbidden, if they were published without the necessary ecclesiastical approbation, of which can. 1385 treats. It is immaterial whether they were published before or after the Code.[85]

II

Can. 1399. — **Ipso iure prohibentur:**

---

80. Sessio IV, *de editione et usu sacrorum librorum.* Cf. also supra, p. 47 ff.

81. Except Catholic translations of the Bible into the vernacular, if published with annotations taken from the Fathers. Cf. supra, p. 107, note 28.

82. Const. *Apostolicae Sedis*, 12 Oct. 1869, §IV, n. 4 (*Fontes*, n. 552).

83. Const. *Officiorum ac munerum*, Jan. 25, 1897, n. 41 (*Fontes*, n. 632).

84. *Annotations* accompany and elucidate the text; a *commentary* constitutes a complete interpretation or explanation of a book of Holy Scripture or of a part of it. Cf. De Meester, *Compendium*, III, n. 1387, 2.

85. De Meester, *o. c.*, n. 1366 and n. 1358, b; supra, p. 106 f.

5⁰ **Libri de quibus in. . . can. 1391. . . si editi fuerint non servatis canonum praescriptionibus.**[86]

In other words, *vernacular translations of the Scriptures, made by Catholics*[87] *are forbidden, if they have not been approved by the Holy See, or have not been published under the supervision of the Ordinary and with annotations taken especially from the holy Fathers of the Church and from learned Catholic writers.*

There were times when the Church was compelled by reason of circumstances to withdraw the use of the Scriptures in the vernacular from the people of those sections where it was abused.[88] For a long time also the permission of the Bishop or of the Inquisitor, under the advice of the pastor or of the confessor, was required for one to read lawfully Catholic translations of the Scriptures in the vernacular. The reason for these restrictions was that more harm than good came from the indiscriminate use of the Scriptures,[89] especially in the hands of ignorant and illiterate people.

After all, St. Peter himself, writing of St. Paul's epistles, says: "In which are certain things hard to be understood, which the unlearned and the unstable wrest, as they do also the other scriptures, to their own destruction."[90] While the Church was compelled thus to restrict the use of the Bible somewhat, she never forbade it absolutely, not even in the vernacular. Rather, she encouraged the study and use of the Written Word of God.[91] Now, as long as a vernacular translation of the Scriptures is made by a Catholic and is approved according to can. 1391, it can be freely read by any one. The

---

86. De Meester, *o. c.*, III, n. 1367; Boudinhon, *o. c.*, p. 108 ff.; Wernz, *o. c.*, III, n. 111 (note 58); Hurley, *o. c.*, p. 73 ff.; Pennacchi, *o. c.*, p. 63 ff.; Arndt, *o. c.*, nn. 110-111.

87. Vernacular translations made by non-Catholics have already been proscribed in can. 1399, n. 1.

88. See supra, pages 36 f., 127.

89. Leo XIII, const. *Officiorum ac munerum*, Jan. 25, 1897, n. 7 (*Fontes*, n. 632); Malou, *De la lecture de la Bible en langue vulgaire;* Pennacchi, p. 67 ff.; supra, pp. 36 f., 127.

90. II Pet. III, 16.

91. See supra, pag. 127.

Church no longer requires the permission or advice of the pastor or confessor.[92]

The Code prescribes, in can. 1391, that "translations of the Holy Scriptures in the vernacular may not be printed unless they have been approved by the Holy See, or are published under the supervision of the Bishops *and* are provided with annotations taken especially from the holy Fathers of the Church and learned Catholic writers." [93] The Code makes no mention of annotations, in dealing with translations approved by the Holy See. In reality, however, no such approval has been granted for a translation without notes for the use of the people.[94] Translations which carry only the approval of the Bishop, must have annotations.[95] The Bishop in this case is any one of the Ordinaries mentioned in Can. 1385, §2. The supervision or vigilance of the Bishops consists not merely in a cognizance of the work but in an active diligence to see that the work is done well and in conformity with the mind of the Church.[96] Augustine[97] suggests a comparison with the Latin Vulgate or with some other translation already approved by the Church.

---

92. While the positive law of the Church does not require such permission or advice, yet, if one is afraid, because of his weakness, that he may expose himself to danger by reading certain portions of the Bible, he should consult his pastor or confessor. The natural law may forbid such a person those portions which are dangerous to him. Moreover, it is advisable to consult a priest before reading the Bible in the vernacular, because the edition which is about to be read may be one of those forbidden by the Church. Cf. De Meester, *o. c.*, III, n. 1367.

93. Leo XIII, Const. *Officiorum ac munerum*, Jan. 25, 1897, n. 7 (*Fontes*, n. 632); De Meester, *Compendium*, n. 1348; Wernz, *Jus Decretal.*, III, n. 111 (note 58); Hurley, *Index Legisl.*, p. 73 ff.; Noldin, *Summa Theol. Mor.*, II, n. 700, 1; Arndt, *De Libr. Prohib.*, nn. 110-111; Bouix, *Tract. de Curia Rom.*, pp. 545-548; Pont. Bibl. Com., Nov. 17, 1921 (*A A S*, XIV - 1922, 27); Augustine, *A Commentary*, VI, p. 447 ff.

94. De Meester, n. 1348 (note 2).

95. The particle "et" in can. 1391 (*sub vigilantia Episcoporum* ET *cum adnotationibus*) is to be interpreted copulatively and not disjunctively, according to a reply given by the Commission for the Interpretation of the Code, May 20, 1923 — *A A S*, XVI (1924), 115.

96. Pennacchi, *o. c.*, p. 65.

97. *O. c.*, VI, p. 448.

The notes, which must accompany the translation before it may be approved by the Ordinary, are to be taken principally from the Fathers of the Church and from approved Catholic authors. It is to be noted that it is not necessary that the annotations report *verbatim* the sayings of the Fathers, but that the Patristic meaning be given so that such notes will convey to the reader the traditional interpretation of the Church.[98] Annotations relating to geographical, ethnographical, topographical, archeological notions, and, in general, to facts of the natural sciences, may be taken from the writings of scholars, regardless of their religion.[99] Paraphrastic translations, Bible histories, are considered as treatises on the Scriptures, not editions. In them no notes are required. The same is true of a Concordance or a Monotessaron of the gospels or any other such work, composed of words or passages taken from the Sacred Scriptures, and arranged so as to form a treatise.[100] Prayerbooks containing the gospels and epistles of the Sundays and Feastdays of the year, or the Psalter, are approved by Bishops, even though they are not accompanied by notes.[101] This exception, however, does not hold for the gospels or epistles or any other books of the Scriptures published separately and under their name in the vernacular without

---

98. Wernz, *Jus Decretal.*, III, n. 111 (note 58); Vermeersch-Creusen, *Ep.*, II, n. 726, 6; De Meester, *Compendium*, III, n. 1348.

99. De Meester, *o. c.*, n. 1348, a; Pennacchi, *o. c.*, p. 66.

100. Vermeersch-Creusen, *l. c.*; Hurley, *Index Legisl.*, p. 75 f.; Boudinhon, *La Nouv. Legisl. de l'Ind.*, p. 109; De Meester, *o. c.*, III, n. 1348; Wernz, *o. c.*, III, n. 111 (nota 58); Van Collie, *Commentarius*, pp. 43-44; Arndt, *De Libr. Prohib.*, p. 129; Genicot-Salsmans, *Inst. Theol. Mor.*, I, n. 453, 1. Heymans in his work *De Ecclesiastica Librorum Aliorumque Scriptorum in Belgio Prohibitione Disquisitio*, p. 195, gives this explanation:

> "... cum voces paraphrastice intercalatae verae sint, ex ss. Patribus catholicisque scriptoribus derivatae annotationes; quae immo in ea, in qua prodeunt forma, legentis intellectum magis iuvant et ab errore felicius preservant, quam annotationes forma ordinaria adhibitae."

101. De Meester, *l. c.*; Noldin, *o. c.*, II, n. 708, 1, b; Vermeersch-Creusen, *l. c.*; Pennacchi, *o. c.*, p. 258; Moureau, *o. c.*, p. 67, 3; Bouuaert-Simenon, *o. c.*, p. 549; Ferreres, *Inst. Can.*, II, p. 154; Van Collie, *o. c.*, p. 44; Genicot-Salsmans, *l. c.*

notes.[102] A translation of the Scriptures in the vernacular
which does not fulfill the requirements of can. 1391[103] as just
explained, is forbidden. However, those translations which
were published before Leo XIII's const. *Officiorum ac munerum*,[104] wherein the *vigilantia Episcoporum* was first introduced,[105] if they are accompanied by annotations taken from
the Fathers of the Church and Catholic scholars and have been
accepted, are permitted, even though they do not bear the explicit approval of the Ordinary.[106]

III

Can. 1399. — Ipso iure prohibentur:
5° ... ex illis (libris) de quibus in cit. cap. 1385, §1, n. 2,
libri ac libelli qui novas apparitiones, revelationes, visiones, prophetias, miracula enarrant, vel qui novas inducunt devotiones,
etiam sub praetextu quod sint privatae, si editi fuerint non servatis canonum praescriptionibus.[107]

Here the Church forbids all *books* and *pamphlets* which
give an account of *new* apparitions, revelations, visions,
prophecies, miracles, or introduce *new* devotions, even under
the pretext that they are private, if they were published without observing the canonical requirements, i. e., previous censorship and approval of the ecclesiastical authorities.

The Church is very slow in accepting any new extraordinary manifestation of God's miraculous intervention, and

---

102. De Meester, *o. c.*, n. 1348.
103. When the book bears the *Imprimatur* of the Ordinary (Can.
1394, §1) it may be safely used.
104. Jan. 25, 1897 (*Fontes*, n. 632).
105. N. 7.
106. Wernz, *o. c.*, III, n. 111 (note 58); De Meester, *o. c.*, III,
n. 1358, b; supra, p. 107, note 2.
107. Decree of the Holy Office, *Sanctissimus*, March 13, 1625
(*Fontes*, n. 719); Urban VIII, Const. *Caelestis Jerusalem*, July 5, 1634
(*Fontes*, n. 213); Leo XIII, Const. *Officiorum ac munerum*, Jan. 25,
1897, n. 13 (*Fontes*, n. 632); De Meester, *Compendium*, III, n. 1368;
Noldin, *Summa Theol. Mor.*, II, n. 708, 5, c; Boudinhon, *La Nouv. Legisl.
de l'Index*, p. 127 ff.; Cocchi, *Commentarium in C. J. C.*, VI, n. 69;
Vermeersch, *De Prohib. et Cens. Libr.*, p. 66 ff.; Pennacchi, *In Const.
Apost. Offic. ac mun.*, p. 103 ff.

this she does only after a long critical and painstaking investigation has shown it to be true. She is also cautious about the introduction of any new devotion. The hurried acceptance and publication of extraordinary events which may or may not be true, on the part of overzealous Catholics, have drawn the ridicule and contempt of the enemies of the Church. The introduction and publication of many new devotions, foreign to the spirit of the Church and sometimes fundamentally erroneous, may do great damage.[108]

Therefore, the Church has on many occasions condemned by name, works narrating new apparitions, revelations, visions, prophecies, miracles or introducing new devotions.[109] In the Code she forbids all such books or pamphlets, unless they have been first examined and approved in accordance with canon law. Thus, the Church clearly gives us her attitude on this matter, not indeed one of skepticism in all that is extraordinary, but rather one of caution and prudence.

Not every form and size of such publications is forbidden, as is usually the case, whenever the word *liber* or *libri* is used in the title of the Code on censorship and prohibition of books.[110] By defining the object of prohibition here as being *libri ac libelli*, the legislator wishes to exclude those kinds of publications which are neither *books* nor *booklets* or *pamphlets* such as single sheets, daily papers.[111] This was already held by some authors[112] under the Leonine legislation which used in the Const. *Officiorum ac munerum*, n. 13, the words *Libri aut scripta*. The Code seems to have taken up this opinion when it changed the very general term *scripta* into *libelli*. Thus, here the word *libri* is not used in the extensive sense given it by can. 1384, §2, because the opposite is clear from

---

108.   Boudinhon, *o. c.*, p. 133, II.

109.   Examples of such decrees may be seen in De Meester, *o. c.*, III, p. 288, n. 5 and p. 290; Pennacchi, *o. c.*, p. 108 ff.

110.   Cf. Can. 1384, §2.

111.   De Meester, *o. c.*, n. 1368; Noldin, *o. c.*, II, n. 708, 5, c, α; Cocchi, *o. et l. c.*; Ayrinhac, *o. c.*, p. 294. Manuscripts are not *published* (editi) and, therefore, could not be included under *libri ac libelli*.

112.   Hurley, *o. c.*, p. 122; Pennacchi, *o. c.*, p. 106 ff.; Moureau, *o. c.*, p. 60.

the use of *libelli* ("nisi aliud constet"). Probably the word *libelli*, also includes magazines and reviews.[113]

1. *Libri ac libelli qui novas apparitiones, revelationes, visiones, prophetias, miracula enarrant.* These extraordinary happenings are called *new*, not alone if they are of recent date, but also if they are new to the readers or hearers, inasmuch as they have not been accepted as yet by the Church through a formal decree or by approved use. In other words, they are *new* if they are recent or have not been accepted by the Church.[114] Moreover, for the prohibition of such books and booklets, it is necessary that the narration of new miracles, visions, etc., be diffuse, almost *ex professo*, that it take up a substantial part of the book or pamphlet, and, besides, that those events be treated as supernatural. Therefore, an occasional reference to some extraordinary things in the life of one who died in the odor of sanctity would not make that work forbidden, especially if nothing is written about their miraculous nature.[115] Likewise, Catholic magazines[116] which might come under *libelli*, are not forbidden because they relate among the news of the times, wonderful happenings, healings, etc., which may take place at Lourdes or elsewhere. This is constantly done and the authorities do not object to it. The commentators of this law, therefore, declare such a practice of our Catholic publications lawful.[117]

---

113. De Meester, *o. c.*, n. 1341, n. 3 (and note 5).

114. De Meester, *Compendium*, III, n. 1341, 3; Cocchi, *Commentarium in C. J. C.*, n. 69, e, γ; Wernz, *Jus Decretal.*, III, n. 111 (note 67); Vermeersch, *De Prohib. et Cens. Libr.*, p. 68; Boudinhon, *La Nouv. Legisl. de l'Index*, p. 131. *Recent* miracles of servants of God whose case of beatification or canonization is before the S. C. of Rites, are included here, until they have received the approval of the Congregation of Rites. Can. 1387. If their case is not pending any more, the approbation of the Ordinary suffices according to can. 1385.

115. Cocchi, *o. c.*, VI, n. 69, e, γ; De Meester, *o. c.*, III, n. 1368, a, γ; Cappello, *De Curia*, I, p. 277; Augustine, *o. c.*, VI, p. 471.

116. Daily or weekly papers are clearly excluded from the meaning of *libelli*.

117. De Meester, *o. et l. c.*; Vermeersch, *De Proh. et Cens. Libr.*, p. 68; Pennacchi, *o. c.*, p. 108; Boudinhon, *o. c.*, p. 132 f. De Meester remarks on pag. 289, note 1: "*Aliter esset resolvendum si ageretur de diario quod ex intento, ad modum objecti principalis, de his materiis age-*

However, the editors of those publications should not declare themselves in favor of the miraculous nature of those events, but await the judgment of the Church.[118]

No one may lawfully read or keep books or booklets narrating those extraordinary events in the manner explained, if they have not been properly examined and approved by the Church authorities in accordance with Canon law. These authorities are the Ordinary in all cases except those relating to pending trials of beatification or canonization of the Servants of God, in which the approval of the S. C. of Rites must be obtained.[119]

2. *Libri ac libelli qui. . . novas inducunt devotiones, etiam sub praetextu quod sint privatae, si editi fuerint non servatis canonum praescriptionibus.*[120] This rule forbids unapproved works which introduce *new* devotions. Devotions are ways of exercising the virtue of religion, i. e., worship of God and the saints. They may be *new* either as regards their *object* (e. g., devotion to the heart of St. Joseph) or as regards their *manner* (e. g., the devotion of the Virgin Priest).[121] The Church, always strict in this matter, is very slow to

---

ret." However, we do not think that a newspaper would come under this law because it could hardly be called *liber* or *libellus*.

118. Pennacchi, *o. c.*, p. 108, 4.

119. Can. 1385, §1, n. 2, §2; 1387; De Meester, *o. c.*, n. 1368, a, β; Urban VIII, in June 5, 1631, ordered that at the beginning and end of every book narrating miracles, visions and other extraordinary events, a declaration be placed wherein the author avows that he states those facts as he believes them to be true, but not on the authority of the Catholic Church. (Cf. Benedict XIV, *De Beatific. et canoniz.*, lib. 2, Cap. 11, n. 6 ff.; Cap. 12, n. 6). Authors generally now regard this law as abrogated since no mention is made of it in the new book legislation. Cf. Vermeersch, *De Prohib. et Cens. Libr.*, p. 67; De Meester, *o. c.*, III, p. 288, note 6; Cocchi, *o. c.*, n. 69, e, γ; Bucceroni, *o. c.*, II, n. 1308.

120. Holy Office, Jan. 13, 1875 (*Fontes*, n. 1037); De Meester, *o. c.*, III, n. 1368, 2; Boudinhon, *o. c.*, p. 133 ff.; Hurley, *o. c.*, p. 155 ff.; Pennacchi, *o. c.*, p. 108 ff.; Van Coillie, *o. c.*, p. 52, II; Gennari, "Circa la nuova disciplina", *Il Mon. Eccl.*, X (1897), 39; Wernz, *o. c.*, III, n. 111 (n. 67); *Perfice Munus!*, III (1928), 179; Vermeersch, *De Proh. et Cens. Libr.*, p. 69 ff.

121. Noldin, *o. c.*, II, n. 708, 5, c, β; Vermeersch, *De Prohib. et Cens. Libr.*, p. 69 f.

approve a devotion whose object is new.[122] She is more le-
nient in approving devotions which are new only in regard
to their manner or method. Many new devotions have been
expressly condemned as, e. g., devotion to the most sacred
blood of Mary, to the Virgin Priest, to the Heart of Penitent
Jesus, etc.[123]

Only books and booklets which *introduce* new devotions
are forbidden; not those which make a passing reference to
some new devotion. The author must treat the matter at
length in an effort to start the devotion.[124] It is immaterial,
for our purpose, whether the devotion is intended for private
use only.

The necessary approbation is to be obtained from the
Ordinary[125] unless the new devotion touches on the sacred
rites; for then the matter is to be referred to the Sacred
Congregation of Rites.[126]

All books just referred to, and contained in Can. 1399,
n. 5, are forbidden if the prescriptions of the Code (Cann.
1385-1394) have not been followed out. These canons as applied to the books in question simply prescribe previous censorship and episcopal approbation for all of them; for vernacular translations of the Bible which are not approved by
the Holy See, that they be made under the supervision of
the Bishop and with annotations; and for works relating to
miracles, visions and other extraordinary events with reference to some servant of God whose case is before the Sacred
Congregation of Rites, that they be submitted to that Congregation for approval. The fact that a priest or a religious
did not secure the necessary permission before he published
a work with the *Imprimatur* of an Ordinary, other than his
own (Cann. 1385, §3; 1386, §1), does not cause the work to
be forbidden.[127] Unless the prescriptions of the Code were fol-

---

122. Boudinhon, *o. c.*, p. 133 f.

123. Other condemned devotions may be seen in De Meester, *o. c.*,
III, p. 290; Boudinhon, *o. c.*, p. 134 f.; Pennacchi, *o. c.*, p. 109 f.; *Perfice
Munus!*, *l. c.*

124. Vermeersch, *De Prohib. et Cens. Librorum*, p. 69.

125. Can. 1385, §1.

126. Vermeersch, *o. c.*, p. 70.

127. Ferreres, *Casus Conscientiae*, I, n. 611.

lowed in publishing works described in can. 1399, n. 5, they are to be considered as forbidden. This is certain if they were published after the Code; and it is equally true, according to the better opinion,[128] if they were published before the Code. In this view, the law embodied in can. 1399, n. 5, affects books printed in the past. Exception is made, however, of Catholic translations of the Bible in the vernacular provided with the proper notes but lacking approval of the Ordinary, unnecessary at the time of their publication (before the const. *Officiorum ac munerum*).[129] They are not forbidden.

The same conclusion holds if we interpret *si editi fuerint non servatis canonum praescriptionibus* to mean that such works as described in can. 1399, n. 5, are forbidden if the prescriptions of canon law *existing at the time of their publication* were not followed out. Since all such works were subject to previous censorship and ecclesiastical approbation long before the Leonine constitution, even as far back as the end of the XV century,[130] if unapproved, they are now forbidden. The only exception is again found in Catholic translations of the Bible in the vernacular published before the promulgation of Leo XIII's constitution in 1897.[131] No obligation existed for these to obtain episcopal approbation,[132] as long as they had annotations taken from the Fathers and Catholic scholars. Therefore they are permitted.

All other Catholic books of piety, religion, theology, etc., which are mentioned in can. 1385, §1 but not in can. 1399, n. 5, may be read even though they bear no ecclesiastical approbation unless they fall under some other part of the same can. 1399.

---

128.   Supra, p. 106 ff.

129.   De Meester, *o. c.*, III, n. 1358, b.

130.   Innocent VIII, const. *Inter multiplices*, Nov. 17, 1497—*Statuta seu Decreta Prov. et Dioec. Syn. S. E. Coloniensis* (Cologne, 1554), p. 280.

131.   Pennacchi, *o. c.*, p. 64 f.

132.   Decr. S. C. Ind., 13 June, 1757 (found in Boudinhon, *o. c.*, p. 366). Cf. also Boudinhon, *o. c.*, p. 107.

Art. VI. *Works subversive of Catholic doctrine
or discipline*

Can. 1399. — **Ipso iure prohibentur:**
**6° Libri qui quodlibet ex catholicis dogmatibus impugnant
vel derident, qui errores ab Apostolica Sede proscriptos tuentur,
qui cultui divino detrahunt, qui disciplinam ecclesiasticam evertere contendunt, et qui data opera ecclesiasticam hierarchiam,
aut statum clericalem vel religiosum probris afficiunt.**[133]

In this paragraph, the Church prohibits in very clear
terms five classes of works which do untold harm to the fold
of Christ by spreading error, discontent and discord, namely,
*books which attack or ridicule any of the Catholic dogmas,
which defend errors condemned by the Holy See, which disparage divine worship, which strive to overthrow ecclesiastical discipline, or which deliberately and systematically use
opprobrious language in treating of the ecclesiastical hierarchy
or of the clerical or religious state.*

Books is a term applied to every size and form of publication, as explained in can. 1384, §4; and there is no indication in this place to the contrary. Moreover, it is clear from
the words of the Code (*impugnant vel derident... tuentur...
detrahunt... evertere contendunt*), that the Church does not
forbid all works which contain any such attack or ridicule
against Catholic dogma, any word of defense for something
declared by the Church to be erroneous, any disparaging remark made against divine worship or any reference against
ecclesiastical discipline. A passing word or remark here and
there in a book, even though offensive to the Church, does not
make the work forbidden. On the other hand, it is not necessary that the *attack, ridicule, defense* or *striving to overthrow* be made *ex professo* as Pennacchi[134] held before the
Code, since the legislator uses that phrase in other parts of

---

133. Benedict XIV, General decrees, n. 13 (Index of Benedict XIV,
158); Leo XIII, const. *Officiorum ac munerum*, Jan. 25, 1897, nn. 11,
14 (*Fontes*, n. 632); De Meester, *Compendium*, III, n. 1369; Cocchi, *Commentarium in C. J. C.*, VI, n. 69 f.; Boudinhon, *La Nouv. Legisl. de l'Index*,
p. 117 ff.; Augustine, *A Commentary*, VI, p. 472; Genicot-Salsmans,
Inst. Theol. Mor., I, n. 452.
134. *O. c.*, pag. 91 ff.

this canon, and purposely omits it here.[135] Hence, the middle position, taken by Wernz[136] and others, is preferable. They hold that this *attack, ridicule, defense, striving to overthrow* must be real and grave and made in some notable way. After all, that is what is meant by saying that a book attacks or ridicules the Virgin birth of Christ, a book attacks the Mosaic authorship of the Pentateuch, a work tries to destroy ecclesiastical discipline by arousing Catholics to rebellion, etc. These things are not usually done in a word or a sentence or even a paragraph. They generally occupy a notable part of a work (a chapter, part of a chapter, or even a page) and are quite serious in the consequences intended.

1. Books are forbidden which *attack* any of the Catholic dogmas by adducing arguments against them; or which *ridicule* them by treating them in a jocose, satirical or comical way. By a *Catholic dogma* is meant a truth revealed by God and solemnly defined or declared as such either by an Ecumenical Council or by the Roman Pontiff speaking *ex cathedra*,[137] e. g., the Immaculate Conception.[138]

---

135.   Van Coillie, *o. c.*, p. 48 f.

136.   *O. c.*, III, n. 111 (note 63); Vermeersch, *De Prohib.*, p. 57 f.; Boudinhon, *o. c.*, p. 118, p. 142; Cocchi, *o. c.*, VI, n. 69 f.; Gennari, *o. c., Il Mon. Eccl.*, X (1897), 37. Wernz writes: "*Hinc media interpretatio videtur legitima, scilicet quod requiratur et sufficiat vera et gravis detractio notabili quodam modo facta.*" While Wernz is referring to *detractio*, the same can be reasonably said of the other verbs, i. e. *impugnant, derident, tuentur, evertere contendunt.*

137.   Can. 1323; Pius IX, letter *Tuas libenter*, 21 December, 1863 (*Fontes*, n. 538; Denzinger, *Enchir.*, nn. 1683-1684). Truths proposed as divinely revealed in the ordinary and universal teaching of the Church are indeed of Catholic faith, but they are *not dogmas* of faith. This term is applied only to truths solemnly defined by the Church, as is clear from the letter of Pius IX *Tuas libenter*, wherein the Holy Father writes:

> Dum vero debitas illis deferimus laudes, quod professi sint veritatem, quae ex catholicae fidei obligatione necessario oritur, persuadere Nobis volumus, noluisse obligationem, qua catholici magistri ac scriptores omnino adstringuntur, coarctare in iis tantum, quae *ab infallibili Ecclesiae iudicio veluti fidei dogmata ab omnibus credenda proponuntur.* Atque etiam Nobis persuademus, ipsos noluisse declarare, perfectam illam erga revelatas veritates adhaesionem, quam agnoverunt necessariam omnino esse ad verum scientiarum progressum assequendum et ad errores confutandos, obtineri posse, *si dumtaxat dogmatibus ab Ecclesia expresse definitis fides et obsequium adhibeatur.* Namque

2. Books are forbidden which *defend errors condemned by the Holy See,*[139] namely doctrines or propositions which have been condemned, at least as *erroneous,* by the Holy See, i. e., either by the Supreme Pontiff personally or by one of his official organs, usually the Holy Office[140] or the Biblical Commission.[141] Errors of this kind condemned in the past are contained in the *Syllabus* of Pius IX,[142] in the decree of the Holy Office *Lamentabili,*[143] and in the encyclical of Pius X,

---

etiamsi ageretur de illa subiectione, quae fidei divinae actu est praestanda, limitanda tamen non esset ad ea, quae expressis oecumenicorum Conciliorum aut Romanorum Pontificum huiusque Sedis decretis *definita* sunt, sed ad ea quoque extendenda, quae ordinario totius Ecclesiae per orbem dispersae magisterio tanquam divinitus revelata traduntur ideoque universali et constanti consensu a catholicis theologis ad fidem pertinere retinentur.

Sed cum agatur de illa subiectione, qua ex conscientia ii omnes catholici obstringuntur, qui in contemplatrices scientias incumbunt, ut novas suis scriptis Ecclesiae afferant utilitates, idcirco eiusdem conventus viri recognoscere debent, sapientibus catholicis haud satis esse, ut *praefata Ecclesiae dogmata recipiant ac venerentur,* verum etiam opus esse, ut se subiciant tum decisionibus, quae ad doctrinam pertinentes a Pontificiis Congregationibus proferuntur, tum iis doctrinae capitibus, quae communi et constanti Catholicorum consensu retinentur ut theologicae veritates et conclusiones ita certae, ut opiniones eisdem doctrinae capitibus adversae quamquam haereticae dici nequeant, tamen aliam theologicam mereantur censuram.

The italics in the quotation are the author's.

Cf. also Tixeront, *History of Dogmas,* I, p. 1-2.

138. Pius IX, const. *Ineffabilis Deus,* 8 Dec., 1854 (*Pii IX Acta,* Pars I, p. 597).

139. Leo XIII, const. *Officiorum ac munerum,* Jan. 25, 1897, n. 14 (*Fontes,* 632) ; S. C. Ind., May 19, 1898 — *A S S,* XXX (1898), 697; De Meester, *Compendium,* n. 1369, b; Boudinhon, *La Nouv. Legisl. de l'Index,* p. 141; Hurley, *Index Legisl.,* p. 123 ff.; Pennachi, *In Const. Apost. Offic. ac muner.,* p. 125 ff.; Wernz, *Jus Decretal.,* III, n. 111 (note 68) ; Moureau, *La Nouv. Legisl.,* p. 63, 4; Bouuaert-Simenon, *Man. Jur. Can.,* p. 555, b; 557, n. 1.

140. Can. 7; Can. 247.

141. Leo XIII, ap. lett., *Vigilantiae,* 30 Oct., 1902 (*Fontes,* n. 649) ; Pius X, motu proprio *Praestantia Scripturae,* 18 Nov. 1907 (*Fontes,* n. 681).

142. Year 1864 (*Fontes,* n. 543; Denzinger, *Enchir.,* nn. 1700 ff.).

143. July 4, 1907 (*Fontes,* n. 1283; Denzinger, *Enchir.,* nn. 2001 ff.).

Pascendi.[144] Among these, are found errors concerning the inspiration of the Scriptures, which were expressly mentioned in the const. *Officiorum ac munerum*, n. 11.[145] Needless to say, only when these errors are defended by means of arguments or reasoning, are the books containing them forbidden.[146]

3. *Books* are forbidden *which disparage divine worship*,[147] that is, try to discredit, or defame, vilify, asperse, divine worship so as to lessen its esteem in others. This must be done in some notable way.[148] By *cultus divinus* is meant the honor with submission which is due to God because of His infinite perfections and man's dependence upon Him (*cultus latriae*), to the Blessed Virgin Mary (*cultus hyperduliae*), to the Angels and to the Saints (*cultus duliae*) because of their close relation to God. Honor belongs also to sacred relics and images on account of their connection with the persons to whom they refer.[149] Divine worship embraces therefore all the acts by which man honors God in Himself or in His Saints. In a special manner, it applies to liturgy which is the sum total of the things, words and actions which have been approved by the Church for rendering external worship to God.[150] There-

---

144. Sept. 8, 1907 (*Fontes*, n. 680, Denzinger, *Enchir.*, n. 2071 ff.).

145. See also Leo XIII, encycl. *Providentissimus Deus*, Nov. 18, 1893 (*Fontes*, n. 621).

146. Boudinhon, *La Nouv. Legisl. de l'Ind.*, p. 142.

147. Leo XIII, const. *Officiorum ac munerum*, Jan. 25, 1897, n. 11 (*Fontes*, 632); De Meester, *o. c.*, III, n. 1369, c; Cocchi, *o. c.*, VI, n. 69, γ; Boudinhon, *o. c.*, p. 118; Wernz, *o. c.*, III, n. 111 (note 63); Pennacchi, *o. c.*, p. 88 ff.; Hurley, *o. c.*, p. 89 ff.; Moureau, *o. c.*, p. 55, 1; Vermeersch, *De Prohib. et Cens. Libr.*, p. 57 f.; Gennari, *o. c.*, *Il Mon. Eccl.*, X (1897), 37; Arndt, *o. c.*, p. 148.

148. Wernz, *o. et l. c.*

149. Can. 1255, §1; De Meester, *o. c.*, III, n. 1247.

150. Cocchi, *o. c.*, V, p. 167; Wernz, *o. c.*, III, n. 314; Van Der Stappen, *Sacra Liturgia* (3. ed., Mechlin, 1911), I, 2; Vermeersch Creusen, *Ep.*, II, n. 572 ff.; Gury-Tummolo, *Compendium Theologiae Moralis*, II, n. 1016. Liturgy, then, is not co-extensive with divine worship, rather it is part of it. Therefore, De Meester (*o. c.*, III, n. 1359, c), and Cocchi (*o. c.*, VI, n. 69, f. γ), are not exact when they describe divine worship as *S S. Ritus* and *actus liturgici*. Both authors, in previous parts of their work (De Meester, *o. c.*, III, n. 1247 ff.;

fore those books which try to discredit or lessen the esteem of the worship due to God, the Blessed Virgin Mary, the Saints, relics, images or other holy things, such as the sacraments, are all forbidden.[151]

4. Books are forbidden which strive *to overthrow or undermine ecclesiastical discipline* in whole or in part. This may be done by attacking the supremacy of the Pope, the authority of Bishops to teach and to rule, the celibacy of the Clergy, the legislation of the Church on the censorship and prohibition of books, the right of the Church to own property, etc.[152]

5. Books are forbidden which *deliberately and systematically use opprobrious language in treating of the ecclesiastical hierarchy or of the clerical and religious state.*[153] This aspersion or opprobrious language must be quite noticeable and the evil intention of the author must be evident throughout the book or a large part of it, since the words *data opera*[154] are used. An occasional or passing remark is not sufficient. The defamation here must be more noticeable than were the attacks, defense, etc., in the cases contemplated in the other four parts of can. 1399, n. 6, just explained, because of the use here of the words *data opera.*[155]

In order that books of this kind may be considered forbidden, their authors must assail the ecclesiastical hierarchy or the religious or clerical state in themselves, as institutions and not simply the men, some or many, who may be members of the hierarchy or of a religious order. A book containing a personal invective against a certain pope, a bishop, a priest or

Cocchi, *o. c.*, V, p. 167 ff.), give the correct interpretation of *cultus divinus* as found in the III Part of the III Book of the Code, and as explained above.

151. Boudinhon, *o. c.*, p. 118; Hurley, *o. c.*, p. 90 f.; Pennacchi, *o. c.*, p. 88 ff. who gives many examples.

152. De Meester, *o. c.*, n. 1369, d; Cocchi, *o. et l. c.*, δ; Augustine, *o. c.*, VI, p. 472 f.

153. Leo XIII, const. *Officiorum ac munerum*, n. 11 (*Fontes*, n. 632); De Meester, III, n. 1369, e; Cocchi, *l. c.*; Boudinhon, *o. c.*, p. 120; Hurley, *o. c.*, p. 97; Pennacchi, *o. c.*, p. 96; Wernz, *o. c.*, III, n. 111 (n. 65); Vermeersch, *De Prohib. et Cens. Libr.*, p. 60; Lehmkuhl, *Theol. Mor.*, II, n. 1330.

154. Supra, p. 133 f.

155. Boudinhon, *o. c.*, p. 120; Vermeersch, *l. c.*

a religious or against a number of popes, bishops, priests or a whole religious order, is not forbidden.[156] Nevertheless, the writers of injurious works of this kind are subject to ecclesiastical punishments, in accordance with can. 2344. A book comes under this class which uses opprobrious language against the Papacy, the Episcopacy, the Priesthood in which the powers of order and jurisdiction reside; or against the Clergy in general or the Religious state; or against the vows of poverty, chastity and obedience taken by religious.[157] The same is true of a book which holds that the ecclesiastical hierarchy opens the way for ambition, the religious state leads to laziness, the clerical life to ambition, avarice, pride, etc.[158]

Art. VII. *Superstitious and Spiritistic Books*

Can. 1399. — **Ipso iure prohibentur:**
7° Libri qui cuiusvis generis superstitionem, sortilegia, divinationem, magiam, evocationem spirituum, aliaque id genus docent vel commendant.[159]

Superstition is described by St. Thomas[160] as "a vice opposed to religion by way of excess; not because in the worship of God it does more than true religion, but because it offers Divine worship to beings other than God or offers worship to God in an improper manner." There are four species of superstition: (1) Improper worship of the true God; (2) idol-

---

156. Pennacchi, *o. c.*, p. 97; De Meester, *l. c.*; Wernz, *l. c.*; Vermeersch, *l. c.* However, cf. Boudinhon, *o. c.*, p. 120.

157. Letter of Leo XIII to Card. Gibbons *Testem benevolentiae*, Jan. 22, 1899 (*Fontes*, n. 640); De Meester, *l. c.*; Boudinhon, *o. c.*, p. 120; Hurley, *o. c.*, p. 104; Pennacchi, *o. c.*, p. 96.

158. Vermeersch, *De Prohib. et Cens. Libror.*, p. 60.

159. Leo XIII, const. *Officiorum ac munerum*, Jan. 25, 1897, n. 12 (*Fontes*, n. 632); De Meester, *Compendium*, n. 1370; Boudinhon, *La Nouv. Legisl. de l'Index*, p. 121 ff.; Pennacchi, *In Const. Apost. Offic. ac muner.*, p. 97 f.; Hurley, *Index Legisl.*, p. 104 ff.; Van Coillie, *Commentarius*, p. 49 f.; Vermeersch, *De Prohib. et Cens. Librorum*, p. 60 f.; Gennari, "Circa la nuova disciplina", *Il Mon. Eccl.*, X (1897), 38 f.; Genicot-Salsmans, *Inst. Theol. Mor.*, I, n. 452, 5; Arndt, *De Libr. Prohib.*, nn. 115-117.

160. *Summa Theol.*, II-II. Quaest. 92, art. 1. Cf. also J. Wilhelm, "Superstition", *Cath Encycl.*, XIV, 339; Noldin, *Summa Theol. Mor.*, II, p. 166 ff.

atry; (3) divination; (4) vain observances, which include magic and occult arts.

Improper worship of God consists in adding something false or foolish to the worship of God. *Idolatry* is a superstition by which divine worship is given to a creature. *Divination* is a superstition by which an attempt is made to extract from creatures knowledge of future events or of things known only to God. Under the head of *vain observances* come all those beliefs and practices, which, at least by implication, attribute supernatural or preternatural powers for good or for evil to causes evidently incapable of producing the expected effects. Many times these extraordinary effects are obtained through the aid of the devil. Black *magic* is one of these vain observances.

Divination,[161] then, is a generic term used to designate all kinds of superstitious practices by which attempts are made to discover future possible events or other unknown things. Persons may strive to know future or hidden things by expressly invoking the devil and using his aid. This is called divination in the strict sense and is divided into many different kinds according to the methods used. If this knowledge is sought from the devil by means of charms we have *praestigia;* if by dreams, *oniromancy;* if by the evocation of the dead, *necromancy* or *spiritism;* if by some appearances in earth, *geomancy;* if in water, *hydromancy;* if in the air, *aeromancy;* if in fire *pyromancy;* if in the entrails of dead animals, *haruspicy.*

Moreover, persons may strive to know the future or hidden things, without expressly invoking the devil, by making use of the most accidental occurrences and the most trifling personal dispositions. Thus, there is the practice of forecasting the future of a child from the moon or star under which it was born, which is called *astrology;* if from the crowing of fowl or the croaking of birds of flight, *augury;* if from accidental words or actions, *omen;* if from the lines of the palm of the hand, *chiromancy* or *palmistry;* if from crystal

---

161. Hurley, *o. c.*, p. 104 ff.; Noldin, *o. c.*, II, n. 153 ff. Cf. also Bouché A.-Leclercq, *Histoire de la divination dans l'antiquité*, 4 vols. (Paris, 1879-1882).

gazing, *crystallomancy*. Other such practices are lucky and unlucky days, numbers, persons, things, actions, etc.

A third kind of divination is that exercised by observing the results of certain actions placed intentionally and seriously by men for the purpose of knowing hidden things. This is what is called *sortilegium* and is usually done by casting dice, cutting cards, melting lead or alum, opening a book, etc.[162]

In the last two classes of divination, even though the devil is not expressly invoked, yet it is often through the aid of the devil that hidden things become known.[163] Hypnotism also, in some of its forms, is superstitious.[164]

All the forms of superstitions just explained and many others were very widespread at the coming of Christianity. The religion of Christ, however, wherever it went, strenuously opposed superstition and the result was that superstition diminished in great measure, but did not disappear entirely. Therefore, the Church has repeatedly throughout the centuries condemned every kind of superstition and has forbidden all works which contain superstitious teachings.[165] Thus the very first mention of Church action against evil books, is the burning of the superstitious books of the new converts at Ephesus.[166] The opposition of the Church to all kinds of superstitions and her absolute unwillingness to make any concession in her legislation against superstitious books, may be seen particularly in the ninth of the Tridentine rules on the Index,[167] in the constitution of Sixtus V, *Coeli et terrae*, of Jan. 5, 1586;[168] in the constitution of Urban VIII, *Inscrutabilis*, of Mar. 31, 1631;[169] in the apostolic letter of Clement XII, *Compertum*, of Aug. 24, 1734;[170] in the decrees of Benedict XIV, *De libris prohibitis nec in Indice nominatim ex-*

---

162. St. Thomas Aquinas, *Summa Theol.*, II-II, Quaest., 95, art. 3.
163. *Ibidem*; Noldin, *o. c.*, II, n. 152, 2.
164. Noldin, *o. c.*, II, n. 168; Hurley, *o. c.*, p. 108 ff.
165. Arndt, *o. c.*, n. 115.
166. *Acts*, XIX, 18. Cf. supra, p. 18.
167. *Fontes*, n. 426 (after Benedict XIV's *Sollicita ac provida*, July 9, 1753).
168. *Fontes*, n. 157.
169. *Fontes*, n. 210.
170. *Fontes*, n. 296.

pressis, §2, n. 14;[171] in the constitution of Leo XIII, *Officiorum ac munerum*, of Jan. 25, 1897, n. 12;[172] and finally in can. 1399, n. 7 of the Code. The Church is still just as severe as ever in condemning not only superstitions of every sort, but all books and other forms of publications which may teach and commend such practices. Therefore, in Can. 1399, n. 7, she forbids *books which teach or encourage any kind of superstition, fortune-telling, sorcery, magic, evocation of or communication with spirits and similar practices.* Not the mere narration of these superstitious practices, but the teaching or recommending thereof causes the book to be forbidden. *To teach* these practices means, to impart the necessary notions regarding them, to give the rules to be followed and to show the way of exercising them; *to recommend* these practices amounts to the same thing as to extol and praise them, to attract favor to them.[173] A book that gives every detail of a certain superstition for the purpose of exposing it and condemning it, is not forbidden.[174] Vermeersch[175] would place here among the superstitious books forbidden, the Talmud and Magazor, which were condemned at various times in the past but are not expressly mentioned in the present law. However, as Boudinhon[176] rightly observes, it is difficult to see any reason for classifying these books with works teaching and encouraging superstitions, divinations, etc. They were originally forbidden, at least the Talmud, because of blasphemies against the Christian religion.[177] This being the case, such books may fall under nn. 3-4 of can. 1399. Nevertheless, if all the ceremonies of the Jews, especially those based on their tradition and not on the Bible, such as the various washings, the sabbatical strictness, etc., for which Our Lord upbraided the Pharisees,[178] are considered superstitious, then

---

171. *Index of Benedict XIV*, 1758.
172. *Fontes*, n. 632.
173. De Meester, *o. c.*, III, n. 1370.
174. Boudinhon, *o. c.*, p. 125; De Meester, *o. c.*, III,. n. 1370.
175. *De Prohib. et Cens. Libr.*, p. 61. Cf. also Moureau, *La Nouv. Legisl. de l'Index*, p. 58.
176. Pag. 126 f.
177. Arndt, *o. c.*, nn. 116-117.
178. Mat. XII, *passim*; XV, 1-11.

there is reason to place the books teaching those ceremonies among the works condemned by can. 1399, n. 7. As a matter of fact there is much contained in them which may properly be called superstition of improper worship of God. In practice, because of this doubt in regard to their superstitious character, the Talmud and Magazor are forbidden only if and insofar as they contain something opposed to the Catholic faith.[179]

Art. VIII. *Books defending duelling, suicide, divorce, Freemasonry or other similar societies*

Can. 1399. — **Ipso iure prohibentur:**
8° Libri qui duellum vel suicidium, vel divortium licita statuunt, qui de sectis massonicis vel aliis eiusdem generis societatibus agentes, eas utiles et non perniciosas Ecclesiae et civili societati esse contendunt.[180]

The law of the Church, therefore, *forbids books which declare duelling, suicide or divorce licit, or, in treating of the masonic or other similar sects, contend that these are useful and not pernicious to the Church and civil society.* This law does not forbid books which only occasionally and perfunctorily mention the matter of duel, divorce, Freemasonry, etc. The matter must be dealt with in some notable way.[181] Otherwise, how could these forbidden institutions and practices be "shown as lawful and not pernicious" or as "useful to the Church and civil society"? This requires statement of facts,

---

179. Can. 1399, n. 4.

180. Leo XIII, const. *Officiorum ac munerum*, Jan. 25, 1897, n. 14 (*Fontes*, n. 632); De Meester, *Compendium*, III, n. 1371; Cocchi, *Commentarium in C. J. C.*, VI, n. 69, h; Vermeersch, *De Proh. et Cens. Libr.*, pp. 61-65; Boudinhon, *La Nouv. Legisl. de l'Ind.*, p. 136 ff.; Noldin, *Summa Theol. Mor.*, II, n. 708, 8; Hurley, *Index Legisl.*, p. 117 ff.; Pennacchi, *In Const. Apost. Offic. ac muner.*, p. 111 ff.; Van Coillie, *Commentarius*, p. 53; Augustine, *A Commentary*, VI, p. 474; Gennari, "Circa la nuova disciplina", *Il Mon. Eccl.*, X (1897), 40; Moureau, *La Nouv. Legisl.*, p. 61 ff.; Wernz, *Jus Decretal.*, III, n. 111 (note 68); Genicot-Salsmans, *Inst. Theol. Mor.*, I, n. 594. Cf. also Quigley, J., *Condemned Societies* (Washington: Catholic University, 1927).

181. Supra, p. 151 f.; De Meester, *o. c.*, III, n. 1371, *Praenotandum;* Hurley, *o. c.*, p. 121 ff.

proofs, answers to objections, which amounts practically to an *ex professo* treatment of the matter.[182] While can. 1399, n. 8, does not contain the clause *ex professo*, yet the verbs used by the legislator amount to the same thing. Accordingly, the text-books of law in those countries in which divorce is granted are not forbidden if they just declare the law on divorce and give a commentary of it; but they are forbidden if expressly and with arguments and reasons they defend the lawfulness of divorce.[183]

1. Libri qui duellum vel suicidium, vel divortium licita statuunt.

Duel is a combat between two persons or two small groups fought with deadly weapons by agreement as to time and place. It is also defined as a combat entered into by two or a few persons in equal numbers, by private authority, by agreement as to time and place and (sometimes) arms, and with danger of death, mutilation or wound.[184] Duelling has always been condemned by the Church[185] and is condemned today, as can be seen in cann. 1240, §1, n. 4; 1241; 2351. The reason is that duelling is contrary to the law of God who gives no one power over his own or other peoples' life.[186] Besides, one should have recourse to the law for reparation of injuries or satisfaction for offenses. Fencing between students in German or other universities is likened to duelling and suffers the same prohibition of the Church as duel it-

---

182. Hurley, *o. c.*, p. 121 ff. Pennacchi (*o. c.*, p. 111) writes: *libros hos ex professo, vel saltem principaliter, de interdictis agere debere, non obiter aut perfunctorie.* Cf. also Bouuaert-Simenon, *o. c.*, p. 556; Noldin, *o. c.*, II, 708, 8; Boudinhon, *o. c.*, p. 136 ff.; Bucceroni, *Inst. Theol. Mor.*, II, n. 1308; Genicot-Salsmans, *o. c.*, I, n. 452, 2.

183. Boudinhon, *o. c.*, p. 138.

184. De Meester, *o. c.*, III, n. 1371, a; Pennacchi, *o. c.*, p. 112; Hurley, *o. c.*, p. 117; Cappello, *De Curia*, I, p. 278.

185. Arndt, *De Libr. Prohib.*, n. 125.

186. Noldin, *o. c.*, II, n. 349. Boudinhon, *o. c.*, p. 137, adds: "...la malice speciale du duel... provient de ce que le duel est choisi comme un moyen de reparer son honneur, d'obtenir satisfaction d'une injure, de terminer une discussion personnelle; et que ce moyen est complètement disproportionné au but à atteindre."

self.[187] A combat between two persons or two small groups, ordered by public authority for the purpose of avoiding or ending a just war, is not a crime.[188] A book defending this kind of duelling which is lawful, is not forbidden. But any work defending private duelling is prohibited.

Suicide[189] is a wilful and direct killing of one's self on one's own authority. God, the sole master and lord of life and death, absolutely forbids the taking of one's own life by suicide.[190] The Church punishes suicides by depriving them of Christian burial[191] and those who have attempted suicide by other punishment.[192] The many suicides which have taken place, especially of late years, prove clearly the wisdom of the Church in forbidding books defending suicide.

Divorce,[193] as taken here, is not simply a separation of husband and wife from bed and board, but that granted by some civil governments whereby the bond of marriage is sacrilegiously declared broken and a new marriage is authorized, while the former partner is still living. This is called perfect divorce as against imperfect divorce or separation, and is directly opposed to the law of God as expressed in the Scripture,[194] and defined and declared by the Church.[195] The pro-

---

187.   Noldin, *o. c.*, II, n. 350; S. C. C. to the Bishop of Wratislavia (Breslau), Aug. 9, 1890 (*Thesaurus Resol. S. C. Concilii,* CXLIX [1890], 769); *Il Mon. Eccl.,* XXXVIII (1926), 267 ff.

188.   Noldin, *o. c.*, II, n. 349, 2.

189.   Noldin, *o. c.*, II, n. 326; Pennacchi, *o. c.*, p. 115 f.; Boudinhon, *o. c.*, p. 139; Hurley, *o. c.*, p. 118 f.

190.   *Ex.* XX, 13; *Gen.* IX, 6; *Deut.* XXXII, 39; *Wis.* XVI, 13 ff.; *Rom.* XIV, 7-9.

191.   Can. 1240, §1, n. 3.

192.   Cann. 985, n. 5; 2350, §2.

193.   De Meester, *o. c.*, III, n. 1371, c; Boudinhon, *o. c.*, p. 138; Pennacchi, *o. c.*, p. 116 f.; Hurley, *o. c.*, p. 119.

194.   *Gen.* II, 24; Mat. XIX, 6; Mark X, 11-12; Luke XVI, 18; *Rom.* VII, 2-3; *I Cor.* VII, 10-11, 39; *Eph.* V, 22.

195.   C. of Trent. Sess. XXIV, *Doctrina de sacramento matrimonii;* Leo XIII encycl. *Arcanum,* 10 Feb., 1880 (*Fontes,* n. 580); Pius XI encycl. *Sacri Connubii,* of Dec. 31, 1930 (*A A S,* XXII [1930], 539). In the words of Leo XIII (*l. c.*),

    "They [these divorces] render the marriage contract infirm; they diminish the good-will between man and wife; they offer ruinous incitements to conjugal infidelity; they prevent the

hibition against literature of this kind is intended to lessen
and, if possible, remove entirely the harm which is being
done by the flood of books, pamphlets, magazines, etc., advocating divorce.

2. Libri qui... de sectis massonicis vel aliis eiusdem ge- neris societatibus agentes, eas utiles et non perniciosas Ecclesiae et civili societati esse contendunt.[196]

That Freemasonry, as a whole, is hostile to Church and
State we know from many sources.[197] This we gather from
the end which it has in view, from the revelations and con-
fessions of many who were its members, from the books and
the laws which the society has published, from the edicts of
those governments which condemned it in the beginning, from
those who have written about the origin and history of the
society, and, finally, from the different constitutions issued
by the Roman Pontiffs for the purpose of condemning the

---

offspring from being properly reared and educated; they sow
the seeds of discord amongst families; and they lower the dignity of woman, who runs the risk of being cast aside when she
has satisfied the lust of man. Now, since there is nothing that
leads to the extinction of families, and to the exhaustion of
kingdoms, so much as corruption of morals, it is quite easy
to see that these divorces — the natural outcome of moral
corruption — are highly injurious to the prosperity of both
families and states; for experience teaches us that, while they
are themselves the results of corruption, they are the cause
of still further corruption. Now, all those evils will appear
the greater if we consider that if once the permission of
divorces be granted, there is nothing to confine them within
fixed and determined boundaries."

196. De Meester, *Compendium*, III, n. 1371, b; 1232, d; Cocchi,
Commentarium in C. J. C., VI, n. 69, h; Boudinhon, *La Nouv. Legil. de
l'Index*, p. 138 ff.; Noldin, *Summa Theol. Mor.*, II, n. 708, 8; Woywod,
A Practical Commentary on the Code of Canon Law, II, p. 484 f.; Hurley,
Index Legisl., p. 123; Pennacchi, *In Const. Apost. Offic. ac muner.*, p.
117 ff.; Vermeersch, *De Prohib. et Cens. Libr.*, p. 62; Van Coillie, *Com-
mentarius*, p. 54; Genicot-Salsmans, *Inst. Theol. Mor.*, I, n. 594; Cappello,
De Curia, I, p. 278; Moureau, *La Nouv. Legisl.*, p. 62.

197. Pennacchi, *o. c.*, p. 117 ff. Cf. Preuss, *A Dictionary of secret
and other societies* (St. Louis: Herder, 1924); *A Study of American
Freemasonry* (St. Louis: Herder, 1924); Quigley, J., *Condemned Societies* (Washington: Catholic University, 1927); Conway, *Question Box*
(1929), p. 210 ff.

society. and inflicting severe punishments on its leaders,[198] and from the Code itself.[199]

What are the other societies referred to in *aliis eiusdem generis societatibus?* From the many documents issued by the Holy See against Freemasonry and kindred societies and from the Code, we learn that the Church here refers to all other societies which *"plot against* the Church or the legitimate civil powers".[200] "The Church" includes her doctrine, her constitution, and ecclesiastical persons; the phrase "legitimate civil powers" refers to the civil government which has been legitimately constituted.[201] A book is forbidden not only when it opposes both Church and State; but also when it attacks either the one or the other. Religious sects, like Protestants, Old Catholics, etc., which do not conspire against Church or State are not included here.[202] Needless to say, the society must be a *true society* in the sense of a body of persons united in the same program "by a solid and impenetrable alliance".[203] Besides these two elements — society, plotting against Church or legitimate civil powers — some authors require that the society be somewhat *secret;*[204] not in the sense that the plotting is done secretly, for Pius IX in

---

198. Clement XII, const. *In eminenti*, 24 Apr., 1738 (*Fontes*, n. 299); Benedict XIV, const. *Providas*, 18 May, 1751 (*Fontes*, n. 412); Pius VII, const. *Ecclesiam*, 13 Sept., 1821 (*Fontes*, n. 479); Leo XII, const. *Quo graviora*, 13 March, 1825 (*Fontes*, n. 481); Gregory XVI, *Mirari vos*, 15 Aug., 1832 (*Fontes*, n. 485); Pius IX, const. *Apostolicae Sedis*, 12 Oct., 1869 (*Fontes*, n. 551); Leo XIII, const. *Humanum genus*, 20 Apr., 1884 (*Fontes*, n. 591).

199. Can. 2335.

200. Pius IX, const. *Apostolicae Sedis*, 12 Oct., 1869, II, 4 (*Fontes*, n. 551); Can. 2335.

201. De Meester, *o. c.*, III, n. 1232, d; Vermeersch, *De Prohib. et Cens. Libr.*, p. 64.

202. Boudinhon, *o. c.*, p. 140.

203. Clement XII, const. *In eminenti*, 24 Apr., 1738 (*Fontes*, n. 299). Leo XIII, in const. *Humanum genus*, 20 Apr., 1884 (*Fontes*, n. 591), expresses it thus: "*sibi homines, tanquam mancipia, tenacissimo nexu, nec satis declarata causa*". Cf. also De Meester, III, n. 1232, d, a; Vermeersch, *De Proh. et Cens. Libr.*, p. 63; Cocchi, *l. c.*

204. Vermeersch, *De Proh. et Cens. Libr.*, p. 62; Vermeersch-Creusen, *Ep.*, II, n. 549, 1; 733, 8; III, n. 535; Boudinhon, *o. c.*, p. 140; Cocchi, *l. c.*; Bouuaert-Simenon, *o. c.*, p. 556.

the const. *Apostolicae Sedis*[205] condemned and punished these societies whether they plot openly or secretly (*palam seu clandestine*);[206] nor that the members of the society take an oath of secrecy, for everyone grants that the existence or lack of this oath would make no difference because of official statements of the Church in this regard;[207] but in the sense that the names of the leaders or the nature of the program and laws or both are kept secret.[208] These authors base their contention on the Papal documents dealing with the subject. Others,[209] however, deny that any secrecy is necessary and base their opinion also on the documents which have been issued by the Holy See on the subject, and on the wording used in the Code whenever these societies are referred to. In fact, the canons in the Code dealing with the societies similar to Freemasonry[210] mention no secrecy, while they mention the other two requirements — society and plotting against the Church or the legitimate civil powers.

While the latter opinion appears better, the probability of the former cannot be denied; therefore, in practice, a certain amount of secrecy should exist before one can liken a society to Freemasonry.[211] In this way, the *Carbonari*,[212] Mazzinians, Fenians,[213] Nihilists, Anarchists, the Internationale and Communistic societies can be classified as similar to Freemasonry. The Odd Fellows, the Sons of Temperance, the

---

205. *l. c.*

206. Cf. also Instr. S. C. of Holy Office, 10 May, 1884, n. 3 (*Fontes*, n. 1085).

207. S. C. of Holy Office, 5 Aug., 1846 (*Fontes*, n. 899); 10 May, 1884, n. 3 (*Fontes*, n. 1085).

208. Vermeersch, *De Prohib et Cens. Libr.*, p. 63.

209. Quigley, *o. c.*, p. 56 ff.; De Meester, *o. c.*, III, n. 1232, d; Cappello, *De Censuris*, n. 298; Van Coillie, *o. c.*, p. 54 f.

210. E. g. cann. 1240, §1, n. 1; 1399, n. 8; 2335.

211. De Meester, *o. c.*, III, n. 1232, d. He notes very wisely in note 7: "*Caeterum adeo indeterminatum est illud requisitum secretum, ut revera in omni societate verificari possit. Inde aegre in eo inveniri potes nota characteristica alicuius societatis.*"

212. Pius VII, const. *Ecclesiam*, Sept. 13, 1821 (*Fontes*, n. 479).

213. S. C. of Holy Office, 12 Jan., 1870 (*Fontes*, n. 1012).

Knights of Pythias,[214] though condemned by the Holy See, do not seem to be likened to Freemasonry. As a matter of fact in the decree of condemnation no excommunication was imposed, as was done for Freemasons, Carbonari, Fenians and other societies, plotting against Church or State. Therefore, the books defending Odd Fellows, the Sons of Temperance and the Knights of Pythias are not forbidden by can. 1399, n. 8.

Is socialism similar to Freemasonry? There are two kinds of *socialists:* extremists and moderates. The *extremists* intend to destroy both Church and legitimate governments with arms and other unlawful means. The *moderates* hold a mitigated form of socialism. Again, they may hold their views as individuals, or they may form a political party, or a society most firmly united. Extreme socialistic societies, if they are also surrounded with a certain amount of secrecy, as required by the opinion of some canonists,[215] are classed with Freemasonry and, as such, they come under can. 1399, n. 8.[216]

Art. IX. *Obscene Books*[217]

Can. 1399. — **Ipso iure prohibentur:**
9° **Libri qui res lascivas seu obscenas ex professo tractant, narrant, aut docent.**[218]

---

214. These three were condemned by the S. C. of the Holy Office, Aug. 20, 1894 (*Fontes*, n. 1171).

215. Supra, p. 164 f.

216. Other forms of socialistic unions cannot be said with certainty to come under this class, but their writings may fall under some other part of can. 1399. However, cf. Van Coillie, *o. c.*, p. 54 f.; Vermeersch, *De Proh. et Cens. Libr.*, p. 64 ff.

217. James J. Walsh, "Sex Instruction, VII, Eliminating Sex Incitements: Reading", *The Homiletic and Pastoral Review*, XXX (1930), 1173; Ford, *Criminal Obscenity;* Lord, *I Can Read Anything, passim;* Shuster, *The Catholic Church and Current Literature*, ch. III.

218. Regulae Indicis Tridentini, reg. VII (*Fontes*, n. 426; at end); Leo XIII, const. *Officiorum ac munerum*, Jan. 25, 1897, n. 9 (*Fontes*, n. 632); Instruction of the Holy Office, May 3, 1927 (*A A S*, XIX [1927], 186); Bethleem, *Romans á lire et Romans á proscrire*, p. 22 ff.; De Meester, *Compendium*, III, n. 1372; Boudinhon, *La Nouv. Legisl. de l'Ind.*, p. 112, ff.; Cocchi, *Commentarium in C. J. C.*, VI, n. 69, i; Sabetti-Barret, *Compendium Theologiae Moralis*, p. 773; Augustine, *A Com-*

Obscene books give much concern not only to the Church but also to civil governments. The abuse of the sex faculties is very detrimental not only to the soul but to the body, and not alone to the individual but to the race. Therefore, the civil rulers in almost every civilized country have enacted some legislation against literature fostering obscenity and immorality. However, civil legislation against obscene literature is disliked by many and acts of censorship and prohibition of noxious literature on the part of civil officials always arouse a certain amount of serious protest or ridicule from a number of people. Undoubtedly, there are many imperfections and shortcomings in every human law, especially in the execution of laws such as these which require much knowledge and prudence, at times absent in some officials. But, the fact is that there is a type of literature that passes the limits of decency and actually becomes a danger for the average reader, especially the young, and which, therefore, the State rightly forbids.

The Church has always protected and defended morality as well as faith. Her book legislation has ever aimed and still aims at the defense of both.[219] This she has done and still does because she is keenly conscious of her duty towards men and their spiritual welfare, according to the mission entrusted to her by God Himself. She realizes full well that, because of the fall of Adam and Eve, human nature is so weak and prone to lust, that immoral writings generally pervert the minds of men and deprave their hearts, lead them to unbridle their passions, cause them to fall into all kinds

---

mentary, VI, p. 474 f.; Bouuaert-Simenon, *Man. Jur. Can.*, p. 556; Genicot, *Inst. Theol. Mor.*, I, n .452, 7; Noldin, *Summa Theol. Moralis*, II, n. 708, 9; *De Sexto*, n. 59; Arndt, *De Libr. Prohib.*, n. 114; Pennacchi, *In Const. Apost. Offic. ac muner.*, p. 84 f.; Vermeersch, *De Proh. et Cens. Libr.*, p. 56; Moureau, *La Nouv. Legisl.*, p. 53 f.; Van Coillie, *Commentarius in Const. Off. ac mun.*, p. 45; Hurley, *Index Legislation*, p. 77 ff.; Heymans, *De Eccl. Libr... Prohibit.*, n. 344; Cappello, *De Curia*, I, p. 275; Gennari, "Circa la nuova disciplina", *Il Mon. Eccl.*, X (1897), 36; Wernz, *Jus Decretal.*, III, n. 111 (note 61); Ayrinhac, *Administr. Legisl.*, p. 295; *Conference Bulletin of the Archdiocese of New York*, V (1927), 25 ff.

219. Cf. brief historical review given above, p. 26 ff.

of crimes and at times even to commit suicide.[220] She knows
that the loss of one's morality leads oftentimes to shipwreck
in the faith. She is mindful also of the words of St. Paul[221]
"Evil communications corrupt good manners" and of those
others:[222]

> "Fornication, and all uncleanness, or covetousness,
> let it not so much as be named among you, as be-
> cometh saints: or obscenity or foolish talking. For
> know you this and understand that no fornicator, or
> unclean or covetous person (which is a serving of
> idols) hath inheritance in the kingdom of God".

It is reasons such as these which make it imperative for the
Church to take severe action against obscene books.

The natural law already forbids every individual the
reading of literature, in whatever degree it may be obscene,
as long as and inasfar as it is dangerous to this individual.
This is quite extensive in application. The positive law of
the Church is not as extensive. It enforces the natural law
only in regard to those books which are dangerous to the
average person.

In Can. 1399, n. 9, are declared forbidden all *books* and
other forms of publications *which treat of, describe or teach
impure and obscene things ex professo.* The words here used
by the Code of Canon Law, go back to the Council of Trent.[223]

1. *Res lascivas seu obscenas* are those things which upon
being seen (in reality or in the imagination) excite the vene-
real appetite,[224] or arouse the lower passions. Such things are
called unclean, dirty, filthy, foul, impure, shameless, pornographic, lewd, libidinous, erotic, salacious, unchaste, dissolute.
A book is not obscene if it merely offends by vulgarity or
against common external propriety.[225]

---

220. Instr. of Holy Office, May 3, 1927 (*A A S*, XIX [1927], 187).
Cf. also St. Thomas, *Summa Theol.*, II-II, quaest. XV, a. 3.

221. *I Cor.*, XV, 33.

222. *Eph.*, V, 3-5.

223. *Regulae Indicis Trid.*, reg. VII (*Fontes*, n. 426, towards end).

224. Vermeersch, *De proh. et Cens. Libr.*, p. 56; De Meester, *o. c.*,
III, n. 1372, a; Cappello, *De Curia*, I, p. 275. Cf. also Vermeersch, *De
Castitate*, nn. 394; 395; 378; 283; 181; 184, 4; 185, 4; 199, 2.

225. *Conference Bulletin of the Archdiocese of New York*, V
(1927), 28.

2. *Ex professo.* If obscenity is contained only in one or several passing remarks, the book is not forbidden by this law.[226] It may however be prohibited by the natural law. But, in order that a book treating of, narrating or teaching obscene things may come under the ban of the positive law of the Church, it must do these things *ex professo.* This means that the attack against morality and decency is made *directly* and in a *notable part of the work* (e. g. a chapter). The author need not declare openly his intention. He may show he is directly aiming at immorality and indecency by the very nature and form of his writing.[227] In other words, the work must be clearly pornographic.[228] It is not necessary that *obscenity* be the principal end of the work.

Those books are said to *treat* of or *discuss* (*tractant*) obscene things which deal with them in such a way as to arouse lust, suggest depraved thoughts and induce the incautious readers to perform immoral actions. Those books are said to *narrate* (*narrant*) obscene things which describe immoralities, real or fictitious, with all their circumstances, in such a realistic way that the reader can almost see them before his eyes. Those books are said to *teach* (*docent*) obscene things which impart and explain how lustful actions are performed, by what means others may be corrupted and led to satisfy one's wicked desires.[229]

The Holy Office, in the Instruction of May 3, 1927,[230]

---

226. If one, while reading a good book, should come across some obscene passage, he may either skip over it or give it a rapid glance, and then continue reading the work. However, no work should be selected with the intention of coming upon such passages. Cf. Vermeersch, *De Castitate,* n. 184, 4.

227. Arndt, *o. c.,* n. 114; De Meester, *o. c.,* III, n. 1372; Boudinhon, *o. c.,* p. 112 f.; Bethleem, *o. c.,* p. 23; Cocchi, *l. c.*; Gennari, *l. c.*

228. Boudinhon, *o. c.,* p. 113; Bethleem, p. 22.

229. De Meester, *o. c.,* n. 1372, c; Boudinhon, *o. c.,* p. 113; Cocchi, *o. c.,* VI, n. 69, i; Vermeersch, *De Proh. et Cens. Libr.,* p. 56; Pennacchi, *o. c.,* p. 84 f.; Cappello, *De Curia,* I, p. 275; Hurley, *o. c.,* 78 ff.; Bucceroni, *Inst. Theol. Mor.,* II, n. 1307.

230. *A A S,* XIX (1927), 186. Bethleem thus writes on pag. 69 of *Romans à lire et Romans à proscrire:* "Ces ecrivains.... justifient les convoitises de la nature; ils insinuent clairement que le mariage est un mal, le divorce un droit, l'adultère une nécessité; ils proclament que

thus describes this class of works:

> Nunc vero satis dolere non licet, ut dictum est, ex hac affluentia librorum in quibus magna cum fascinatione nugacitatis par inest turpitudo, gravissimam animarum iacturam existere. Etenim quam plures huius generis scriptores fulgentissimis imaginibus impudica facta depingunt; obscenissima quaeque, modo tecte, modo aperte et procaciter, omni castimoniae lege neglecta, enarrant; subtili quadam analysi vitia carnalia vel pessima describunt eaque cunctis orationis luminibus et lenociniis exornant, adeo ut nihil iam in moribus inviolatum relinquatur...Nam quis ignorat litteris eiusmodi phantasiam fortiter excitari, effrenatam libidinem vehementer accendi et cor in coenum turpitudinum trahi?

Therefore, pornographic works, like Zola's, are forbidden by this rule. However, *legal, medical, scientific* and *moral* books dealing with immoral subjects are not forbidden by the positive law of the Church.[231] For, while the book treats of obscene or immoral matters, the purpose of the author, as expressed by him or as evidenced in the contents and method of the work, is a scientific one, to enable men in different professions to understand sexual problems and to apply the

---

l'amour voluptueux est un chaste ardeur, ses manifestations un entraînement pardonnable, un peche mignon ou un cas pathologique; ils prêchent que les lois de la chasteté ne sont pas plus obligatoires que celles du mariage, que la fidelité conjugal est une absurdité et une imposibilité. Ils tournent en ridicule l'honnête femme et réhabilitent la courtisane, ils mettent sur la même ligne les enfants legitimes et les enfants de la débauche. En un mot, ils appellent bien ce qui est mal et mal ce qui est bien, ils exaltent le vice et flétrissent le devoir, ils renversent les notions les plus élémentaires de la morale evangelique et du droit naturel, ils corrompent les moeurs en faussant les idées..."

231. De Meester, *o. c.*, III, n. 1372; Hurley, *o. c.*, p. 84 f.; Noldin, *o. c.*, II, n. 708, 9; Cocchi, *l. c.*; Boudinhon, p. 113. Among those books can be classed the works which reverently impart knowledge of sexual matters to people who have reached the age and maturity when such knowledge is necessary or useful, provided this be done in the spirit of the Church, expressed recently by Pius XI in his encyclical on *the Christian Education of Youth*, Dec. 31, 1929 (*The Eccl. Rev.*, LXXXII [1930], 358). Cf. also decree of the S. C. of the Holy Office on sexual education, March 21, 1931 (*A A S.* XXIII [1931], 119); Kirsch, F. M., *Sex education and Training in Chastity* (New York: Bengiger Bros., 1930).

proper treatment. Since the aim is not to attack morality and decency, the book does *not* discuss, narrate or teach obscene things *ex professo*, and therefore does not come under the positive law of the Church expressed in can. 1399, n. 9. However, even these scientific treatises are dangerous to some people, especially the young, the innocent, the impressionable, etc. For such persons the prohibition to read those books exists, and it arises from the natural and positive divine law.

No general rule can be given in regard to *novels, romances, love-stories* and how far they are affected by this law of the Church. No doubt many of them discuss or narrate obscene things *ex professo* (profusely and with the intention to arouse the lower passions), as the recent instruction of the Holy Office[232] testifies. These are certainly prohibited by can. 1399, n. 9. However, the greater number of novels, romances or love-stories are not forbidden by the positive law of the Church, but the reading of at least some of them may be forbidden by the natural and positive divine law.[233]

Obscene pictures are not classed among obscene books if published alone and by themselves. For the Code in can. 1384, §2, explicitly extends the meaning of "book" to "all other published *writings*" and not to pictures.[234] But, if they are part and parcel of a book, review, or other publication, then they become subject to this law. Should the work, illustrated by the pictures, be *ex professo* obscene, then the pic-

---

232. May 3, 1927 — *A A S*, XIX (1927), 186.

233. *Acta et Decreta Concilii Provincialis Mechliniensis Quarti anno MCMXX Mechliniae habiti* (Mechlin, 1923), Sectio Moralis, n. 57; St. Alphonsus, *De Proh. Libr.*, Cap. I, n. 9; De Meester, *o. c.*, III, n. 1372; Cocchi, *o. c.*, VI, n. 69, i; Van Coillie, *o. c.*, p. 46 f.; Bethleem, *o. c.*, p. 67 ff.; Bucceroni, *o. c.*, II, n. 1307; Ayrinhac, *o. c.*, p. 295.

234. For the same reason *moving pictures* cannot be said to come under the positive laws of the Church on books as contained in Cann. 1384 - 1405. However, the *written part* of a film may be of itself and in conjunction with the pictures portrayed, *ex professo obscene*. In that case the words "aliis editis *scriptis* quibuslibet" of can. 1384, §2, would be verified, and the whole film would be forbidden by the positive law of the Church. Cf. Boudinhon, who on p. 113 (*o. c.*), writing about pictures, states: "le plus souvent elles seront englobées dans la prohibition... cela est vrai surtout quand aux gravures est joint un text explicatif mauvais."

tures share in the positive prohibition of the Church.[235] In any case, the natural law always forbids not only books, in the ecclesiastical sense, but all other things which may endanger the salvation of the reader.

Before the publication of the Code, the positive law of the Church in forbidding obscene works made some exceptions with regard to *classical writings*. Thus in the seventh Rule of the Council of Trent we read:

> Antiqui vero [libri] ab Ethnicis conscripti, propter sermonis elegantiam et proprietatem, permittuntur: nulla tamen ratione pueris praelegendi erunt.[236]

Art. 10 of Leo XIII's constitution *Officiorum ac munerum*[237] reads thus:

> Libri auctorum sive antiquorum, sive recentiorum, quos classicos vocant, si hac ipsa turpitudinis labe infecti sunt, propter sermonis elegantiam et proprietatem, iis tantum permittuntur, quos officii et magisterii ratio excusat: nulla tamen ratione pueris vel adolescentibus, nisi solerti cura expurgati, tradendi out praelegendi sunt.

Classical works, then, both ancient and modern, even though obscene, were permitted to professors and adult students of literature, men of letters, literary critics, heads of institutions of learning, and others who needed them because of their office or of teaching. But in no case were such books to be given or read to boys or young people.[238] However, the Code makes no mention whatever of any exception to the gen-

---

235. Boudinhon, *o. c.*, p. 113. The instruction of the Holy Office of May 3, 1927 (*A A S*, XIX [1927], 186) refers to these works thus: "*Etenim quamplures huius generis scriptores fulgentissimis imaginibus impudica facta depingunt.*"

236. *Fontes*, n. 426. Cf. also Gretser, *De Jure et More Proh.*, lib. I, Cap. V, F and G; Arndt, *o. c.*, n. 147.

237. Jan. 25, 1897, *Fontes*, n. 632. Cf. also Pennacchi, *o. c.*, p. 85 ff.; Wernz, *o. c.*, III, n. 111 (10). Wernz gives as examples of such classics: among the ancient, *Ovid, Juvenal;* among the modern, *Boccaccio, Heine, Byron, Voltaire.*

238. For a more detailed interpretation of art. 10, cf. Vermeersch, *De Prohibitione et Censura Libr.*, p. 77 ff.; Pennacchi, *In Const. Apost. Offic. ac Mun.*, p. 85 ff.; Van Coillie, *De Prohib. et Cens. Libr.*, p. 45 ff.; Boudinhon, *La Nouvelle Legisl. de l'Index*, p. 114 ff.; Hurley, *Index Legisl.*, p. 85; Wernz, *Jus Decretal.*, III, n. 111, 10.

eral prohibition by the Church of obscene books, in favor of
obscene classical works. This omission would seem to indicate that the Church has not renewed her former concession,
contained in art. 10 of the constitution *Officiorum ac munerum*. For Can. 6, n. 6 abrogates all general disciplinary
laws promulgated before the Code and not contained therein,
unless they are found in the approved books of liturgy, or
they are natural or positive divine laws. The law in question
is neither liturgical nor natural nor positive divine. It is indeed in conformity with the natural law, which permits certain persons books, which, though dangerous to others, are not
dangerous to themselves, or, if somewhat dangerous, are necessary for other reasons. But art. 10 of the constitution *Officiorum ac munerum* appears to be an ecclesiastical law giving
a permission and making restrictions which, though intended
to safeguard the natural law, are not identical with it. Therefore, there does not seem to be any ground for considering
the former concession in favor of obscene classical works still
in force.

Accordingly, when the necessity arises of using a classical
work which is obscene, permission must be obtained from the
Ordinary or the Holy Office, if this can be done without grave
inconvenience. If it be too difficult or impossible to secure
permission, the law of the Church ceases to bind and one is
to be guided only by the natural law.

Of the canonists who have written since the publication
of the Code, many[239] hold the view just presented, namely,
that art. 10 of the constitution *Officiorum ac munerum* was

---

239 De Meester, *Compendium*, III, n. 1372; Vermeersch-Creusen,
Ep., II, n. 735, N. B.; Noldin, *Summa Theol. Mor.*, II, n. 711, 2, b; Cocchi,
Commentarium in C. J. C., VI, n. 69, i; Blat, *Commentarium Text. C.
J. C.*, III, p. 362 f.; Bouuaert-Simenon, *Man. Jur. Can.*, p. 556; Ferreres,
Instit. Can., II, p. 159; Woywod, *A Practical Commentary*, II, p. 133;
Ayrinhac, *Administrative Legisl.*, p. 295; Gury-Tummolo, *Compendium
Theologiae Moralis*, II, n. 1018; Marc-Gestermann-Raus, *Institutiones
Morales Alphonsianae*, I, p. 862; Augustine, *A Commentary*, VI, p. 482;
Conference Bulletin of N. Y., V (1927), 23; *Theologisch-praktische
Quart.* (Linz), LXXVII (1924), 724 ff.

abrogated by the Code. Others,[240] however, hold that the declaration of Leo XIII in favor of classical works which are obscene, is still in force, even though not mentioned in the Code. In practice, because of the weight of authority (though not of arguments) in favor of the milder opinion, the stricter view cannot be imposed on any one. Therefore, professors of literature and others, who, by reason of their office or of teaching, must use classical works which are obscene, may do so. However, they must always have a serious reason, and they must not give or read those works, unless expurgated, to boys or young people. Moreover, all other precautions, dictated by the natural law, must be observed.

Art. X. Liturgical works

Can. 1399. — Ipso iure prohibentur:

10° **Editiones librorum liturgicorum a Sede Apostolica approbatorum, in quibus quidpiam immutatum fuerit, ita ut cum authenticis editionibus a Santa Sede approbatis non congruant.**[241]

The liturgy of the Church is a sure guide to her teaching, as the ancient axiom, first enunciated by St. Celestine, pithily expresses: *"Legem credendi lex statuat supplicandi."*[242]

240. A Coronata, *Institutiones Juris Canonici*, II, p. 343; Badii, *Institutiones Juris Canonici*, II, p. 162, n. 1; Boudinhon, *o. c.*, p. 116; Bargilliat, *Praelectiones Juris Canonici*, I, n. 633.

241. Pius V, const. *Quod a nobis*, July 9, 1568 (*BRT*, VII, 685); const. *Quo primum*, July 14, 1570 (*Fontes*, n. 135); Clement VIII, const. *Cum sanctissimum*, July 7, 1604 (*Fontes*, n. 191); Urban VIII, const. *Si quid est*, Sept. 2, 1634 (*Fontes*, n. 214); const. *Quamvis alias*, June 17, 1644 (*Fontes*, n. 228); Benedict XIV, encycl. *Demandatam*, Dec. 24, 1743, §21 (*Fontes*, n. 338); Leo XIII, const. *Officiorum ac munerum*, Jan. 25, 1897, n. 18 (*Fontes*, n. 632); *Codex Juris Can.*, Cann. 1257; 1390. Cf. also De Meester, *Compendium*, III, n. 1347; n. 1373; Cocchi, *Commentarium in C. J. C.*, VI, n. 69, 1; Nodin, *Summa Theol. Moralis*, II, n. 708, (10); Boudinhon, *La Nouv. Legisl. de l'Ind.*, p. 171 ff.; Augustine, *A Commentary*, VI, 190 f., 475 f.; Vermeersch-Creusen, *Ep.*, II, n. 726, 5; n. 733, 10; Hurley, *Index Legislation*, p. 139 ff.; Pennacchi, *In Const. Apost. Offic. ac muner.*, p. 152 ff.; Van Coillie, *Commentarius in Const. Off. ac mun.*, p. 61; Gennari, "Circa la nuova disciplina", *Il Mon. Eccl.*, X (1897), 67; Wernz, *Jus Decretal.*, III, n. 111 (note 72); Arndt, *De Libr. Prohib.*, n. 128-132.

242. Pope St. Celestine, Ep. 21, Cap. XI, 12 (*MPL*, L, 535).

Above all else, the Church prizes the integrity of the faith of which she is the guardian. She cannot, therefore, allow her official prayer and worship to be in contradiction with her doctrine. She has watched the development of her liturgical books with the utmost care, lest anything tainted with error might be incorporated in them. The liturgical books are, therefore, an authentic expression of the Catholic faith, and are, in fact, a source from which theologians, may draw confirmatory arguments in defense of the faith.[243]

This fact as well as the wish of the Church to preserve liturgical uniformity have led her to forbid *all editions of liturgical books, approved by the Holy See, in which any alterations have been made, in such wise that they are no longer the same as the authentic editions approved by the Holy See.*

The *liturgical books* approved by the Holy See are:[244] the Missal and the Roman Breviary with which are closely connected the Roman Martyrology and the Roman Calendar, the Roman Pontifical, the Ceremonial of Bishops, the "Caeremoniale Romanum", the Roman Ritual and the "Memoriale Rituum."[245]

The *Missal* is the book used by the Church for the sacrifice of the Mass. The *Breviary* contains the prayer of the Church which is recited by her priests, as well as by other clerics in major orders and certain religious. Both of these works were promulgated by Pope St. Pius V, the Breviary in the constitution *Quod a nobis,* July 9, 1568,[246] the Missal in the constitution *Quo primum,* July 14, 1578.[247] Improvements and changes were made by his successors from time to time and revised editions of both the Missal and the Breviary

---

243. Dom Cabrol, O. S. B., *The Roman Missal in Latin and English* (New York: 1921), p. XI; Tanquerey, *Sinopsis Theologiae Dogm.,* I, p. 644 f.

244. Leo XIII, const. *Officiorum ac munerum,* Jan. 25, 1897, n. 18 (*Fontes,* n. 632); Wernz, *o. c.,* III, n. 341 ff.; Vermeersch-Creusen, *o. c.,* II, n. 575; De Meester, *o. c.,* III, nn. 1249, 2; 1347, a; Boudinhon, *o. c.,* p. 171 ff.; Pennacchi, *o. c.,* p. 153 ff.; Hurley, *o. c.,* p. 139 ff.

245. Liturgical works of the Oriental rite are not considered here, as is clearly stated in can. 1.

246. *BRT,* VII, 685.

247. *Fontes,* n. 135.

were published. The last important changes in the Roman Breviary were made by Pius X. The new edition became obligatory on Jan. 1, 1913.[248] The most recent approved typical edition of the Roman Missal is the one promulgated by Benedict XV in the decree of the S. C. of Rites, July 25, 1920.[249] The Holy See has also approved and allowed the use in some churches of certain ancient Breviaries and Missals, other than the Roman. Thus, in Spain liturgical books of the Mozarabic rite may be used and in Milan books of the Ambrosian rite.[250]

Closely connected with the Missal and the Breviary are the *Roman Martyrology*, which contains the names of the martyrs and other saints honored on the altars of the Church, and the *Roman Calendar*. The last typical edition of the Martyrology was published in 1922.

Additions are made from time to time by the S. C. of Rites to the Missal, Breviary, Calendar and Martyrology due to the establishment of new feasts. These additions approved and published by the Holy See are to be considered as parts of the liturgical books to which they are added.

The *Roman Pontifical* and the *Ceremonial of Bishops* are concerned only with functions reserved to Bishops. The Pontifical was made of universal obligation by Clement VIII, through the constitution *Ex quo*, 10 Feb., 1597[251] while the Ceremonial was published by the same Pope through the constitution *Cum novissime*, 14 July, 1600.[252] This latter has been revised a few times by other Popes.[253] The *Roman Ceremonial* is proper to the Holy See as it contains only papal functions or ceremonies.[254] The *Roman Ritual* contains the prayers and ceremonies used in the administration of the Sacraments and in other sacred functions. It was promulgated by Paul V through the constitution *Apostolicae Sedi*, June 17, 1614.[255] The latest typical edition of the Ritual is the one approved

----

248. Const. *Divino afflatu*, Nov. 1, 1911 (*Fontes*, n. 696).
249. Placed at the beginning of the Missal.
250. Vermeersch-Creusen, *Ep.*, II, n. 575.
251. *Fontes*, n. 180.
252. *BRT*, X, 597.
253. Wernz, *o. c.*, III, n. 343.
254. Wernz, *o. c.*, n. 344.
255. At the beginning of the Ritual and in *Fontes*, n. 198.

by Pius XI, June 10, 1925. Finally, the *Memoriale Rituum* gives the rites prescribed for some important sacred functions when they are performed in small churches. This was first approved by Benedict XIII for Rome in the year 1725,[256] then by other popes for the whole world.[257] Benedict XV by a decree of Jan. 14, 1920, promulgated a revised edition of the Memoriale.[258]

These books whether published in their entirety or in part, with the *Gregorian chant*[259] accompanying the words or without it, always retain their sacred character. All new editions of these must represent exactly the authentic editions published by the Holy See.

By a decree of the S. Congregation of Rites, of May 17, 1911,[260] the following must also be considered as liturgical books: the *offices and masses proper* to some diocese, order or religious congregation: the *Clementine Instruction* for the exposition of the Forty Hours, *and the Collection of Decrees of the S. C. of Rites.*

All new editions of any of the liturgical books of the Church or of any of their parts must conform to the editions approved by the Holy See[261] which serve as a type or model.[262] The Code also requires that the concordance of the new edition with the typical edition be attested to by the Ordinary of the place where the book is printed or published.[263] How-

---

256. Wernz, *o. c.*, III, n. 346; Vermeersch-Creusen, *Ep.*, II, n. 575.

257. S. C. of Rites, July 31, 1821, 1 (*Decr. Auth. C. S. R.*, n. 2616); Mar. 16, 1876 (*Decr. Auth. C. S. R.*, n. 3390); Dec. 9, 1899 (*Decr. Auth. C. S. R.*, n. 4049); Aug. 22, 1902 (*Decr. Auth. C. S. R.*, n. 4101).

258. *A A S*, XII (1920), 448.

259. Thus the *Kyriale* (typical ed. 1905), the *Graduale* (1907), the *Officium pro Defunctis* (1909); the *Cantorinus seu Toni communes Officii et Missae cum regulis et exemplis* (1911); *Antiphonale Diurnum* (1912, 2nd ed. 1919); *Officium Majoris Hebdomadae* (1922). Cf. De Meester, *o. c.*, III, 2 f.

260. *A A S*, III (1911), 242.

261. Can. 1390.

262. For that reason they are called *editiones typicae.*

263. Can. 1390. Cf. also decree of S. C. R., Aug. 4, 1877 (*Decr. Auth. S. C. R.*, n. 3427), which requires the same for translations of parts of the Mass into the vernacular.

ever, the mere lack of this testimony of the Bishop does not make the new edition forbidden.[264] But if in the new edition something was changed, even though of small importance, whether the change consists in interpolation, mutilation or transposition, so that the new edition is different from the typical edition, then such a new edition is forbidden. It is immaterial whether these modifications were introduced purposely or not. It suffices that they be there and that they affect the sense or the order determined by the Holy See. Typographical errors or repetion of some parts to render the reading of, e. g., the Breviary easier, or omission of some parts for which the reader is referred to another place, are not considered modifications.[265]

In practice, when a liturgical book bears the episcopal attestation to its conformity with the typical edition, it is certainly permitted, unless its nonconformity to the typical edition be evident.

The rule just explained does not apply to prayer-books in which some parts of the Missal or the Breviary are contained.[266] The reason is that an ordinary prayer-book is not a liturgical book, and can. 1399, n. 10, deals only with liturgical books.

Art. XI. *Works of Spurious or Revoked Indulgences*

Can. 1399 — **Ipso iure prohibentur:**

---

264. The only books forbidden because of lack of episcopal approbation are enumerated in can. 1399, n. 5. Cf. also De Meester, *o. c.*, III, nn. 1347, 1373; Mothon, *Institutions Canoniques*, I, p. 886, n. 24.

265. De Meester, *o. c.*, III, n. 1373; Vermeersch-Creusen, *Ep.*, II, n. 733, 10; Noldin, *o. c.*, II, n. 708, 10; Cocchi, *o. c.*, VI, n. 69, e; Boudinhon, *o. c.*, p. 175 ff.; Ferreres, *Institutiones Can.*, II, p. 159; Bouuaert-Simenon, *o. c.*, p. 557; Bucceroni, *Institutiones*, n. 1306. If one in major orders uses a forbidden Breviary to recite the divine office, he fulfills his obligation. Cf. Ferreres, *l. c.*; Ubach, *Compendium Theol. Mor.*, I, p. 386.

266. Vermeersch-Creusen, *Ep.*, II, n. 726, 5°; De Meester, *o. c.*, III, n. 1347.

11° Libri quibus divulgantur indulgentiae aprocryphae vel a Sancta Sede proscriptae aut revocatae.[267]

By this decree are forbidden all those *works spreading a knowledge of apocryphal indulgences or indulgences proscribed or withdrawn by the Holy See.*

This is not a new law, for many times the Supreme Pontiffs in the course of the centuries have spoken vigorously against abuses in the matter of indulgences.[268] By a decree of the S. C. of Indulgences of Apr. 14, 1856,[269] the Ordinaries were requested to use all the power in their hands to take away spurious indulgences from among the faithful. Leo XIII in n. 16 of his constitution *Officiorum ac munerum*[270] forbids in words almost identical with can. 1399, n. 11, the spreading of indulgences which are false or have been proscribed or revoked.

An *indulgence,* according to can. 911, is the remission (partial or total) of the temporal punishment due, before God, for sins whose guilt has been blotted out. It is granted by ecclesiastical authority from the treasury of the Church to living members by way of absolution, and to the deceased by way of suffrage. Indulgences can be granted by the Su-

---

267. Decree of S. C. of Indulgences, Apr. 14, 1856 (*Decreta Authentica S. Cong. Ind.,* n. 571) ; Leo XIII, const. *Officiorum ac munerum,* Jan. 25, 1897, n. 16 (*Fontes,* n. 632) ; De Meester, *Compendium,* III, n. 1374; Boudinhon, *La Nouv. Legisl. de l'Ind.,* p. 158 ff.; Cocchi, *Commentarium in C. J. C.,* VI, n. 69, m; Ayrinhac, *Administr. Legisl.,* p. 296; Hurley, *Index Legislation,* p. 133 ff.; Pennacchi, *In Const. Apost. Offic. ac muner.,* p. 134 ff.; Moureau, *La Nouv. Legisl.,* p. 65; Wernz, *Jus Decretal.,* III, n. 111 (notes 70-71) ; Van Coillie, *Commentarius in Const. Off. ac mun.,* p. 58 f.; Gennari, "Circa la nuova disciplina", *Il Mon. Eccl.,* X (1897), 66 f.; Arndt, *De Libr. Prohib.* ,n. 121; Beringer, F., *Les Indulgences, Leur Nature et Leur Usage* (4th French ed., Paris: P. Lethielleux, 1925) ; Lepicier, A., *Indulgences, Their Origin, Nature and Development* (London: Burns Oates and Washbourne, Ltd., 1928) ; Hagerdon, F. E., *General Legislation on Indulgences* (Washington: Catholic University, 1924) ; Fanfani, L., *De Indulgentiis,* 2 ed. (Turin: Marietti, 1926).

268. Boudinhon, *o. c.,* p. 158 ff.; Pennacchi, *o. c.,* p. 154 ff.; Arndt, *o. c.,* n. 121.

269. *Decreta Authentica S. Cong. Ind.,* n. 571.

270. Jan. 25, 1897 (*Fontes,* n. 632).

preme Pontiff, to whom Christ our Lord has committed the disbursement of the whole spiritual treasure of the Church and by those persons to whom this power is expressly given,[271] such as Cardinals,[272] Metropolitans,[273] and Bishops.[274] However, these persons, inferior to the Pope, cannot delegate their power to grant indulgences to others; they cannot grant indulgences applicable to the dead nor can they grant other indulgences to an act of piety or a society to which the Holy See or some other, according to law, has already granted some indulgence, unless new conditions are prescribed for the new indulgences.[275] An indulgence is called spurious or *apocryphal* ("apocrypha") which was never validly granted; it is called *proscribed* ("proscripta") if it was condemned by the Holy See on account of some abuses; it is called *revoked* ("revocata") if, after having been granted, it was, for good reasons, withdrawn or abrogated.[276]

All books spreading a knowledge of indulgences which are spurious, or have been proscribed or revoked by the Holy See, are condemned. Clearly, such books are not forbidden unless they offend against this law either in their entirely or in a notable part. A book, mentioning in passing some spurious indulgence or one which was condemned or withdrawn by the Holy See, could hardly be said to "spread the knowledge" of such indulgences.[277]

---

271.   Can. 912.

272.   Can. 240, §1, n. 24.

273.   Can. 274, n. 2.

274.   Can. 349, §2, n. 2.

275.   Can. 913.

276.   Cappello, *De Curia*, I, p. 284; Ferraris, *Bibliotheca Canonica*, "Indulgentia", a. 4; Hurley, *o. c.*, p. 135 f.; Cocchi, *o. c.*, VI, n. 69, m. Examples of indulgences which are apocryphal, proscribed or revoked, are to be found in the decree *Delatae sepius* of Innocent XI, March 7, 1678 (Ferraris, *o. c.*, IV, 249); De Meester, *o. c.*, III, p. 296, note 5; Boudinhon, *o. c.*, p. 159 ff.; Beringer, *Les Indulgences, Leur Nature et Leur Usage* (4th French ed., Paris: P. Lethieleux, 1925), I, p. 116 f.

277.   Supra p. 151 f. Cf. also Genicot-Salsmans, *Institutiones Theol. Mor.*, I, n. 422, 9; Cocchi, *l. c.* These authors would consider the books described forbidden only when they treat the matter *ex professo*. However, the Code does not mention an *ex professo* treatment.

An indulgence is certainly *authentic*[278] which is contained in the *Raccolta,*[279] or in the *Acta Apostolicae Sedis,*[280] or which has been recognized as such by the Sacred Congregation of the Indulgences or, from Nov. 3, 1908, to March 25, 1917, by the Sacred Congregation of the Holy Office or, since then, by the Sacred Penitentiary.[281]

Art. XII. *Sacred Images*

Can. 1399.— Ipso iure prohibentur:
12° Imagines quoquo modo impressae Domini Nostri Iesu Christi, Beatae Mariae Virginis, Angelorum atque Sanctorum vel aliorum Servorum Dei ab Ecclesiae sensu et decretis alienae.[282]

---

278. Cf. decree of the S. C. of Indulgences, Aug. 10, 1899 (*ASS*, XXXII [1899], 241-249); Pius X, motu proprio *Cum per Apostolicas,* April 7, 1910 (*Fontes,* n. 685); Beringer, *Les Indulgences,* I, p. 119 ff.

279. The full title is: *Raccolta di orazioni e pie opere, per le quali sono state concesse dai Sommi Pontefici le Sante Indulgenze.* It is a collection of prayers and good works to which the Supreme Pontiffs have attached indulgences. At first it appeared as a private compilation of Telesphorus Galli in 1807. After the death of Galli, new editions were published by Aloysius Prinzivalli. In 1877 the first official edition of the *Raccolta* was published by order of Pius IX. Other official editions were published in 1886 and 1898. The *Raccolta* of 1898 contained all general indulgences granted up to that time. The latest edition of this work was published in 1929 with the title: *Collectio Precum Piorumque Operum Quibus Romani Pontifices in Favorem Omnium Christifidelium aut Quorumdam Coetuum Personarum Indulgentias Adnexuerunt* (Rome, Vatican Polyglot Press, 1929). It contains the indulgences granted in favor of all the faithful or certain groups of persons from 1899 to 1928. There are several approved English translations of it. *The Raccolta or Collection of Indulgenced Prayers and Good Works,* by Ambrose St. John (11. ed., New York: Benziger Bros., 1930) comprises the indulgences contained in the authentic editions of the *Raccolta* of 1898 and 1929.

280. Can. 9.

281. Whatever concerns indulgences is now within the province of the Sacred Penitentiary. Before Nov. 3, 1908, the Sacred Congregation of Indulgences dealt with them; but from that day (cf. Pius X, const. *Sapienti Consilio,* June 29, 1908 [*Fontes,* n. 682]) until Mar. 25, 1917, the S. C. of the Holy Office was entrusted with them. (Cf. Benedict XV, motu proprio *Alloquentes,* March 25, 1917 [*Fontes,* n. 710]).

282. Council of Trent, Sessio XXV, *De invocatione, veneratione, et reliquiis sanctorum, et sacris imaginibus;* S. C. of the Holy Off., decree

The teaching of the Church concerning sacred images was clearly set forth in the Council of Trent[283] which decreed as follows:

> And the Bishops shall carefully teach this, — that, by means of the histories of the mysteries of our Redemption, portrayed by paintings or other representations, the people is instructed, and confirmed in (the habit of) remembering, and continually revolving in mind the articles of faith; as also that great profit is derived from all sacred images, not only because the people are thereby admonished of the benefits and gifts bestowed upon them by Christ, but also because the miracles which God has performed by means of the saints, and their salutary examples, are set before the eyes of the faithful; that so they may give God thanks for those things; may order their own lives and manners in imitation of the saints; and may be excited to adore and love God, and to cultivate piety. But if any one shall teach, or entertain sentiments, contrary to these decrees; let him be anathema.
>
> And if any abuses have crept in amongst these holy and salutary observances, the holy Synod ardently desires that they be utterly abolished; in such

---

Sanctissimus, 13 Mar., 1625 (*Fontes,* n. 719); Urban VIII, const. *Coelestis Jerusalem,* 5 July, 1634 (*Fontes,* n. 212); const. *Sacrosancta,* 15 Mar., 1642 (*Fontes,* n. 223); Benedict XIV, const. *Sollicitudini,* 1 Oct., 1745 (*Fontes,* n. 362); Leo XIII, const. *Officiorum ac munerum,* Jan. 25, 1897, n. 15 (*Fontes,* n. 632); *Codex Judis Canonici,* Cann. 1279; 1385, §1, n. 3. Cf. also De Meester, *Compendium,* III, nn. 1267; 1341, 5; 1375; Vermeersch-Creusen, *Ep.,* II, nn. 605; 726, 3; 733, 12; Cocchi, *Commentarium in C. J. C.,* VI, n. 69, n; Boudinhon, *La Nouv. Legisl. de l'Ind.,* p. 145 ff.; Wernz, *Jus Decretal.,* III, n. 111, note 69; Hurley, *Index Legislation,* p. 125 ff.; Pennacchi, *In Const. Apost. Offic. ac muner.,* p. 127 ff.; Moureau, *La Nouv. Legisl.,* p. 63 ff.; Van Coillie, *Commentarius in Const. Off. ac mun.,* p. 56 f.; Gennari, "Circa la nuova disciplina", *Il Mon. Eccl.,* X (1897), 63 ff.; Augustine, *A Commentary,* VI, p. 241; Bouuaert-Simenon, *Man. Jur. Can.,* p. 510, 557; Vermeersch, "De Prohibitione Imaginum", *Periodica de Relig.,* XIV (1926), (93) ff.; Arndt, *De Libr. Prohibit.,* p. 146.

283. *Sessio XXV, De invocatione, veneratione, et reliquiis sanctorum et sacris imaginibus.* Cf. also the Second Nicene Council, *Actio* VII and VIII (*Fontes,* n. 5); Fourth Council of Constantinople, can. 3 (*Fontes,* n. 6); St. Thomas Aquinas, *Summa Theol.,* II-II, Quaest. 94, art. 2, ad primum; Quaest 103, art. 3, ad tertium; Hurley, *o. c.,* p. 125 f.

wise that no images, (suggestive) of false doctrine, and furnishing occasion of dangerous error to the uneducated, be set up.

While, therefore, the Church encourages the use of images because of the many benefits derived therefrom, she is very watchful lest such representations be misleading. And, as she knows of the existence in the present and of the possibility in the future of such dubious or dangerous images, she forbids the use of them in can. 1399, n. 10.

Images, therefore, *in whatever manner printed, of our Lord, the Blessed Mother, the Angels, the Saints and other Servants of God, if they depart from the meaning and decrees of the Church*, are forbidden.

1. *Imagines quoquo modo impressae* are all kinds of representations or images printed or stamped. This phrase applies to all those ways in which, by means of impression, effigies are mechanically multiplied. It makes no difference whether this impression is made by means of a plate, a cut, or the negative of a photograph or by any other process. This law, therefore, affects engravings, photographs, litographs, phototypes, and daguerrotypes but not images made by hand such as paintings or statues.[284] Pictures, like books, must be *published*. Otherwise they do not fall under this prohibition.[285] Authors generally[286] exclude also *medals*. The reason is that while medals bear an image impressed on metal and are spread very easily, yet they can hardly be said to be printed; rather they are *struck*. Furthermore, this title of the Code deals with books and other forms of literature. Pictures have some connection with books, but medals have not. Therefore, it can be safely said that medals are not *imagines impressae*.

---

284. De Meester, *o. c.*, III, n. 1341, 5, c; Vermeersch-Creusen, *Ep.*, II, n. 725, 3°; Hurley, *o. c.*, p. 126 f.; Noldin, *o. c.*, II, n. 708, 12, a; Boudinhon, *o. c.*, p. 148 f.; Pennacchi, *o. c.*, p. 127 f.; Cocchi, *l. c.*; Van Coillie, *o. c.*, p. 56 f.; Bouuaert-Simenon, *o. c.*, p. 547, 3; Ferreres, *Instit. Can.*, II, p. 158; Cappello, *De Curia*, I, p. 280; *Periodica de Religios.*, XIV (1926), (98).

285. Can. 1384, §2. Cf. also *Periodica de Religios.*, XIV (1926), (93) f.

286. De Meester, *l. c.*; Vermeersch-Creusen, *l. c.*; Noldin, *l. c.*: Boudinhon, *o. c.*, p. 149; Pennacchi, *o. c.*, p. 128; Cocchi, *l. c.*; Vermeersch, *De Prohib et Cens. Libr.*, p. 89.

2. Imagines....*Domini Nostri Jesu Christi, Beatae Mariae Virginis, Angelorum atque Sanctorum vel aliorum Servorum Dei ab Ecclesia sensu et decretis alienae.*

This certainly applies to images which *represent a false dogma*, e. g., the Son being inferior to the Father; or which are apt to *provoke sensuality* or which may easily *lead the ignorant people into error.*[287]

Many examples of images which are not in conformity with the mind and practice of the Church are enumerated in the decree of the S. C. of the Holy Office, *Sanctissimus*,[288] in the constitutions of Urban VIII, *Caelestis Jerusalem*[289] and *Sacrosancta*,[290] in the fourth book of the work of Benedict XIV, *De Beatificatione et canonizatione Servorum Dei*, P. II, c. 21, as well as in his constitution *Sollicitudini*[291] and in his General Decrees, §3,[292] and in many decrees of the Sacred Congregation of the Holy Office.[293]

Canon 1399, n. 12, mentions only images of "our Lord, the Blessed Virgin Mary, the Angels, the Saints and other Servants of God." Therefore, since the laws of prohibition are to be interpreted strictly, pictures of the Holy Trinity, of the Father and of the Holy Ghost are not affected by this law. There are some decrees prohibiting the representation of, e. g., the Holy Trinity in the womb of the Blessed Virgin Mary, or in the form of one man with two heads and one dove, or one man with three heads, or three distinct men sim-

---

287.   Can. 1279, §3; Vermeersch-Creusen, *Ep.*, II, n. 605, 3; De Meester, *o. c.*, III, n. 1267, 2 b.   However Bucceroni, *Inst. Theol.*, II, n. 1310, states: *Excipe, nisi retineantur uti merum historicum artis monumentum.*

288.   Mar. 13, 1625 (*Fontes*, n. 719).

289.   July 5, 1634 (*Fontes*, n. 213).

290.   Mar. 15, 1642 (*Fontes*, n. 223).

291.   Oct. 1, 1745 (*Fontes*, n. 362).

292.   Contained in his Index of 1758. These decrees have no more force of law, but serve as examples of what the Church disapproves in religious imagery.

293.   E. g., Feb. 28, 1875 (*ASS*, VIII [1875], 361); Apr. 3, 1895 (*ASS*, XXVIII [1895], 61); Apr. 8, 1916 (*Fontes*, n. 1300); Mar. 30, 1921 (*AAS*, XIII [1921], 197); Mar. 16, 1928 (*AAS*, XX [1928], 103).

ilar and equal to each other;[294] the Holy Ghost in human form,[295] etc. Certainly the decrees issued after the publication of the Code are binding. Pre-Code legislation in this matter is also still in force, even though not contained in the Code, at least as far as public worship is concerned, since Can. 2 states that all liturgical laws retain their force unless some of them should be expressly corrected in the Code.[296] Nevertheless, owing to the explicit treatment in the Code of *printed images* and to the express mention of "images of our Lord, the Blessed Virgin Mary, the Angels, the Saints and other Servants of God", it must be concluded that printed images of the Holy Trinity, the Father and the Holy Ghost, even though contrary to the meaning and the decrees of the Church, are not forbidden by the general law.[297]

Christ our Lord may be depicted in all the stages of human development, because "The Word was made flesh, and dwelt amongst us",[298] but always in accordance with the tradition of the Church. He can also be represented as a lamb, as He is thus called in the Scriptures.[299] The Sacred Congregation of the Holy Office with a decree of Feb. 23-24, 1921, declared as prohibited by law some pictures depicting the Stations of the Cross in a new way.[300]

Images of the Blessed Virgin Mary must represent her in the form and dress customary in the Catholic Church from olden times. Images showing her in the habit of a partic-

---

294. Benedict XIV, const. *Sollicitudini*, Oct. 1, 1745 (*Fontes*, n. 362).

295. Decree of the S. C. of the Holy Office, March 16, 1928 (*AAS*, XX [1928], 103).

296. *Periodica de Religious.*, XIV (1926), (95).

297. *Periodica de Religios.*, XIV (1926), (96). Nowadays pictures of the Holy Trinity, the Father and the Holy Ghost are very rare.

298. John I, 14.

299. John I, 29.

300. *AAS*, XIII (1921), 197. Those pictures are contained in the work of Cyrille Verschaeve, *La Passion de Notre Seigneur Jésus Christ Ornée de Compositions d'Albert Servaes* (Brussels and Paris: G. Van Oeste et Cie., 1920).

ular religious order or congregation are forbidden.[301] Benedict XIV[302] quotes a statement of Sarnelli[303] to show that from apostolic times it has been customary to represent the Blessed Virgin clothed in a garment of a rosy or purple color, with a mantel of azure blue. Bernardette saw her at Lourdes in a snow-white garment and mantel, with an azure girdle.[304]

Angels have always been represented in the Church under the forms in which, Holy Scripture records, they have appeared to men. Hence, they are generally shown as youths, beautiful in appearance, clad in white, girt round the loins, and sometimes as supplied with wings. They are also represented as children wrapt in contemplation or as heads of children with two wings. The wings indicate their spiritual nature. Angels sometimes have their hands joined in contemplation, at other times they carry the instruments of God's anger, as a sword, or of His mercy, as the cross and other insignia of the passion of our Lord.[305] Canonized saints must also be represented in the traditional way and with diadems or aureolas; the beatified are not to be shown with diadems but only with rays of glory; the servants of God who are neither canonized nor beatified, are not to be represented with either diadems, aureolas or rays or with suppliants at their feet, because such would betoken honor and invocation.[306]

Stamped or printed pictures contrary to these decrees of the Church are forbidden. But pictures which do not carry

---

301.   Urban VIII, const. *Sacrosancta*, Mar. 15, 1642, n. 1 (*Fontes*, n. 223). This prohibition applies also to images of Our Lord, the Angels and Saints, unless a certain saint actually wore that habit in his life, e. g. St. Francis.

302.   *De Beat. et Can. Serv. Dei.*, lib. IV, part II, cap. XXI, n. 8.

303.   *Epistolae ecclesiasticae*, tom. IV, ep. 46.

304.   Fourth lesson of the Feast of Our Lady of Lourdes, Feb. 11.

305.   Pennacchi, *o. c.*, p. 133; Hurley, *o. c.*, p. 131; Boudinhon, *o. c.*, p. 147.

306.   Urban VIII, const. *Caelestis Hierusalem*, July 5, 1634, n. 1 (*Fontes*, n. 213); Pennacchi, *o. c.*, p. 133; Hurley, *o. c.*, p. 131; Boudinhon, *o. c.*, p. 154.

the episcopal approbation required in Can. 1385, §1, n. 3, if
they represent our Lord, the Blessed Virgin, the Angels, the
Saints or any other Servants of God in accordance with the
tradition and decrees of the Church are not forbidden.[307]

---

307. De Meester, *o. c.*, III, n. 1341, d; Mothon, *Institutions Canoniques*, I, p. 886, n. 26.

CHAPTER VII

BOOKS FORBIDDEN BY SPECIAL DECREE AND
THE INDEX OF PROHIBITED BOOKS[1]

In the preceding chapter a study was made of the classes
of books which are forbidden by the general law of the Church.
In those rules practically all dangerous works are contained
but no forbidden book is mentioned by name. It is left to the
individual to apply the laws to particular books to determine
whether they are forbidden or not. Generally speaking, these
rules should suffice for the proper guidance of readers. Unfortunately, however, extraordinary cases arise in which the
extraordinary measure must be taken of condemning a work
by name. This special condemnation is issued only when very
serious reasons make it imperative[2] and it comes either from
the Ordinary or from the Holy See.[3]

The Index of Prohibited Books is a list of all the works
which have been condemned *nominatim* by the Holy See[4] and
which are still considered as such.[5]

---

1. De Meester, *Compendium*, III, nn. 1359 and 1376; Vermeersch-
Creusen, *Epitome*, II, n. 734; Ayrinhac, *Administr. Legisl.*, p. 297 f.

2. *"Gravioribus causis postulantibus"*, Instr. of the S. C. of the
Holy Office, May 3, 1927 (*A A S*, XIX [1927], 189). Cf. supra, pag.
63 f., for some of those reasons.

3. Can. 1395.

4. Only the Holy See can publish an Index of Prohibited Books
(cf. Vermeersch-Creusen, *o. c.*, II, n. 734). However, there is nothing
to prevent Ordinaries, in case of necessity, from issuing for their subjects a list of books which are forbidden by the general law of the
Church. Cf. Instr. of the S. Congr. of the Holy Office, May 3, 1927
(*A A S*, XIX [1927], 189).

5. For the history of the *Index of Prohibited Books* cf. supra, p. 46
ff. There can be no question about the binding force of the Index after
the Code. This is evident from the editions published after the Code,
especially the last one (1929) issued by Pius XI. Cf. also Vermeersch-

The title of each forbidden book is given in its original
language. Moreover, some books are marked with a cross,
others with an asterisk, so that it may be seen at a glance
which have been forbidden in the most solemn manner, by
means of Apostolic letters, and which less solemnly by means
of decrees with the clause *donec corrigatur* (until such time
as corrections are made). This distinction, however, concerns
only the method but not the effect of the prohibition.[6] Nevertheless, it is a help in finding the books condemned *nominatim*
by means of Apostolic letters, works which one is forbidden
to defend, **read or keep** under pain of excommunication specially reserved to the Holy See.[7]

Occasionally in the *Index of Prohibited Books*, the name
of an author is followed by the phrase *Opera Omnia*[8] ("All
works"), or *Omnes fabulae amatoriae*[9] ("All love stories").
By condemning "all the works" (*Opera omnia*) of an author
the Church does not intend to forbid each individual work
of that author, but to cast the shadow of suspicion upon all
of them. If, therefore, such an author be a non-Catholic and
he has written a book which does not treat of religion,[10] except perhaps in passing, and which is not forbidden by the
general law nor by special decree, his book may lawfully be
read. The same mitigation applies to the work of a Catholic,

Creusen, *Ep.*, II, n. 734; Bouuaert-Simenon, *o. c.*, p. 557 f. Pruemmer,
Man. Iuris Eccl., q. 419, incorrectly holds that the Index binds now only
inasfar as the books contained therein come under can 1399.

6. Cf. *Index of Prohibited Books* (English ed., 1930), p. XXXI.
Regardless of the manner in which a book has been condemned, the condemnation always "entails the prohibition without special permission,
either to publish, to read, to keep, to sell, to translate it, or in any way
to pass it on to others." (Can. 1398, §1). A book forbidden by name
cannot be republished, even though corrected, without the permission of
the one who condemned it, his Superior or his successor. (Can. 1398, §2).
Cf. supra, p. 120 f.

7. Can. 2318, §1. Cf. *infra*, p. 227 ff.

8. E. g. **France**, Anatole. *Opera omnia.*

9. E. g. **Sand**, George (*pseudonyma*). *Omnes fabulae amatoriae.*

10. A work on religion by a non-Catholic whose works are "all"
forbidden, remains prohibited until it is certain that it contains nothing
against the Catholic faith, according to can. 1399, n. 4. Cf. also De
Meester, *o. c.*, III, p. 277, note 3.

if it is evidently not forbidden by general law or by special decree.[11]

No official interpretation is available for the phrase *Omnes fabulae amatoriae*, but authors generally[12] interpret it to mean that all the love stories of the author in question are forbidden unless *it be certain* that one or the other of them is not condemned by the general rules of the Code nor by special decree. This interpretation is based on the explanation given by the Church[13] of the other phrase *Opera Omnia*, which in reality, is even more universal and severe. Accordingly, love-stories[14] which do not deal of impure love, or obscenity are not forbidden.[15] Thus, the Count of *Monte-Cristo, The Three Mus-*

---

11. Preface to *Index Librorum Prohibitorum Leonis XIII, S. P.* (ed. 1925), pp. XVI-XVII. Cf. also De Meester, *o. c.,* III, n. 1359, a, α; Vermeersch-Creusen, *Ep.* II, n. 734, 4; Cocchi, *Comment. Cod. Jur. Can.,* VI, n. 67, N.B.; Noldin, *Summa Theol. Mor.,* II, n. 710, c; Betten, *The Rom. Index,* p. 41, n. 1; Bethleem, *Romans à lire et Romans à proscrire,* p. 20. De Meester, *o. c.,* III, p. 277, note 3, gives as examples some works which are not included in the phrase *Opera omnia: Essai de grammaire général* of Groudhon, *Le Rêve* of Zola and *Le Crime de Sylvestre Bonnard* of Anatole France. In the recent edition of the *Index* published by order of Pius XI (1929), the preface, just referred to, is omitted. However, it must still be considered as interpretation of the *Index* as long as it does not conflict with any new law; and in the topic now under discussion no conflicting new law or interpretation has been issued. Cf. also Cann. 21-22.

12. De Meester, *o. c.,* III, n. 1359, b; Bethleem, *o. c.,* p. 20; Bouuaert-Simenon, *Man. Jur. Can.,* p. 558; Genicot-Salsmans, *Inst. Theol. Mor.,* I, n. 451; Betten, *o. c.,* p. 41, n. 1.

13. Preface to the *Index Librorum Prohib. Leonis XIII S. P.,* pp. XVI, XVII.

14. De Meester, *l. c.,* notes that *fabulae amatoriae* means what *opera romanensia* meant in the old *Index.* Therefore, dramas and comedies are not included. This is confirmed by the special decree prohibiting D'Annunzio's works (S. C. Ind. May 8, 1911 — cf. *Index of Proh. Books*). It explicitly condemned *Omnes fabulae amatoriae* and *Omnia opera dramatica.* Therefore dramatic works are not included in the phrase *Omnes fabulae amatoriae.*

15. It is well at this point to note from Betten, p. 41, n. 1: "The number of such exceptions cannot be great, because if it were the terms *Opera omnia* or *Omnes fabulae amatoriae* would not have been chosen, but the few really bad books would have been enumerated individually. In practical life we cannot figure with such exceptions. The books so designated must be left alone."

keteers of Alexander Dumas, *Francois le Champi*, *La Petite Fadette* and *La Mare au diable* of George Sand, are permitted, according to Bethleem.[16]

It happens at times that after the first volume or volumes of a work have been placed in the Index, other volumes are published; so also after a periodical publication has been condemned, it continues to be published; also after "all the works" of an author have been forbidden, new works are published by the same author. In all these cases, the volumes of a forbidden work, the numbers of a forbidden periodical, as well as, the new works of a forbidden author, published *after* the decree of condemnation, are not included in that decree. However, they are open to suspicion and are rightly considered to be prohibited by one or several of the general rules contained in Can. 1399, unless the irreproachable character of the work gives evidence of amendment by the author.[17]

---

16. *Romans à lire et Romans à proscrire*, p. 20. This work is very valuable, for it classifies the principal love stories and their writers according to the laws of God and of the Church.

17. Preface to the *Index Libr. Proh. Leonis XIII P. M.*, p. XX. Cf. also De Meester, *o. c.*, III, n. 1359, a *β*; Ayrinhac, *o. c.*, p. 296; Betten, *o. c.*, p. 41, n. 1.

CHAPTER VIII

EXEMPTIONS AND EXCEPTIONS

It has been pointed out in an earlier chapter[1] that the laws and decrees forbidding books bind all Christians, even those who do not consider it dangerous for themselves to read a condemned work. However, the law itself exempts some classes of people and makes provision for the granting of permission to others to read forbidden books in cases of necessity. This matter is all treated in canons 1400-1405.

Art. I. *Exemptions*

Can. 1400: — **Usus librorum de quibus in can. 1399, n. 1 ac librorum editorum contra praescriptum can. 1391, iis dumtaxat permittitur qui studiis theologicis vel biblicis quovis modo operam dant, dummodo iidem libri fideliter et integre editi sint neque impugnentur in eorum prolegomenis aut adnotationibus catholicae fidei dogmata.**

Can. 1401: — **S. R. E. Cardinales, Episcopi, etiam titulares, aliique Ordinarii, necessariis adhibitis cautelis, ecclesiastica librorum prohibitione non adstringuntur.**

In these two canons the Code itself authorizes the persons mentioned to use books which are forbidden to all others.

1. *Persons engaged in theological or biblical studies* may lawfully use editions of the original text or of the ancient Catholic versions of the Sacred Scriptures published by non-Catholics as well as any non-Catholic translations of the Bible (forbidden by can. 1399, n. 1). They may use also Catholic translations of the Scriptures into the vernacular which were published without the necessary canonical requirements, i. e.

---

1. Supra, p. 73 ff.

approval of the Holy See or of the Ordinary with annotations taken particularly from the works of the Fathers of the Church and of learned Catholic writers.[2] There is another class of Scriptural works, which are forbidden in Can. 1399, n. 5, but which are not expressly mentioned in Can. 1400, i. e. Catholic editions of the text or of the ancient Catholic versions of Holy Scripture, and notes or commentaries on the same, if they were published without the previous ecclesiastical censorship and approval required by Can. 1385, §1, n. 1. Boudinhon[3] rightly extends the exemption of Can. 1400 to those works also. For, if non-Catholic Scriptural works are allowed to persons engaged in theological or biblical studies, there is at least as much reason for allowing Catholic unapproved editions, provided the other conditions, i. e. integrity, fidelity, orthodoxy, are fulfilled.

In order that these forbidden Scriptural editions may be read they must be *faithful to the originals and complete, and in the prefaces or notes to them, no attack must be made on the dogmas of the Catholic faith.* The "fidelity and integrity" required, when there is question of old non-Catholic versions *seems* to refer not to the Scriptural text itself but to the original form in which they were published by a non-Catholic author, even though they contained some false statements.[4] Otherwise, most Protestant Bibles would be forbidden even to those who are engaged in theological and biblical studies, since they are known to lack fidelity and integrity, as far as the text of the Scripture is concerned. In fact, some passages have been distorted, and all the deuterocanonical parts of the Old Testament have been omitted.[5]

The other condition for the lawful use of forbidden Scriptural works is that in them *no attack be made on the dogmas of the Catholic faith,* i. e., truths solemnly defined by the

------

2. Books forbidden by Can. 1399, n. 5.

3. *O. c.,* p. 98.

4. Schaepman, Dr. A. B. M., "Over libri prohibiti.", *Nederlandsche Katolieke Stemmen,* 1929, pp. 151-154; Vermeersch-Creusen, *Ep.,* II, n. 735, 2; Cocchi, *Comment. in C. J. C.,* VI, n. 70, c; Pennacchi, *In Const. Apost. Off. ac mun.,* p. 83 f.

5. Pennacchi, *l. c.*

Church.[6] If a Catholic opinion[7] or a doctrine theologically certain[8] is attacked, or errors are defended which are not opposed to a dogma, the exemption still holds. Moreover, to *attack* a dogma of Catholic faith means to give reasons, proofs for the attack. A simple denial of a dogma is not sufficient.[9]

Who are the persons affected by this exemption? *Iis dumtaxat permittitur qui studiis theologicis vel biblicis quovis modo operam dant.* Any person who in any way whatever, whether in an institution of learning or privately at home,[10] is engaged in theological or biblical studies, may lawfully read forbidden Scriptural works which are faithful to the original, and integral and do not attack any Catholic dogma. Therefore, this permission applies to all scholars given to these sciences, students of theology or Scripture[11] in colleges, theological seminaries and universities; also to all priests, who in accordance with the prescriptions of Canon Law[12] continue their sacred studies after their ordination; finally it applies to any one, cleric or layman, who gives himself seriously to theological or biblical studies in any way whatever, e. g. to prepare for an examination, to write an essay, etc.[13]

---

6. Supra, p. 152.

7. Boudinhon, *o. c.*, pp. 100-101, 103.

8. Gennari, "Circa la nuova disciplina", *Il Mon. Eccl.*, X (1897), 34.

9. Gennari, *l. c.*; Bucceroni, *Instit. Theol. Mor.*, II, n. 1304.

10. S. C. Ind., May 23, 1898 (*ASS*, XXX [1898], 697 f.).

11. In many ecclesiastical colleges certain portions of theology or Sacred Scriptures are studied simultaneously with Hebrew and Greek. It is allowed in such cases to use non-Catholic editions of the Hebrew or Greek text of the Scriptures, provided they are faithful to the originals and integral, and in no way attack any Catholic dogma. The same is not permitted to students of Greek and Hebrew who do not study theology nor Sacred Scripture. For these, the Bishop needs a special indult. Cf. S. C. Ind., June 21, 1898 (*ASS*, XXX [1898], 749); Boudinhon, *La Nouv. Legislation de l'Index*, p. 100 f.; Hurley, *Index Legisl.*, p. 69 ff.; Wernz, *Jus Decretal.*, III, n. 111 (note 57).

12. Can. 129.

13. Noldin, *Summa Theol. Mor.*, II, 711, 2, a; Hurley, *l. c.*; Boudinhon, *l. c.*; Bouuaert-Simenon, *Man. Jur. Can.*, p. 558; Cocchi, *o. c.*, VI, n. 70, c; Pennacchi, *In Const. Apost. Offic. ac muner.*, p. 61 f.; Van Coillie, *Commentarius in Const. Off. ac mun.*, p. 42; Wernz, *l. c.*; Betten,

2. Cardinals of the Holy Roman Church, Bishops both residential and titular, and other Ordinaries, are excused, when taking the necessary precaution, from observance of the ecclesiastical prohibition of books.[14]

It was always understood in the Church that the ecclesiastical prohibition of books did not bind equally the people and the hierarchy. The reason is that the hierarchy must be on the lookout for evil literature to be able to warn the people in time against it and, whenever necessary, to refute error. Besides, the knowledge that they have of religion and their piety usually makes them less vulnerable than others.

A canon of the fourth Council of Carthage, which took place towards the end of the 4th century, thus reads: *"Episcopus libros gentilium non legat, haereticorum autem pro necessitate aut tempore."*[15] This principle in favor of Bishops and other members of the hierarchy was always recognized by the Church. Only in extremely difficult times did she extend her prohibitions to them also, as, e. g., in her condemnation of Iconoclast literature at the Second Nicene Council in 787,[16] and in her proscription of Luther's writings in 1520.[17] This extraordinary measure seems to have been the rule also from the time of the Protestant reformation to the time of the Code.[18] In these exceptional times, even members of the hierarchy had to secure permission to read books forbidden by the positive law of the Church.

The Code has revived the principle of exemption in this matter as applied to Cardinals, Bishops and other Ordinaries.

The Roman Index, p. 43 (n. 10) ; Augustine, *A Commentary,* VI, p. 475 ff.; De Meester, *Compendium,* III, n. 1377, b; Genicot-Salsmans, *Inst. Theol. Mor.,* I, n. 453, 1, and note 1; Blat, *Commentar. Textus C. J. C.,* III, n. 289; *The Ecclesiastical Review,* LXXVIII (1928), 184 f.

14. St. Alphonsus, *Theol. Mor.,* VII, n. 299; Lugo, *De Virtute fid.,* disp. 21, sect. 2, n. 70; Augustine, *o. c.,* VI, p. 477 f.; Blat, *o. c.,* III, n. 290; Boudinhon, *o. c.,* p. 194 f.; Pennacchi, *o. c.,* p. 171; Betten, *o. c.,* p. 36.

15. C. 1, D.XXXVII.

16. Mansi, XIII, 429 (c. 9).

17. Leo X, const. *Exsurge Domine,* of June 15, 1520 (*Fontes.* n. 76).

18. St. Alphonsus, *Theol. Mor.,* VII, n. 299; Lugo, *l. c.;* Pennacchi, *o. c.,* p. 171; Boudinhon, *o. c.,* p. 194 f.

The other Ordinaries, besides the Supreme Pontiff and residential Bishops, are[19] Abbots and Prelates *nullius* and their Vicars General, Administrators of vacant dioceses, Vicars and Prefects Apostolic, and their Vicars Delegate,[20] and those who, in the absence of the aforesaid assume the reins of government in the interim, according to the prescription of law or approved constitutions, such as the Chapter of Canons or, as in the United States of America, the Diocesan Consultors, the Vicar Capitular, the Pro-vicar and Pro-prefect Apostolic; also the Major Superiors of clerical exempt religious orders or congregations. Now, as long as these persons take the necessary precautions prescribed by the natural and positive law of God against injuring themselves or others through dangerous books, they are not bound by the ecclesiastical prohibition of books as contained in the general rules of the Code, in the *Index of Prohibited Books* and in all special decrees of the Holy See. This exemption is very general and there is no basis for restricting it to works which are not obscene. Whenever, then, and inasfar as an obscene book is forbidden *only* by ecclesiastical law, Cardinals, Bishops and other Ordinaries may read it, for a good reason and with the necessary precautions. However, as a rule, this class of works is forbidden by the natural law which binds all equally.

Art. II. *"Licentia" or Permission to Read Prohibited Books*

"The condemnation of a book entails the prohibition, *without special permission*, either to publish, to read, to keep, to sell, to translate it, or in any way to pass it on to others".[21] This applies to every one who is not expressly exempted.[22] No matter what a man's position in life or learning may be, if he

---

19. Can. 198.

20. Letter of the S. C. of the Propag. of the Faith, Dec. 8, 1919 (*A A S*, XII [1920], 120).

21. Can. 1398, §1.

22. Persons engaged in theological or biblical studies are exempted from the ecclesiastical prohibition of some biblical works (Can. 1400); Cardinals, Bishops and other Ordinaries are exempted from all the rules and decrees of ecclesiastical prohibition (Can. 1401).

is baptized, he is bound by this law. One must either abstain
from using forbidden books or he must secure the permission[23]
necessary to read them.

Sect. I. *Authorities who can grant permission to read
forbidden books.*

Permission to read, keep or in any way use books forbidden either by the general rules of the Code or by special decrees of the Holy See, can be granted only by the Holy See and
by those to whom the Holy See gives that faculty[24] according
to the principle: *"Omnis res per quascumque causas nascitur
per easdem dissolvitur".*[25]

1. If the Pope himself condemned a work, then he is the
only one who can give permission to use that work, unless he
gives that power also to others.[26] For all other books condemned by the Apostolic See, permission is granted by the
Holy Office.[27]

A petition sent to the Holy Office must be recommended
by the Bishop, if the petitioner be a secular priest or cleric,

---

23. This permission is at times called a dispensation. This is not
quite correct. A dispensation implies that the law is suspended in a
particular case, while a permission (*licentia*) denotes the application of
a law which is conditional, a law, namely, which gives the option, either
to observe the law or to obtain permission to do what is otherwise forbidden. A dispensation is *contra ius*, a permission is *iuxta ius*. Cann.
1401-1405 offer a clear example of *permission*. Cf. Chelodi, *Jus de Personis*, n. 86 (note 1); Vermeersch-Creusen, *Ep.*, II, n. 736, 2. However,
the word dispensation is not infrequently used not only by authors but
also by the Code itself. Cf. can. 247, §4.

24. Leo XIII, const. *Officiorum ac munerum*, Jan. 25, 1897, n. 23
(*Fontes*, n. 632).

25. C. 1, X, *De Reg. Jur.*, V, 41.

26. This principle was clearly expressed by Pius XI when he gave
faculty to Cardinal Dubois and the other Bishops of France to grant
permission to read *L'Action Française: "Cum Summus ipse Pontifex
memoratum Commentarium Indici librorum prohibitorum insenuerit, idem
unus huiusmodi interdictione ac vetito exsolvere potest."* (*A A S*, XIX
[1927], 185). Cf. Vermeersch-Creusen, *Ep.* II (ed. 1930), n. 736, 1; *Il
Mon. Eccl.*, XXXVIII (1927), 129.

27. Can. 247, §4. Cf. also Vermeersch-Creusen, *l. c.*; De Meester,
o. c., III, n. 1379, a.

by the Superior, if he be a religious. For a lay person the recommendation of the confessor is sufficient. Moreover, the petition should state the reason for the request and the position and occupation of the petitioner. Thus, if one asks permission to read forbidden books *ratione studiorum*, he must state that he is professor or teacher of such and such a subject, a student of such a university, the writer of such a work, employed in such a library, etc. In the rescript granting the permission, works which are *ex professo* obscene are always excepted. Moreover, when the petitioner is a woman, it is generally committed to her confessor to permit each forbidden book which she may need.[28]

Examples of formulas to be used by persons asking for permission from the Holy See to read forbidden books and of others used by the Holy See in granting the requested permission, may be read in Cappello, *De Curia Romana*, I, p. 304 ff and 309.[29] The beginning of the formulas used by the Holy See has been changed recently. It now reads: "*SSmus D. N. . . . Divina Providentia Pp. per facultates R. P. D. Assessori S. Officii impertitas, si vera sunt exposita, benigne annuit pro gratia ut liceat oratori, etc.*"[30]

Nuncios, Internuncios and Apostolic Delegates, have wide powers delegated to them for the countries in which they represent the Supreme Pontiff. Among their faculties[31] there is one (Chapter I, n. 14) which empowers them to grant permission to keep or read forbidden books and newspapers, with those precautions and limitations which will be deemed necessary or useful in each case, as is done by the Holy Office.[32]

---

28. Vermeersch-Creusen, *Ep.*, II, n. 736.

29. Cf. also Arndt, *De Libris Prohibitis*, n. 182.

30. Vermeersch-Creusen, *l. c.*

31. Vermeersch-Creusen, *Ep.*, I, Appendix I.

32. "*Concedendi ad normam Const. Officiorum et munerum facultatem retinendi ac legendi prohibitos libros et ephemerides, cum cautelis et sub limitationibus quae necessaria vel utilia in singulis casibus videbuntur, et in usu penes S. Congr. S. Officii sunt.*" This faculty seems to have been drawn up in pre-code language, and even then, rather negligently. For, the const. *Officiorum ac munerum* was superseded by the Code, and apparently there is no reason why the defunct constitu-

Therefore, in the United States, permission to read forbidden books may be sought from the Apostolic Delegate, instead of writing to the Holy See.

2. *Ordinaries* also have been given special powers to permit their subjects the use of books forbidden by the Holy See. The Code empowers them to give permission in individual cases only. Besides that, many Ordinaries have obtained the faculty to give general permission.

A) Can. 1402. — §1 **Ordinarii licentiam ad libros quod attinet ipso iure vel decreto Sedis Apostolicae prohibitos, concedere suis subditis valent pro singulis tantum libris atque in casibus dumtaxat urgentibus.**[33]

Before the publication of Leo's const. *Officiorum ac munerum*, there was no express authorization given to Bishops or other Ordinaries to permit the use of condemned works. It was indeed admitted by moralists, led by St. Alphonsus[34] that in case of necessity the Bishop could give such a permission. But this was based more on the use of *epikeia* than on any official document.[35] However, in the constitution *Officiorum ac munerum* (n. 25), Bishops and other Prelates with quasi-episcopal jurisdiction received ordinary power to grant permission to read individual books for urgent cases; and now the Code, in very similar words, empowers all Ordinaries to grant permission to their subjects to read single books prohibited by the general law or by a decree of the Apostolic See, but only in cases of urgent necessity.

Ordinarii are all those listed in Can. 198, as explained

---

tion and not the Code should be the pattern to which papal legates must conform their permissions. (Cf. Boudinhon, *o. c.*, p. 205, note 1). Moreover, the constitution was not *Officiorum* ET *munerum*, but *Officiorum* AC *munerum*.

33. Leo XIII, const. *Officiorum ac munerum*, Jan. 25, 1897, n. 25 (*Fontes*, n. 632); St. Alphonsus, *De Prohib. Libr.*, cap. V, n. 2; *Theologia Mor.*, VII, n. 299; Suarez, *De Fide*, disp. 20, sect. 2, n. 28; Lugo, *De Virt. Fid.*, disp. 21, sect. 2, n. 71; Boudinhon, *La Nouv. Legisl. de l'Ind.*, pp. 197, 206; Wernz, *Jus Decretal.*, III, n. 111 (note 78); Augustine, *A Commentary*, VI, p. 479; Blat, *Commentar. Textus C. J. C.*, III, n. 291, §1.

34. *Theol. Mor.*, VII, n. 299.

35. Wernz, *l. c.*; Boudinhon, *o. c.*, p. 197 ff.

above.[36] This power is *ordinary* and therefore may be delegated.[37]

Ordinaries can permit the use of any book which is forbidden either by general law or by special decree. No distinction is here made between irreligious and immoral or obscene books. Therefore, an Ordinary can grant permission to read even an obscene book,[38] if there is a just reason for it.[39] In any case, the Ordinary can give permission *only* for certain specified books (not necessarily one), and in urgent cases: *"pro singulis tantum libris atque in casibus dumtaxat urgentibus"*.[40] A case is urgent in which a person cannot do or obtain something without reading a forbidden book. This would happen, e. g., if one could not prepare for an examination or give a prompt answer to an objection against the Church, without reading a forbidden book.[41]

B) **Can. 1402. — §2. Quod si generalem a Sede Apostolica facultatem impetraverint suis subditis permittendi ut libros proscriptos retineant ac legant, eam nonnisi cum delectu et iusta ac rationabili causa concedant.**[42]

In the first paragraph of this canon the Ordinaries are

---

36. Pag. 197. This is the only power which Ordinaries in Missionary countries have with regard to forbidden books. No other faculty is contained in the Quinquennial Faculties given by the S. C. for the Propagation of the Faith. However, wider powers, if considered necessary, may be obtained from the Holy Office through the S. C. for the Propagation of the Faith. Cf. Vermeersch, *De Formulis Facultatum S. C. de Propaganda Fide Commentaria*, p. 114.

37. Vermeersch-Creusen, *Ep.*, II, n. 736, b; Wernz, *o. c.*, III, n. 111 (note 78); Augustine, *o. c.*, VI, p. 479; Betten, *o. c.*, p. 36.

38. Vermeersch-Creusen, *Ep.*, II, n. 735, N. B.; Augustine, *o. c.*, VI, p. 480; Bouuaert-Simenon, *Man. Jur. Can.*, p. 559.

39. Arndt, *De Libris Prohibitis*, p. 86.

40. Can. 1402, §1.

41. Pennacchi, *In Const. Apost. Off. ac mun.*, p. 173.

42. Leo XIII, const. *Officiorum ac munerum*, Jan. 25, 1897, n. 25 (*Fontes*, n. 632); De Meester, *Compendium*, III, n. 1379, c; Vermeersch-Creusen, *Ep.*, II, n. 736, b; Boudinhon, *o. c.*, p. 197 ff.; Pennacchi, *o. c.*, p. 173 f.; Moureau, *La Nouv. Legisl.*, p. 78 f.; Gennari, "Circa la nuova disciplina", *Il Mon. Eccl.*, X (1897), 82 f.; Blat, *o. c.*, III, n. 291, §2; Arndt, *o. c.*, n. 183.

authorized to give permission in individual urgent cases to read some specified forbidden books. But that is not sufficient in some dioceses of very large dimensions and in those where institutions of learning, such as universities, frequently request permission to read forbidden books. Therefore, the Holy See gives to many Ordinaries[43] general faculties to permit their subjects to read and keep[44] forbidden books. These faculties, given by the Holy Office[45] are now worded as follows:[46]

> Concedendi non ultra triennium, licentiam legendi ac retinendi, sub custodia tamen ne ad aliorum manus perveniant, libros prohibitos et ephemerides, exceptis operibus haeresim vel schisma ex professo propugnantibus, vel etiam ipsa religionis fundamenta evertere nitentibus nec non operibus de obscenis ex professo tractantibus, sigulis Christi fidelibus sibi subditis, non nisi tamen cum delectu et iusta ac rationabili causa (cfr. can. 1402 P. 2 Cod. I. C.), iis scilicet tantum qui eorumdem librorum et ephemeridum lectione sive ad ea impugnanda sive ad proprium legitimum munus exercendum, vel iustum studiorum curriculum peragendum, *vere* indigeant.
>
> Adnotandum-Recensita facultas Episcopis conceditur per se ipsos personaliter exercenda seu memini deleganda; et graviter onerata ipsorum conscientia super reali omnium memoratarum conditionum concursu.

The permission granted in virtue of these faculties is a general permission. It applies to all[47] books forbidden by the

---

43. This general faculty of permitting the use of forbidden books was given before the Code even to Rectors of seminaries and colleges, to professors and to librarians, with certain restrictions. Cf. Cappello, *De Curia Romana*, I, p. 303 f.

44. The Ordinary cannot give permission to publish, to sell, to translate a forbidden work or in any way to pass it on to others.

45. Only the S. C. of the Holy Office has ordinary power to grant these general faculties (Can. 247, §4) and no other Congregation, not even de S. C. of the Propagation of the Faith. However, the Holy Office may grant the permission through the Congregation of the Propagation of the Faith (Vermeersch, *De Formulis Facultatum S. C. de Propaganda Fide Commentaria*, p. 114). Papal legates cannot give these general faculties to Bishops. They do not come under the term Apostolic See or Holy See, as explained in Can. 7.

46. Vermeersch-Creusen, I (1929), Appendix III.

47. Noldin, *o. c.*, II, n. 713.

Holy See, except those which *ex professo* advocate heresy or
schism, those which try to undermine the very foundations
of religion, and those which are *ex professo* obscene. No
general permission may be given for these works.[48]

These general faculties must be exercised by the Ordinary
personally. He cannot delegate them. This exceptional re-
striction is expressed in the faculties themselves. The Vicar
General is an Ordinary. Therefore, he can exercise these special powers.[49] The successor of an Ordinary inherits the ha-
bitual faculties which his predecessor had.[50]

Ordinaries can use these faculties for their own subjects
only, regardless of the place where either they themselves
or their subjects may be temporarily residing.[51] The Ordinary
will make use of these faculties with discretion,[52] using dis-
crimination as regards the books which he permits and the
persons to whom he grants permission. Thus, he will permit
only those classes of books for which the petition was made
and he will grant the permission only to those to whom it will
be of advantage and not of harm.[53] Formerly, the general
faculties expressly prescribed that general permission be given
only to *men of sound character and learning*, and if there was
question of works which defend heresy or schism or undermine the very foundations of religion, the Bishop could give
such a permission only to *those whom he knew to have more
than ordinary learning, piety and zeal for the faith.*[54] While
these words are not found in the new faculties, they certainly

---

48.   Vermeersch-Creusen, *o. c.*, II, n. 735, N. B.; Wernz, *o. c.*, III,
n. 111 (note 77).

49.   Moreover, according to can. 66, §2, *facultates habituales...
concessae Episcopo competunt quoque Vicario Generali.* The Vicar General had this power, already under Leo XIII's legislation contained in
the constitution *Officiorum ac munerum* (n. 25). Cf. Pennacchi, *o. c.*,
p. 172.

50.   Can. 66, §2.

51.   Can. 201, §3.

52.   Can. 1402, §2.

53.   Cocchi, *o. et l. c.*, n. 71, c; Boudinhon, *o. c.*, p. 202 f.; Hurley,
o. c., p. 172 ff.; Moureau, *o. c.*, p. 78; Van Coillie, *o. c.*, p. 72; Gennari,
*Quistioni Teologico-Morali di Materia Riguardanti specialmente i nostri
tempi*, p. 644.

54.   Cf. Cappello, *De Curia Rom.*, I, p. 302 ff.

serve as a commentary on the phrase *cum delectu* of can. 1402, §2, which regulates all such faculties.

Moreover, there must be a *just and reasonable cause*[55] before this permission may be granted. In the words of the faculties,[56] the petitioner must really need to read forbidden books either to attack them and refute the errors contained therein, or as a necessary help to his sacred ministry, his office or his studies. Mere curiosity or one's simple interest in a certain kind of reading is not a sufficient reason for obtaining permission to read forbidden books.

Ordinaries who have these faculties must observe all the conditions placed in the rescript, otherwise they act unlawfully and at times even invalidly.[57] However, the faculties themselves are to be interpreted widely because there is question of a privilege *praeter ius*[58] and of power delegated by the Holy See *ad universitatem negotiorum.*[59] No fee may be asked for giving permission to read and keep forbidden books.[60]

As for the time limit of the permission which the Ordinaries may grant, in virtue of their faculties, there can be no doubt that in view of the three-year term which is now expressly given as the maximum in the faculties, they cannot grant any permission to last more that three years.[61] On the

---

55. Can. 1402, §2, Cocchi, *o. et l. c.,* gives as the reason for that requirement *"ad vitandam acceptionem personarum et arbitria quae maxime noxia sunt."*

56. See supra, p. 202; Boudinhon, *o. c.,* p. 204.

57. Can. 39; 203: *"Delegatus qui sive circa res sive circa personas mandati sui fines excedit, nihil agit."* Cf. De Meester, *o. c.,* III, n. 1380, d.

58. Cann. 66, 68, 50.

59. Can. 200.

60. Cf. Faculties of Bishops in Vermeersch-Creusen, *Ep.* I (1929), Appendix III.

61. If no time limit should be contained in the faculties, then the Ordinary may grant permission *in perpetuum,* even though his faculties are quinquennial. Cf. Wernz, *Jus Decretal.,* III, n. 111 (note 79). This cannot be done if the faculties empower him to grant permission only *ad tempus.* Cf. Reiffenstuel, *Jus. Can. Un.,* lib. V, tit. VII, n. 59; Schmalzgrueber, *Jus Eccl. Un.,* lib. V, Pars I, tit. VII, n. 39; De Meester, *Compendium,* III, n. 1380, d. Any permission which is limited in time and not extended to the lifetime of the petitioner is *ad tempus.* Many

other hand, the Ordinary may grant such a three-year permission any time during the five years that his faculties last. Therefore, even though his faculties expire on the next day, he may grant permission to read forbidden books for three years. The reason is that the three-year's permission does not depend on the length of time for which the Ordinary has faculties, but on whether he has faculties the moment he grants permission. This is the clear meaning of the words of the faculties: *"Concedendi, non ultra triennium, licentiam"*.[62]

Finally, Ordinaries in granting permission, must mention the apostolic faculty in virtue of which they are acting.[63]

---

authors consider the permission granted *usque ad revocationem* as being *ad tempus.* Cf. Arndt, *De Libr. Prohib.*, p. 252, c; Vermeersch, *De Prohib. et Cens. Libr.*, p. 113; De Meester, *o. c.*, III, n. 1380, d.

62. Reiffenstuel, *o. et l. c.*, n. 59, asks the question as to whether a Bishop who in virtue of his quinquennial faculties has *permission to read and keep forbidden books* and *communicate it to other priests*, may communicate that permission for a period of time which goes past the five years for which he himself has it. In answering, he gives arguments for the negative, namely he believes that a Bishop cannot communicate to others a permission for any greater length of time than he has it himself. However, he admits that the matter is doubtful and leaves it to the Roman authorities to decide. Schmalzgrueber, *o. et l. c.*, n. 39, seems to agree with him. The question raised by these two eminent canonists has no direct bearing upon what was said above, viz., that an Ordinary having quinquennial faculty to give permission of reading prohibited books *non ultra triennium*, may give such a permission for three years even the moment before his faculties expire. For in the old faculties, about which Reiffenstuel and Schmalzgrueber wrote, the Bishop was *permitted to read and keep forbidden books himself and to communicate that permission to other priests*. If, therefore, the bishop's permission lasted only five years, he could only communicate what he had for as long as he had it. Accordingly, if his permission expired within a year he could not pass it on to others for four or five years. Now, however, the basis for these author's doubts does not exist. For Bishops are exempt from the Church law on prohibition of books according to Can. 1401. The special faculties of Ordinaries now have no reference to any personal permission given them for reading or keeping books. They simply authorize them to give their subjects permission to read books, for no more than three years. This authorization lasts five years. In every moment of those five years, they can give a three-year permission.

63. De Meester, *o. c.*, I, n. 468, III, n. 1380, e; Vermeersch, *De Prohib. et Cens. Libr.*, p. 113.

Sect. II. *Interpretation and use of permission to read
forbidden books.*

Can. 1403. — §1. **Qui facultatem apostolicam consecuti
sunt legendi et retinendi libros prohibitos, nequeunt ideo legere
et retinere libros quoslibet a suis Ordinariis proscriptos, nisi in
apostolico indulto expressa iisdem facta fuerit potestas legendi
et retinendi libros a quibuslibet damnatos.**[64]

The permission to read forbidden books is to be interpreted *widely*, because there is question of a privilege and
privileges are widely interpreted.[65] In doubts, therefore, the
grantee must be favored. However, the permission granted
by the Holy See does not make it lawful for one to read books
condemned by his Ordinary, unless the Apostolic grant empower him to read or keep books prohibited by any authority
whatsoever.[66] An exempt regular who has Apostolic permission may read works condemned by the local Ordinary,[67] but
not those of *his own* Ordinary, unless the opposite is stated.

The permission to read forbidden books applies to all
forms of publications, pamphlets, magazines, weekly and daily

---

64. Reg. 81, *Reg. Juris*, in VI°; S. Cong. Ind., Dec. 6, 1895 (*ASS*,
XXVIII [1895], 314 f.); Leo XIII, const. *Officiorum ac munerum*, Jan.
25, 1897, n. 26 (*Fontes*, n. 632); Pius X, encycl. *Pascendi*, Sept. 8, 1907
(*Fontes*, n. 680); motu proprio *Sacrorum Antistitum*, Sept. 1, 1910, n.
111 (*Fontes*, n. 689); Boudinhon, *La Nouv. Legisl. de l'Index*, p. 208;
Pennacchi, *In Const. Apost. Offic. ac mun.*, p. 178 ff.; Moureau, *La
Nouv. Legislation*, p. 80; Gennari, "Circa la nuova disciplina", *Il Mon.
Eccl.*, X (1897), p. 83; Blat, *Comment. Text. C. J. C.*, III, n. 292; Arndt,
De Libris Prohibitis, n. 184.

65. Cann. 68 and 50. Cf. also Reg. 15, *Reg. Juris*, in VI°; De
Meester, *o. c.*, III, n. 1380, 2, a; Vermeersch-Creusen, *Ep.* II, n. 736, 2;
Van Coillie, *o. c.*, p. 74; Bouuaert-Simenon, *o. c.*, p. 559, note.

66. "*A quibuslibet damnatos*" is different from "*libros quoscum-
que prohibitos*" (Cf. Bouuaert-Simenon, *o. c.*, p. 559): the former phrase
includes books condemned by the Bishop, but not the latter. Moureau,
o. c., p. 80, 2, thinks that "*libros quocumque modo damnatos*" is equivalent to libros "*a quibuslibet damnatos.*"

67. Decrees of local Ordinaries do not bind exempt regulars. See
supra, p. 88 f.

papers, etc.[68] However, if the permission is given for newspapers only, then condemned books may not be read.[69]

Persons receiving permission to read prohibited books, must read carefully and carry out all the conditions contained therein, especially those which regard the works excepted and the length of time for which the permission is given. Unless, the opposite is expressly stated in the rescript, the permission is a *personal* favor and therefore may be used everywhere, even though it is granted by the Bishop.[70] The clause *ad effectum eos impugnandi* does not mean that one must set out at once to attack those books. It is sufficient that the petitioner read forbidden works to prepare himself for attacking them whenever the occasion may present itself. According to a probable opinion, the clause indicates the reason on account of which the permission was granted, and not a condition, so that the grantee may use those works for any good purpose.[71] If, however, such a person read forbidden books for mere curiosity he certainly sins, but not grievously.[72] Gennari[73] practically declares that, once the permission is obtained, the ecclesiastical law of prohibition ceases to bind, except in regard to those works excluded by the rescript. The natural law alone must then be considered. Can. 1405, §1, seems to confirm this.

Can. 1403. — §2. **Insuper gravi praecepto tenentur libros prohibitos ita custodiendi, ut hi ad aliorum manus non perveniant.**[74]

---

68. Vermeersch-Creusen, *Ep.*, II, n. 736, 2.

69. De Meester, *o. c.*, III, n. 1380, 2, c; Ferreres, *Institutiones Canonicae*, II, p. 161; Cappello, *De Curia Rom.*, I, 289.

70. Putzer, *Commentarium in Facultates Apostolicas*, n. 55 (note); De Meester, *o. c.*, III, n. 1380, 2, d, γ; Vermeersch-Creusen, *Ep.*, II, n. 736, 2; Bouuaert-Simenon, *o. c.*, p. 559.

71. De Meester, *o. c.*, III, n. 1380, 2, d, δ.

72. Putzer, *o. c.*, n. 174; Heymans, *De Ecclesiast. Libror... Prohib.*, n. 345; St. Alphonsus, *Theol. Mor.*, VII, n. 291; Genicot-Salsmans, *Inst. Theol. Mor.*, I, n. 457; Arndt, *De Libris Prohibitis*, n. 182, d; De Meester, *l. c.* Accordingly, if the books read are forbidden under pain of excommunication, this is not incurred by such a person.

73. *Quistioni Teologico-Morali*, p. 644.

74. Leo XIII, const. *Officiorum ac munerum*, Jan. 25, 1897, n. 26 (*Fontes*, n. 632); Van Coillie, *Commentarius*, p. 75; De Meester, *Com-*

This obligation, which is generally mentioned also in the faculties of Ordinaries, and in the rescripts granting permission, comes from the natural law against scandal.[75] Besides, the permission is given only to keep and read forbidden books, but not to pass them on to others. Accordingly, all those who are not bound by the ecclesiastical prohibition of books either because of exemption or because of permission obtained, must so guard these books that they may not fall into the hands of others who have no permission. The safest way, though not the only way, of accomplishing this is to place them under lock and key.[76]

The greatest care should be taken by librarians in this regard so that no one may read forbidden literature, available at the library, without the necessary permission.[77] Books of this kind should be placed in a separate section, accessible only to those who show the required permission or are known by the librarian to have it.[78] While this can be easily done in Catholic libraries, and other libraries owned by Catholics, it is almost impossible in public libraries. A librarian in such public institutions is allowed to use some discretion as to the persons to whom he gives books and as to the kind of books he lends. A Catholic librarian is bound, as far as he is permitted, to use this power for the observance of the laws of God and of the Church in this matter. However, since he is a servant of the library, when he has used all that discretion which the library statutes permit him, he cannot be obliged further. Therefore, he need not ask every one who requests a forbidden book whether he has permission or not;

---

pendium, III, n. 1380, e; Boudinhon, *La Nouv. Legisl. de l'Index*, p. 210 f.; Pennacchi, *In Const. Ap. Offic. ac mun.*, p. 179; Moureau, *La Nouv. Legisl.*, p. 80, 3; Gennari, "Circa la nuova disciplina", *Il Mon. Eccl.*, X (1897), 83; Blat, *Comment. Text. C. J. C.*, III, n. 292.

75. Boudinhon, *l. c.*

76. Boudinhon, *o. c.*, p. 211.

77. Boudinhon, *o. c.*, pp. 211 and 293; Hurley, *Index Legislation*, p. 175; Pennacchi, *o. c.*, p. 179 f.; Van Coillie, *o. c.*, pp. E5 and 93; Gennari, *Quistioni Teologico-Morali*, p. 737 f.; Reiffenstuel, *Jus Can. Un.*, lib. V, tit. VII, n. 131; Augustine, *A Commentary*, VI, p. 478; De Meester, *o. c.*, III, n. 1380, e.

78. Pennacchi, *o. c.*, p. 179 f.; Hurley, *o. c.*, p. 175. Cf. *infra*, p. 213.

if he did so, he might lose his position. Besides, it is impossible to know whether every person coming to the public library is baptized and, therefore, bound by the laws of the Church; it is also impossible for him to know all the publications which are forbidden.[79] Priests and others who have obtained permission to keep prohibited books in their libraries, ought to provide during their lifetime for the destination of these books after their death. Negligence in this matter may cause much harm.[80]

Can. 1405. — §1. Licentia a quovis obtenta nullo modo quis eximitur a prohibitione iuris naturalis legendi libros qui ipsi proximum spirituale periculum praestant.[81]

Permission to read forbidden books, or exemption from the ecclesiastical prohibition of books, does not excuse the recipient from the prohibition of books based on the natural law, which forbids every one all works, whatever be their language, shape or size, if they place him in the proximate danger of sinning. A work which places one in the remote danger of a serious sin, or in the proximate danger of a slight sin, may be read for any good reason,[82] which generally exists when one has obtained permission. A work which places one in the proximate danger of a serious sin may be read only in case of grave necessity, provided the danger is rendered remote by the use of all the means of self-protection, natural and supernatural, that are reasonably in one's power, such as a firm purpose of not sinning, fervent prayer, good and pious thoughts, confession, Communion and spiritual reading.[83] A work which will *certainly* lead one to mortal sin, may not be

---

79. Cf. Gennari, *Quistioni Teologico-Morali*, p. 736 f.
80. Vermeersch, *De Prohib. et Cens. Libr.*, p. 116.
81. St. Alphonsus, *De Prohib. Libr.*, Cap. IV, n. 31; De Meester, *Compendium*, III, n. 1380, f; Blat, *Commentar. Textus C. J. C.*, III, n. 294; Boudinhon, *La Nouv. Legisl. de l'Ind.*, p. 209; Betten, *The Roman Index*, p. 45 (n. 14), p. 18 ff.; Van Coillie, *Commentarius in Const. Off. ac mun.*, p. 75 f.; D'Annibale, *In Constitutionem Apostolicae Sedis*, n. 34 (note 3); Arndt, *De Libr. Prohib.*, p. 88 f.; *Acta et Decreta Conc. Prov. Mechlin.*, (1920), sectio moralis, n. 57.
82. Noldin, *Summa Theol. Mor.*, I, n. 326, 3.
83. *Ibidem*, n. 326, 2; Betten, *o. c.*, p. 19.

read,[84] regardless of any excuse, permission or exemption. Accordingly, if a person knows, from experience, that a certain class of books always, or nearly always, leads him to sin, or to serious doubts regarding the faith, doubts which, because of his ignorance, he is unable to solve, he is bound to abstain from such works, even though he has permission to read forbidden books or is exempt from the ecclesiastical prohibition.

Art. III. *Booksellers*

Can. 1404. — Librorum venditores libros de obscenis ex professo tractantes ne vendant, commodent, retineant; ceteros prohibitos venales ne habeant nisi debitam licentiam a Sede Apostolica impetraverint, neve cuiquam vendant nisi prudenter existimare possint ab emptore legitime peti.[85]

The legislator has already prohibited *the sale* of forbidden books in Can. 1398, §1,[86] but due to the vast importance of the matter, he dedicates a special canon to bookselling. Accordingly, in virtue of can. 1404, *booksellers may not sell, or lend or keep in stock books explicitly dealing with lewd and licentious matters; they are not to expose for sale other prohibited books unless they have obtained permission from the Holy See, nor are they to sell them to any customer unless in their own prudent judgment they are led to suppose that the buyer is lawfully entitled to have them.*

---

84.   Noldin, *o.* et *l. c.,* n. 326, 2, d.

85.   Leo XIII, const. *Officiorum ac munerum,* Jan. 25, 1897, n. 46 (*Fontes,* n. 632); Pius X, encycl. *Pascendi,* Sept. 8, 1907 (*Fontes,* n. 680); motu proprio *Sacrorum Antistitum,* Sept. 1, 1910, n. III (*Fontes,* n. 689); S. C. Holy Office, Aug. 6, 1856 (*Fontes,* n. 938); S. C. Prop. F., June 26, 1820 (*Collect. P. F.,* n. 745). Cf. also De Meester, *o. c.,* III, n. 1381; Boudinhon, *o. c.,* p. 289 ff.; Hurley, *o. c.,* p. 237 f.; Pennacchi, *o. c.,* p. 243 ff.; Van Coillie, *o. c.,* p. 94 f.; Gennari, "Circa la nuova disciplina", *Il Mon. Eccl.,* X (1897), p. 136; Noldin, *o. c.,* II, n. 126; Blat, *o. c.,* III, n. 293; Arndt, *o. c.,* nn. 172, 212-215; Vermeersch, *De Prohib. et Cens. Libr.,* p. 46 f.; Vermeersch-Creusen, *Ep.,* II, n. 732; Betten, *o. c.,* p. 36, 3.

86.   See supra, p. 119.

This rule binds all baptized booksellers, Catholics and non-Catholics.[87] However, here the Church refers particularly to Catholic booksellers. Under the term *booksellers* come also sellers of all kinds of publications, periodicals, newspapers, etc.[88]

Booksellers are forbidden to *sell, lend* or *keep* in stock books which are *ex professo* obscene, in the sense explained above.[89] Commentators[90] of Leo XIII's constitution *Officiorum ac munerum*[91] which in n. 46 contained expressions practically identical with can. 1404, made an exception in favor of obscene classical books. Since in art. 10 of the same constitution it was made lawful for certain people to read such works, it must have been lawful also to keep them and sell them or lend them to those people. Otherwise, how could such books be procured by them? The Code makes no explicit exception in favor of classical works which are obscene. However, there are some good authorities who maintain that the Code did not abrogate the exception in favor of obscene classical works contained in the pre-Code legislation.[92] This opinion is sufficiently probable to be followed in practice. After all, the laws under consideration are restrictive and therefore must be interpreted strictly.[93] In accordance with this view, booksellers are not forbidden to keep, sell or lend an obscene classical work to one who can be presumed to ask legitimately for it.

Although this rule mentions specifically only booksellers, it applies also[94] to owners of hotels and others who place read-

---

87. Cf. supra, p. 73 f.; De Meester, *Compendium*, III, n. 1381, 1.

88. Can. 1384, §2. Cf. also De Meester, *Compendium*, III, n. 1381, 3, 4; Van Coillie, *Commentarius*, p. 94 f.; Gennari, "Circa la nuova disciplina", *Il Mon. Eccl.*, X (1897), p. 80 f.

89. Supra, p. 169.

90. E. g. Vermeersch, *De Prohib. et Cens. Libr.*, p. 46; Hurley, *Ind. Legisl.*, p. 239; Pennacchi, *In Const. Apost. Off. ac mun.*, p. 244.

91. *Fontes*, n. 632.

92. Supra, p. 174.

93. Can. 19.

94. If not on the strength of the words of can. 1404, certainly in virtue of can. 1398, §1, which forbids all kinds of communications of prohibited books.

ing matter at the disposal of their customers.[95]

Concerning all other prohibited books, those, namely, which are not *ex professo* obscene, the legislator forbids booksellers to *keep* or *expose* them *for sale*, without permission from the Holy See. A book is said to be *kept or exposed for sale* (*venalis habetur*) which is so shown to the public in a store, at an auction, in the streets, in a catalogue, or in some other way, that the public may know that it is on sale.[96] That is clearly forbidden. However, a bookseller is allowed to *sell* those prohibited books to any one whom he can reasonably presume to have permission.[97] For this purpose, he may *procure* for his customers any forbidden book which they lawfully request of him,[98] or he may *keep*[99] a number of such books secretly so as to be able to furnish them promptly upon lawful request. This conclusion seems to follow logically from the contrast, in can. 1404, between *"ne vendant, commodent, retineant"* as applied to obscene books, and *"venales ne habeant"* as applied to other forbidden books. Evidently the legislator does not forbid booksellers to sell, lend or keep secretly prohibited books which are not obscene, provided they are not kept or exposed for sale.

---

95.   Supra, p. 118; De Meester, *Compendium*, III, n. 1381, 4; Bouuaert-Simenon, *o. c.*, p. 559. A confessor who has no hope that a penitent guilty of this crime will abstain from it, may omit a clear admonition so that he may not place the man in bad faith. However, he must try to diminish the harm by having good literature made available. Cf. De Meester, *l. c.*

96.   Cocchi, *Commentar. in Cod. J. C.*, VI, n. 73; De Meester, *Compendium*, III, n. 1381, 1; Vermeersch, *De Prohibit. et Cens. Libr.*, p. 46; Blat, *Commentar. Text. C. J. C.*, III, p. 368; Boudinhon, *La Nouvelle Legisl. de l'Index*, p. 292.

97.   Vermeersch-Creusen, *Ep.*, II, n. 732, 1; Augustine, *A Commentary*, VI, p. 482; Bouuaert-Simenon, *Man. Jur. Can.*, pp. 553, 559; A Coronata, *Instit. Jur. Can.*, II, p. 348; Ubach, *Compendium Theol. Mor.*, I, p. 380.

98.   Besides the authors referred to in the preceding note, cf. Noldin, *Summa Theol. Mor.*, II, n. 715, a; De Meester, *o. c.*, III, n. 1381, 2; Boudinhon, *o. c.*, p. 292; Vermeersch, *o. c.*, p. 46; Cipollini, *De Cens. Lat. Sent.*, p. 107; Van Coillie, *Commentarius*, p. 93.

99.   A Coronata, *o. c.*, II, p. 348; Augustine, *A Commentary*, VI, p. 482. Cipollini, *o. c.*, p. 107, denies that.

A man employed by another to sell his goods and books at auction, cannot be said to have those things on sale *himself.* Rather he is selling them for another and in another's name. Therefore, he is not forbidden by the positive law in this canon to auction off all the books which his employer asks him to auction off, even though some of them are condemned. The natural law is to be his guide here. There is question of cooperating towards something evil. This cooperation is never lawful in regard to books which are entirely and seriously obscene or irreligious.[100] It is, however, permitted for other kinds of condemned books, provided there is a sufficiently grave reason, e. g. a grave loss if this man refused to do it, while others would easily be found to take his place.[101] A civil officer in charge of an auction sale certainly does not come under this ruling. He has nothing to do with the sale proper. Moreover, there is a decision of the Holy See that he is not even obliged to find out whether, among the goods to be sold, there are books against faith or morals or not. However, if he knows that there are some such works and he is in a position to prevent their sale to persons who have no permission to use them, he is obliged to do so.[102]

Can. 1404 applies also to circulating and other libraries which lend books.[103] They may not keep or lend books which are *ex professo* obscene. They may not expose other forbidden books to the public, without permission of the Holy See. However, they are permitted to keep condemned works which are not obscene in a separate secret compartment, without special permission.

A local Ordinary cannot give the permission to booksellers to keep forbidden books for sale, even though he has special faculties. For, his faculties empower him only to permit his subjects to "read and keep"[104] forbidden books but

---

100. De Meester, *l. c.*; Van Coillie, *o. c.*, p. 94; Noldin, *o. c.*, II, n. 126, a; Boudinhon, *o. c.*, p. 293; Vermeersch, *De Prohib. et Cens. Libr.*, p. 46. Vermeersch (*l. c.*) remarks that, at least, a more serious reason is needed for such a cooperation.
101. De Meester, *l. c.*
102. *Coll. S. C. de Pr. Fid.*, n. 745.
103. Boudinhon, *o. c.*, p. 293; Pennacchi, *o. c.*, p. 245.
104. See faculties above. p. 202.

not to have them for sale. The Holy See alone grants this special permission.

No bookseller may sell or lend a prohibited work unless he has good reasons to suppose that the person asking for it has permission. This prudent judgment may be formed from the circumstances of the case, the character of the buyer and the nature of the book requested. It is not necessary to ask each buyer or borrower whether he has permission to read that book or not.[105]

Art. IV. *Presumed Permission*[106]

Occasions will arise when it becomes necessary to read some forbidden work and it is not possible to obtain permission in time. Thus, the reading of a forbidden book may become an urgent necessity for a judge who is called upon to decide on its legality, according to civil law; or for a professor or for the editor of a paper who has to refute its errors immediately; or for a priest who must answer its attacks against the Church. In these and many other similar cases of urgent necessity the rule to be followed is this: if it is possible to obtain permission from the Holy See or from the Ordinary in time, then permission must be obtained; otherwise, forbidden works may be read as far as the necessity requires and with due precautions. Telephone and telegraph are not considered proper means to ask permission.

---

105. De Meester, *Compendium*, III, n. 1381, 2; Cocchi, *l. c.*; Gennari, "Circa la nuova disciplina", *Il Mon. Eccl.*, X (1897), 135 f. Noldin, *Summa Theol. Mor.*, II, n. 715, 2, a, would only require that, considering the circumstances, the bookseller is not morally certain that the buyer has no permission. This opinion is certainly practical. However, it seems to do injustice to the text "*nisi prudenter existimare possint ab emptore legitime peti*", which seems to require a *positive* prudent judgment that the buyer *has* the necessary permission.

106. De Meester, *Compendium*, III, n. 1378, 1; Suarez, *De Fid. Div.*, disp. 20, sect. 2, n. 28; Lugo, *De Virt. Fid.*, disp. 21, sect. 2, nn. 66 and 69; Wernz, *Jus Decretal.*, III, p. 121 (note 77); Lehmkuhl, *Theol. Mor.*, II, n. 1337; Arndt, *De Libris Prohib.*, n. 185; Betten, *The Rom. Ind.*, p. 43 f.

CHAPTER IX

DUTIES OF LOCAL ORDINARIES AND OTHERS
IN CARE OF SOULS

**Can. 1405. — §2. Ordinarii locorum aliique curam anima-
rum habentes opportune moneant fideles de periculo et damno
lectionis librorum pravorum, praesertim prohibitorum.**[107]

All the legislation of the Holy See, all the laws of the
Code, all the works of canon law would be useless, at least
as regards the prohibition of books, if the Bishops and their
priests did not bring the message of the Church in this matter to the faithful. For that reason the Church has always
insisted that Bishops take an active part in this battle waged
by her against evil literature.[108] Before closing the title dealing with the legislation on books, she again reminds *local
Ordinaries and others entrusted with the care of souls of their
duty to warn the faithful in an opportune manner of the
danger to which they are exposed and the evil they may derive from reading obnoxious literature and in particular prohibited books.*

This duty belongs first to Bishops, then to pastors and
their assistants and finally to other priests with care of souls.
They should know the laws of the Church concerning prohibition of books. They should put those laws into practice

---

107. Clement XIII, const. *Christianae reipublicae*, Nov. 25, 1766
(*Fontes*, n. 461); Leo XIII, const. *Officiorum ac munerum*, Jan. 25, 1897,
n. 21 (*Fontes*, n. 632); Instruction of the S. C. of the Holy Office, May
3, 1927 (*A A S*, XIX [1927], 187); Pennacchi, *In const. apost. Offic. ac
muner.*, p. 164, 189; Moureau, *La Nouv. Legisl.*, p. 71, 3; Betten, *The
Rom. Index*, p. 45, n. 13; Boudinhon, *La Nouv. Legisl. de l'Index*, p.
190 f.; Wernz, *Jus Decretal.*, III, n. 107; Cocchi, *Commentarium in C.
J. C.*, VI, n. 73, *scholion*.

108. Supra, p. 86 ff.

themselves.[109] They should make the laws of the Church known to their people, warning them against all dangerous literature and not simply against what is certainly forbidden.[110] They are to see that no books against faith or morals be used in the public or private schools under their jurisdiction.[111] They should try to keep objectionable books out of circulating or public libraries,[112] or at least see that they are safely guarded. Finally, priests in care of souls could prevent much harm by tactfully and prudently asking booksellers, newspaper and magazine sellers to abstain from selling forbidden matter.

Ordinarily it is not wise to mention from the pulpit the names of books or papers which are to be avoided. A general description together with an explanation of the laws of the Church on prohibition of books should usually suffice. However, if the danger is so serious that the Ordinary considers it necessary to forbid a work by name or simply to declare publicly that such a book is forbidden by the general law of the Church, he has the power and duty[113] to do so. Pastors and other priests in such extreme cases must consult their Ordinaries.

Prohibition of evil books is not the only means available to prevent the harm. It is only a negative means. Shepherds of souls, to keep their flocks from poisonous literature must follow the example as well as the orders and suggestions of the Supreme Pontiffs. The Popes have never stopped at forbidding evil literature; they have always encouraged and fostered good literature.[114] Today most people read. Unless they

---

109.   Ferreres, *Institutiones Canon.*, II, p. 157, reproaches those priests who read publicly, e. g. on a train, forbidden or dubious newspapers.

110.   Can. 1405, §2.

111.   Can. 469.

112.   Augustine, *A Commentary*, VI, 462 f.

113.   Can. 1395, §1.

114.   Cf. Pius IX, encycl. *Inter multiplices* to the Bishops of France, Mar. 21, 1853 (*Pii IX P. M. Acta*, Pars I, p. 439); Leo XIII, encycl. *Pergrata nobis*, Sept. 14, 1886 (*Fontes*, n. 595); encycl. *Paternae Providaeque*, Sept. 18, 1899 (*Fontes*, n. 643); Pius X, a letter for Hungary of Jan. 10, 1908 (*Le Canoniste Contemporain*, XXXI [1908], 382 ff.); letter to the Bishops of Brazil, June 11, 1911 (*A A S*, III [1911], 261); letter to the Bishops of Lombardy, July 1, 1911 (*A A S*, III [1911], 475);

have good literature at their disposal, it is not likely they
will abstain from dangerous publications. Therefore, local
Ordinaries and others in care of souls should do their utmost
to encourage the production and publication of sound and in-
teresting literature, books, pamphlets, magazines, newspapers,
etc. Every effort should be made to induce the people to read
these good publications.[115]

In this regard the book-reviews given in nearly all the
Catholic magazines and papers are very helpful. In these
reviews of current literature Catholics will find a safe guide
to their reading. Moreover, in nearly every language are
found Catholic catalogues of some of the best books of past
and modern authors.[116] Finally, Catholic libraries are of the
greatest value for a wide circulation of good and wholesome
books.

In the archdiocese of New York there is a committee
on literature known as *Cardinal Hayes Literature Committee.*
It was established by His Eminence Cardinal Hayes in 1928.
Its object is:

1) To cultivate, especially among Catholics, a sound critical sense, which will foster the reading of good books
and discourage the reading of bad books.
2) To impress upon publishers the value and importance
of the Catholic point of view.
3) To encourage Catholics to take their rightful place in
the world of letters.
4) To stem the tide of pernicious literature.

The means used to achieve this end are various. First
of all, the Committee publishes every week an article on literary subjects. It appears not only in the Catholic newspapers
of the United States of America but is sent also to publishers,
Catholic schools and colleges, to the literary editors of secular

---

letter of the Secretariate of State of Mar. 30, 1915, for the creation of
the association "Opera nazionale per la buona stampa" (*A A S*, VII
[1915], 246).

115. Cf. *La Civiltà Catholica,* 18th series, XI (1903), 9-23; Wernz,
Jus Decretal., III, n. 107; Boudinhon, *La Nouvelle Legisl. de l'Index,*
p. 190 f.

116. E. g., John C. Reville, S. J., *My Bookcase,* 4. ed. (New York:
The American Press, 1928).

papers and to the sectarian press by the National Catholic Welfare Conference News Service.

This article deals with recent books and periodicals, with current literary tendencies and with individual authors. The policy pursued is a constructive one, i. e., an effort is made to select from publishers' lists such books as can be recommended in order to show what books should be read, to create a demand for them, to induce authors to write books which can be recommended, to persuade publishers to produce them. The recommendation is based on the moral tone and literary value of the book. No book is praised merely because Catholic or religious. As a general rule condemnation of specific books is avoided, but the principles on which such books should be condemned are clearly defined. Another part of the program of Cardinal Hayes Literature Committee is to publish occasional lists of books recommended. Early in March, 1931, a list of one hundred books was issued by the Committee and published in Catholic and secular papers. It contains works of art, biography, fiction, essays, history, philosophy, poetry, religion and travel. No one can fail to see what a great help this is for people who wish to know and read what is best in literature.

Among other means, devised and put to practice in this country, towards the fulfilment of the same end, — to cultivate and encourage good literature and to discourage and stem pernicious publications— are the *Catholic Writers' Guild*, the *Catholic Book Club, Parish Libraries* and *Bookracks*. The Catholic Writers' Guild is an association of prominent Catholic writers who meet every month for the purpose of examining current literature and of devising means and ways to elevate the faith and morals of writers and editors. The Catholic Book Club chooses every month what is considered by its prominent editors, under the supervision of the Ordinary, to be the best Catholic book of the month. Many parishes have a library of their own for the free use of the people, while most parishes have a bookrack through which Catholic books, pamphlets, magazines and papers are made accessible to all at a very low price.

CHAPTER X

Penalties for the Violation of the Ecclesiastical Laws on Prohibition of Books

Can. 2318. — §1. In excommunicationem Sedi Apostolicae speciali modo reservatam ipso facto incurrunt, opere publici iuris facto editores librorum apostatarum, haereticorum et schismaticorum, qui apostasiam, haeresim, schisma propugnant, itemque eosdem libros aliosve per apostolicas literas nominatim prohibitos defendentes aut scienter sine debita licentia legentes vel retinentes.[1]

---

1. C. 2, *de reliquiis et veneratione sanctorum*, III, 12, in Extravag. com.; John XXII, const. *Super illius*, year 1326, §3 (*Fontes*, n. 37); Leo X, const. *Exsurge Domine*, June 10, 1520, §5 (*Fontes*, n. 76); Pius IV, const. *Dominici gregis*, Mar. 24, 1564, §3 (*Fontes*, n. 105); Sixtus V, const. *Coeli et terrae*, Jan. 5, 1586, §4 (*Fontes*, n. 157); Urban VIII, const. *Inscrutabilis*, Mar. 31, 1631, §2 (*Fontes*, n. 210); Pius VII, const. *Ecclesiam*, Sept. 13, 1821, §11 (*Fontes*, n. 479); Pius IX, const. *Apostolicae Sedis*, Oct. 12, 1869, §1, n. 2 (*Fontes*, n. 552); Leo XIII, const. *Officiorum ac munerum*, Jan. 25, 1897, n. 47 (*Fontes*, n. 632); S. C. of the Holy Office, Jan. 13, 1891, ad 1 (*Fontes*, n. 1147); (C. G.-Ceylan), Aug. 23, 1852, ad 7 (*Coll. S. C. de Prop. Fid.*, I, n. 1080); S. C. of the Index, encycl. Aug. 24, 1864 (*Coll. S. C. de Prop. Fid.*, I, n. 1261); Apr. 27, 1880 (*A S S*, XX [1887], 368). Cf. also De Meester, *Compendium*, III, n. 1384 ff.; Cappello, *De Censuris*, n. 224 ff.; Vermeersch-Creusen, *Ep.*, III, n. 517; Boudinhon, *La Nouvelle Legisl. de l'Index*, p. 294 ff.; Hurley, *Index Legisl.*, p. 246 ff.; Chelodi, *Jus Poenale*, p. 74 f.; Noldin, *De Censuris*, nn. 61-62; Pennacchi, *In Const. Apost. Off. ac mun.*, p. 246 ff.; Moureau, *La Nouvelle Legisl.*, p. 99 ff.; Van Coillie, *Commentarius in const. Off. ac mun.*, p. 95 ff.; Gennari, "Circa la nuova disciplina", *Il Mon. Eccl.*, X (1897), 153 ff.; St. Alphonsus, *De Prohib. Libr.*, V, n. 3 ff.; Suarez, *De Fide Div.*, disp. 20, sect. 2; Reiffenstuel, *Jus. Can. Un.*, lib. V, tit. VII, n. 34 ff.; Schmalzgrueber, *Jus Eccl. Un.*, lib. V, pars I, tit. VII, n. 27 ff.; Farrugia, *Commentarium in Censuras Latae Sententiae Codicis Juris Canonici*, n. 168 ff.; Pighi, *Censurae Latae Sententiae*, n. 54 ff.; Cerato, *Censurae Vigentes*, n. 70 ff.; Sole, *De Delictis et Poenis*, n. 326 ff.; Cipollini, *De Censuris Latae Sententiae*, p. 103 ff.;

Can. 2318. — §2. **Auctores et editores qui sine debita licentia sacrarum Scripturarum libros vel earum adnotationes aut commentarios imprimi curant, incidunt ipso facto in excommunicationem nemini reservatam.**[2]

Many had been the punishments inflicted by the Church upon violators of her laws on books, until Pius IX, through the constitution *Apostolicae Sedis,* of October 12, 1869,[3] reduced them to two only,[4] namely, an excommunication reserved in a special way to the Supreme Pontiff for those who would knowingly read, keep, publish or defend books of heretics and apostates, upholding heresy, or any other books forbidden by name through Apostolic letters; and an excommunication, reserved to no one, for those who would print or have others print Scriptural works without the approval of the Ordinary. Leo XIII, in his constitution *Officiorum ac munerum,* of Januaray 25, 1897, nn. 47-48[5] retained the same punishments in practically the same words. The only difference was this that the words of Pius IX *Libri de rebus sacris tractantes* were changed by Leo XIII to *Sacrarum Scripturarum libri, vel earundem adnotationes vel commentarii,* in accordance with an explanation given by the S. C. of the Holy Office to the Bishop of Ratisbon, December 22, 1880.[6] Can. 2318 now restates those penalties, as expressed by Pius IX and Leo XIII with only a few slight variations. The present law, then, must

---

Lehmkuhl, *Theologia Moralis,* II, n. 1183 ff.; Genicot-Salsmans, *Institutiones Theologiae Moralis,* II, n. 588, n. 610; Arndt, *De Libr. Prohib.,* n. 165 ff.; Bouix, *De Curia Rom.,* p. 523 ff.; Ferraris, *Bibliotheca,* V, 141 ff.

2. Council of Trent, sess. IV, *de editione et usu sacrorum librorum;* Pius IX, const. *Apostolicae Sedis,* Oct. 12, 1869, §IV, n. 4 (*Fontes,* n. 552); Leo XIII, const. *Officiorum ac munerum,* Jan. 25, 1897, n. 48 (*Fontes,* n. 632); S. C. of the Holy Office, (Ratisbon) Dec. 22, 1880 (*Fontes,* n. 1068). Cf. also all the authors referred to in note 1.

3. §1, n. 2 and §IV, n. 4 (*Fontes,* n. 552).

4. "*Omnes aliae poenae antiqui iuris hac in re statutae* (cfr. v. g. Reg. X Indic.) *sive spirituales sive temporales, medicinales vel vindicativae nunc sunt penitus abrogatae.*" — Wernz, *Jus Decretal.,* III, n. 110, (IV).

5. *Fontes,* n. 632.

6. *Fontes,* n. 1068, ad II.

be understood according to the interpretation given to it by the Church or by approved authors before the Code, with due regard for the changes introduced in the Code.[7]

Art. I. *Excommunication reserved in a special way to the Holy See*

Publishers of the works of apostates, heretics and schismatics which advocate apostasy, heresy and schism, incur *ipso facto* an excommunication specially reserved to the Apostolic See from the date of publication. The same penalty is incurred by those who defend, or knowingly and without the necessary permission read, or keep these works or others prohibited by name in Apostolic letters.

I. The **penalty incurred** for the violation of this law is an *excommunication reserved in a special way to the Holy See.* Accordingly, no one except the Holy See and those whom it may delegate for the purpose, have power to absolve the culprit from it. The sin committed by violating that law is reserved by reason of the excommunication. No priest can forgive it unless the censure is first taken away.[8]

II. The **writings forbidden** under pain of excommunication specially reserved to the Holy See are the *books of apostates, heretics and schismatics* which *advocate apostasy, heresy and schism and those prohibited by name in Apostolic letters.*

A. First, then, it is required that the work be a *book* in the strictest sense of the word. For, penalties,[9] especially when there is question of reserved censures,[10] must be interpreted strictly. Besides, the wide and extensive meaning given to the word *liber* or book in can. 1384, §2, applies only to title XXIII of Part IV of Book III of the Code. It does not apply to this canon.[11] A book, thus strictly understood, is what men generally call a "book", namely, a volume of

---

7. Can. 6, nn. 2-3.

8. Can. 2250, §2.

9. Can. 2219.

10. Can. 2246, §2.

11. De Meester, *Compendium*, III, n. 1385, 1, a; Vermeersch-Creusen, *Ep.*, III, n. 517, 1.

considerable *size* and having a certain *unity*.[12] Authors generally accept the figures of Schmalzgrueber[13] as to the size of a book, namely, 10 folio pages, or 160 pages in octavo (the average book page), or 320 pages in 16mo.[14] This element must not be judged mathematically, but morally,[15] together with the element of unity; unity of subject or at least of tendency.

Besides these two elements, some authors[16] require that the work be *printed*, thus excluding not only manuscripts but also writings produced by means of typewriter, polygraph, lithography, mimeograph or photography. And, indeed, people apply the term "book" only to that which is printed. Moreover, here it is a question of *published* works (as the word *editores* implies), and printing is practically the only way a work is published nowadays. Theoretically, however, it is possible that a work be published in a manner other than by printing, e. g., by means of lithograph, mimeograph, etc. Such a work could be truthfully called a "book".[17] Nevertheless, since the opinion requiring printing is at least probable, no excommunication would be incurred unless the work is printed. Accordingly, the following are not[18] books and therefore are not affected by can. 2318:

---

12. Lugo, *De Virt. Fid. Div.*, disp. 21, sect. 2, n. 38; Vermeersch-Creusen, *l. c.* Cf. also supra, p. 78 f.

13. *Jus Eccl. Un.,* lib. V, pars I, tit. VII, n. 55. Cf. also Vermeersch-Creusen, *Ep.*, II, n. 723; III, n. 517, 1; De Meester, *Compendium*, III, n. 1339, 3, a; Augustine, *A Commentary*, VI, 431; Ayrinhac, *Administrative Legislation*, p. 275.

14. Even though a book is printed in minute letters and thin paper (e. g., a vest-pocket edition), it still retains the nature of a book. Cf. Cipollini, *De Cens. Latae Sent.*, p. 104.

15. Lugo, *l. c.*

16. Cappello, *De Censuris*, n. 226, 1; Noldin, *De Censuris*, n. 61; Bouuaert-Simenon, *Manuale Juris Canonici*, p. 769, n. 55; Sole, *Censurae Vigentes*, n. 328, 2; Cipollini, *De Censuris Latae Sententiae*, p. 104.

17. Vide supra, p. 81 f. Cf. also Ferreres, *Institutiones Can.*, II, p. 149 (n. 381, a); Pighi, *Censurae Latae Sententiae*, n. 55; Cavigioli, *De Censuris Latae Sententiae*, p. 70.

18. De Meester, *Compendium*, III, n. 1385, 1, a; Cappello, *De Censuris*, n. 226; Vermeersch-Creusen, *l. c.*; Farrugia, *Commentarium in Censuras*, n. 171; Arndt, *De Libr. Prohib.*, n. 166, 5; Chelodi, *Jus Poenale,*

1. Booklets and pamphlets, even though bound together into a volume, unless, in that case, they have the unity required for a book;
2. Newspapers;[19]
3. Leaflets;
4. Calendars;
5. Sermons and letters, unless they are published in form of a book with the size and unity required;
6. Manuscripts and all non-printed works.

Authors do not agree with regard to *periodicals, reviews, magazines.* The S. C. of the Holy Office on Jan. 13, 1892[20] answered in the affirmative to the question: *"Utrum scienter legentes publicationes periodicas in fasciculos ligatas, habentes auctorem haereticum et haeresim propugnantes, excommunicationem incurrant, de qua Bulla Apostolicae Sedis...?"* Most canonists, who have written on Can. 2318, refer to this decision of the Holy Office, but not all of them interpret it in the same way. Some hold that reviews, periodicals and magazines as such come under the term book.[21] Others would liken these publications to books, only if they are bound into volumes.[22] A third group, more correctly, denies that periodicals, magazines or reviews come under the word *book* of can. 2318, even though bound into volumes, unless such volumes have that unity of subject or at least of tendency required for the notion of a book.[23] Accordingly, if a periodical, magazine or review given to science, philosophy, religion or some other subject, has apostates, heretics or schismatics for

n. 60, 2; St. Alphonsus, *De Prohib. Libr.*, V, nn. 7-8; Schmalzgrueber, *Jus Eccl. Un.*, lib. V, pars I, tit. VII, n. 54; Lugo, *De Virt. Fid. Div.*, disp. 21, sect. 2, n. 33; Reiffenstuel, *Jus Can. Un.*, lib. I, tit. XXXI, n. 144 (he changed his view in lib. V, tit. VII, nn. 41-45).

19. S. C. of the Index, Apr. 27, 1880 (*A S S*, XX [1887], 368).

20. *Fontes*, n. 1147.

21. Chelodi, *l. c.*; Van Coillie, *Commentarius*, p. 31 f.

22. Woywod, *A Practical Commentary*, II, p. 469; Pighi, *Censurae Latae Sententiae*, n. 55, 1, a; Cipollini, *De Censuris Latae Sententiae*, p. 104; Cappello, *De Censuris*, n. 226, 2; Lehmkuhl, *Theologia Moralis*, II, n. 1184.

23. De Meester, *Compendium*, III, n. 1339, 3, b; n. 1385, 1, a, and note 2; Vermeersch-Creusen, *Ep.*, II, n. 723; III, n. 517; Augustine, *A Commentary*, VI, 431.

authors, a volume or series of issues advocating apostasy, heresy, or schism is forbidden under pain of excommunication specially reserved to the Holy See. However, it is contended by some that, the words of the decision of the Holy Office of Jan. 13, 1892, simply mean that to read in a volume or series of a periodical publication articles of a *heretic* advocating *heresy*, is forbidden under pain of excommunication.[24] In practice, very often periodicals or magazines or reviews will escape this penalty[25]

B. Secondly, a book must either be the work of one or more apostates, heretics, or schismatics who in it advocate apostasy, heresy or schism, or it must have been condemned by name in Apostolic letters. No other kind of books are condemned under pain of excommunication specially reserved to the Holy See. The prohibition of obscene books, then, has no censure attached to it.

An *Apostate* is a baptized person who completely abandons the Christian faith,[26] whether he embraces another religion such as Mohammedanism and Buddhism, or becomes an unbeliever, a rationalist, a materialist or an atheist.[27] A *heretic* is one who has received baptism and, while retaining the name of Christian, *obstinately* denies or doubts one or more of the truths of divine Catholic faith.[28] Here there is question only of a *formal* heretic.[29] A *schismatic* is a baptized person

------

24. Boudinhon, *La Nouvelle Legisl.*, p. 300 f. Cf. also De Meester, *Compendium*, III, p. 309, note 2.

25. De Meester, *Compendium*, III, n. 1385, 1, a.

26. Can. 1325, §2. Cf. also Pennacchi, *In Const. Apost. Off. ac. mun.*, p. 53; Hurley, *Index Legisl.*, p. 58; Suarez, *De Fid. Div.*, disp. 20, sect. 2, n. 11.

27. Ayrinhac, *Administrative Legislation*, p. 196.

28. Can. 1325, §2. Cf. also Pennacchi, *l. c.*; Hurley, *l. c.*; St. Alphonsus, *Theol. Mor.*, VII, n. 282, n. 302; Schmalzgrueber, *Jus Eccl. Un.*, lib. V, Pars. I, tit. VII, n. 36; Reiffenstuel, *Jus Can. Un.*, lib. V, tit. VII, n. 36.

29. De Meester, *Compendium*, III, n. 1285, 1; Wernz, *Jus Decretal.*, III, p. 111 (note 55); Cappello, *De Curia Rom.*, I, p. 274; Pighi, *Censurae Lat. Sent.*, nn. 52 and 55; Cerato, *Censurae Vigentes*, n. 70, 1, d; Farrugia, *Comment. in Cens. Lat. Sent.*, n. 170; Cipollini, *De Cens. Lat. Sent.*, pp. 96 and 104; Lehmkuhl, *Theol. Mor.*, II, n. 1183; Arndt, *De Libr. Prohib.*, n. 166, 4; Avanzini, De Const. "Apost. Sedis", p. 11.

who refuses to recognize the authority of the Supreme Pontiff and be subject to him, or to communicate with the members of the Church who are subject to him.[30]

It is not necessary that an apostate, heretic or schismatic be declared such in an ecclesiastical court. It suffices that his crime of apostasy, heresy or schism be of common knowledge or that it be clearly evident from the work itself in which he *obstinately* upholds apostasy, heresy or schism, even though so far he has been known to be a Catholic.[31]

The penalty is incurred even though the work is the product of both Catholics and apostates, heretics or schismatics; also when a work is made of a text and a commentary when either of them is written by an apostate, a heretic or a schismatic and it is the larger part of the work. The fact that there is a smaller part written by a Catholic does not take away the punishable character of the work.[32] Nor does a work of this kind cease to be prohibited with excommunication, if its author is now a Catholic.[33]

The following[34] are not considered as apostates, heretics or schismatics in the sense explained and therefore their works are not forbidden under the pain of excommunication: 1) Non baptized persons, e. g., Jews, Pagans, Buddhists or Mohammedans; 2) people suspected of heresy and material heretics; 3)

---

30. Can. 1325, §2.

31. De Meester, *Compendium*, III, n. 1385, 1, b; Suarez, *l. c.*; Lugo, *De Virt. Fid. Div.*, disp. 21, sect. 2, n. 40; Reiffenstuel, *o. c.*, n. 108; Aichner, *Compendium Juris Canonici* (Brixen, 1887), p. 520, n. 6; Gury, *Compendium Theologiae Moralis* (Lyons, 1899), II, n. 981, quest. 2; Avanzini, *De Constitutione "Apost. Sedis"*, p. 11. However, D'Annibale, *In const. Ap. Sed.*, n. 40 (note 32) in defining a heretic requires that he belong to some sect or that he be so declared by the Church. Nevertheless, since the definition of heretic in can. 1325, §2, requires neither affiliation with a sect nor a declaration from the Church, certainly one's heresy may be known in other ways, e. g., from the obstinate attack in his book against a doctrine of faith.

32. De Meester, *Compendium*, III, n. 1385, 1, b; St. Alphonsus, *De Prohib. Libr.*, V, n. 10; *Theol. Mor.*, VII, n. 286; Suarez, *De Fid. Div.*, disp. 20, sect. 2, n. 13; Schmalzgrueber, *Jus Eccl. Un.*, lib. V, pars I, tit. VII, n. 36; Lugo, *De Virt. Fid. Div.*, disp. 21, sect. 2, nn. 46-47. Cf. also supra, p. 135 f.

33. De Meester, *l. c.*

34. De Meester, *Compendium*, III, n. 1385, 1, b.

persons whose apostasy, heresy or schism is not certainly known; 4) old heretics like Tertullian and Origen, whose works are allowed, as mentioned above.[35]

Not all works written by apostates, heretics or schismatics, are forbidden under pain of excommunication but only those which, in their entirety or to a large extent (e. g. in a chapter), advocate apostasy[36] heresy and schism.[37] A book is not forbidden if it simply denies a doctrine of faith, or ridicules it; nor if an occasional attack is made.[38] This is true not only of works which treat of religion *ex professo*: but also of those which treat of philosophy, history or any other subject. If the objectionable parts are all taken out from such a work; or if the volume containing arguments in favor of apostasy, heresy or schism is removed from a set made up of several volumes; the remainder may be read or kept without incurring an excommucation.[39]

Authologies, readers, historical source books or other similar works, containing selections taken from books of apostates, heretics or schismatics in which apostasy, heresy or schism is noticeably propounded, are all forbidden under pain of excommunication as long as they retain those objectionable parts, and provided they have unity, as required in a "book" in the strict sense.[40] Otherwise, no excommunication is incurred.[40a]

---

35. P. 139 f.

36. Can. 1399 prohibits "works advocating apostasy", not explicitly by that name, but implicity under "books which try to undermine the very foundations of religion".

37. In the sense of Can. 1325, §2. Cf. also supra, p. 129 f.

38. Sabetti-Barrett, *Compendium Theologiae Moralis* (New York: Pustet, 1926), n. 976; Lugo, *De Virt. Fid. Div.*, disp. 21, sect. 2, nn. 51-52; Gury, *Compend. Theol. Mor.*, II, n. 979; Lehmkuhl, *Theol. Mor.*, II, n. 1183; Bucceroni, *Institutiones Theologiae Moralis* (Rome, 1893), II, n. 1165; D'Annibale, *In Const. Apost. Sedis*, n. 40; Bouuaert-Simenon, *Manuale Juris Can.*, p. 555, a; De Meester, *Compendium*, III, n. 1363; supra, p. 130.

39. Cf. supra, p. 109 ff.; De Meester, *Compendium*, III, n. 1385, 1, c.

40. Cf. supra, p. 221 ff.

40a. Probably because often this class of works lacks the necessary unity, it is excluded from Can. 2318 by Cappello, *De Censuris*, n. 226; Cocchi, *Comment. in C. J. C.*, VIII, n. 143; Cipollini, *De Cens. Lat. Sent.*, p. 104.

In addition to works of apostates, heretics and schismatics advocating apostasy, heresy and schism, there is another class of works forbidden under pain of excommunication specially reserved to the Holy See, namely works prohibited *by name through Apostolic Letters*. For a work to be considered as certainly belonging to this class of books, three conditions must be fulfilled, namely:

1) It must have been prohibited through an *Apostolic Letter,* coming directly and immediately from the Supreme Pontiff. The penalty is not incurred when the condemnation comes from a Congregation, even though the decree is approved by the Pope or issued at his command.[41] An Apostolic Letter may take the form of a Brief, a Bull, an Encyclical or some other form. However expressions such as these: *de apostolicae Nostrae auctoritatis plenitudine,* or *Apostolica auctoritate,* must be found in it.[42] The books condemned through Apostolic Letters are marked with a cross (†) in the *Index of Prohibited Books.*[43]

2) It must have been prohibited *by name* i. e., name or title of the work. Condemnation of works in groups, unless the title of each work is given, is not sufficient to incur the censure of which there is question here, because the Code requires that the work be condemned *nominatim.*[44] It does not matter *when* those works were thus prohibited. Therefore,

---

41. The Pope himself condemned the paper *L'Action Française* (Dec. 29, 1926 — *A A S,* XVIII [1926], 529) through a decree of the Holy Office. There is no question here of an Apostolic Letter.

42. De Meester, *Compendium,* III, n. 1385, 2, a; Cappello, *De Censuris,* n. 228; *De Curia Rom.,* I, p. 301; Bouuaert-Simenon, *Manuale Jur. Can.,* p. 769; Hilgers, *Der Index,* p. 96 ff.; *Die Bücherverbote in Papstbriefen,* p. 6 ff.; Boudinhon, *La Nouvelle Legisl.,* p. 304; Bucceroni, *Inst. Theol. Mor.,* II, n. 1165; Lega, *Praelectiones in Textum Juris* (Rome, 1910), III, n. 418; Arndt, *De Libr. Prohib.,* n. 167; Avanzini, *De Const. Apost. Sedis,* p. 13 f.; Santi-Leitner, *Praelectiones Juris canonici* (New York, 1904), V, 98.

43. New English edition, 1930, "Explanatory notes", p. XXXI.

44. De Meester, *Compendium,* III, n. 1385, 2, b; Avanzini, *De Const. "Apost. Sedis",* p. 15, d; Santi-Leitner, *l. c.*

works forbidden through Apostolic Letters before the constitution *Apostolicae Sedis*[45] are affected.

3) It must have been prohibited *under pain of excommunication reserved to the Roman Pontiff.* The phrase "libri per Apostolicas literas nominatim prohibiti", was first used by Pius IX in the constitution *Apostolicae Sedis* of Oct. 12, 1869.[46] The purpose of the Pope in issuing this constitution was to reduce the censures *latae sententiae.* With this in view, nearly all the commentators of this famous document interpreted the phrase *libri per Apostolicas literas prohibiti* to apply only to works which had been forbidden through Apostolic Letters under penalty of excommunication reserved to the Supreme Pontiff.[47] Otherwise, Pius IX, at least as far as that part of his constitution is concerned, would not have reduced but increased and rendered more severe the already severe penalties which the book legislation contained. That opinion was almost general before the Code. Now, the words of the Code are identical in this matter with those of Pius IX. Therefore, they are to be interpreted according to the interpretation given by commentators of the *Apostolicae Sedis*, as can. 6, n. 2 directs us. For that reason modern authors generally[48] teach that unless an Apostolic letter of whatever date con-

---

45.   Oct. 12, 1869 (*Fontes*, n. 552). Cf. also Wernz, *Jus Decretal.*, III, p. 135 (note 117) ; Avanzini, *De Const. "Apost. Sedis"*, p. 14.

46.   *Fontes*, n. 552.

47.   E. g., Pennacchi, *Commentaria in Constitutionem Apostolicae Sedis*, I, p. 127; Aichner, *Compendium Jur. Can.*, p. 520 f.; Gury, *Compendium Theol. Moralis*, II, n. 981, quest. 4; D'Annibale, *In Const. Apost. Sedis*, n. 40 (note 34) ; Lehmkuhl, *Theol. Mor.*, II, n. 1184; Avanzini, *De Const. "Apost. Sedis"*, p. 15, e. Bucceroni, *Inst. Theol. Mor.*, II, n. 1165, held that as long as the Apostolic letter inflicted excommunication, with no mention of reservation, that penalty became *specialiter reservata* after the constitution of Pius IX.

48.   Cappello, *De Censuris*, n. 229; Chelodi, *Jus Poenale*, n. 60, 2; Sabbetti-Barrett, *Comp. Theol. Mor.*, n. 976; Vermeersch-Creusen, *Ep.*, III, n. 517, 1; Bouuaert-Simenon, *Man. Juris Can.*, p. 769; De Meester, *Compendium*, III, n. 1385, 2, c; Cerato, *Censurae Vigentes*, n. 70, 1, i; Farrugia, *Comment. in Cens. Lat. Sent.*, n. 171, 2, c; Santi-Leitner, *Praelect. Juris Can.*, V, p. 98. However, Cipollini, *De Cens. Lat. Sent.*, p. 105, holds that no mention of punishment or reservation is necessary for a book condemned through Apostolic letters to come under can. 2318, §1.

demns a book under pain of excommunication reserved to the Supreme Pontiff or the Holy See, no excommunication is incurred now for the use of such a book.[49] However Chelodi[50] would not require the mention of excommunication reserved to the Supreme Pontiff, for such condemnations posterior to the Code.

Therefore, not all the books listed in the Index with a cross are forbidden under the severe penalty inflicted in can. 2318, §1, but only those which fulfil the three conditions given.

III. The **actions prohibited** under pain of excommunication specially reserved to the Holy See are *publication* of books of apostates, heretics and schismatics which advocate apostasy, heresy or schism, as well as *defense* of them, knowing and wilful *reading* and *keeping* without the necessary permission of such works or others forbidden by Apostolic letters. What is meant by publishing, reading and keeping a book was explained at length in pp. 113-119.[51] Suffice it to call to mind that only the person or group of persons who publish the work in their own name are *editors*. Neither the author as such nor the printer as such are publishers.[52] However, if they were accomplices, with full culpability, for the publication of the work or if the work could not have been published without their cooperation, they incur the same punishment as the editors.[53]

---

49. Hilgers, *Der Index*, p. 89, states that only four out of all the books condemned *nominatin* by Apostolic Letters have been forbidden under pain of excommunication reserved to the Supreme Pontiff.

50. *Jus Poenale*, n. 60, 2 (note 5).

51. Cf. also Boudinhon, *La Nouvelle Legisl.*, p. 314 ff.; Cappello, *De Censuris*, nn. 225, 230-234; Noldin, *De Censuris*, n. 62; Chelodi, *Jus Poenale*, n. 60, 2; Cerato, *Censurae Vigentes*, p. 147 f.; Pighi, *Censurae Lat. Sent.*, n. 55; Vermeersch-Creusen, *Ep.*, III, n. 517, 2; Leech, *A Comparative Study of the Constitution "Apostolicae Sedis" and the "Codex Juris Canonici"* (Washington: Catholic University, 1922), p. 20; Woywod, *A Practical Commentary*, II, p. 470; Augustine, *A Commentary*, VI, p. 432; Bouuaert-Simenon, *Manuale Juris Can.*, p. 769; Farrugia, *Commentarium in Cens. Lat. Sent.*, n. 172 f.; Sole, *De Delictis et Poenis*, n. 328; Lugo, *De Virt. Fid. Div.*, disp. 21, sect. 2, n. 94 ff.; Bucceroni, *Instit. Theol. Mor.*, II, n. 1165; Arndt, *De Libr. Prohib.*, n. 168 ff.

52. Cappello, *De Censuris*, n. 225.

53. Cann. 2209, §§1-3 and 2231.

Thus, an author guilty of apostasy, heresy or schism may incur two excommunications, one because of the errors held,[54] the other because of editing a work in which he propounds his errors.[55] Those who distribute or sell works already published are not editors.[56] Republication of books prohibited through Apostolic letters is forbidden without permission of the Holy See;[57] but no penalty is attached to this particular violation, unless the work is written by heretics, apostates, or schismatics and it defends heresy, apostasy or schism. This is clear from the wording of canon 2318, §1.[57a]

A person *defending* any of the works described in can. 2318, §1 is excommunicated, whether his defense is *material*[58] (e. g., he hides it or prevents it in some other way from being denounced or destroyed) or *moral*, i. e., by his words, writings or actions he strives to show that the doctrine in the book is good and opportune and therefore the book is not to be condemned. No censure is incurred by one who praises the style, the language, the literary ability and even the intention of the author, as long as this is not done to commend the work.[59] Chelodi[60] with others, would excuse from the censure, a person who defends a work only materially, e. g., hides it so that it may not be burned. Cappello,[61] calls that opinion probable.

The excommunication directed against *retinentes* generally does not apply to librarians, bookbinders and servants who keep forbidden books for those who employ them.[62] It applies to booksellers who keep forbidden books for sale (but not to those who keep them secretly to sell them or lend them to

---

54. Can. 2314.

55. Supra, p. 224 ff.

56. Cappello, *De Censuris*, n. 224; Cerato, *Censurae Vigentes*, n. 70, 1 f.

57. Can. 1398, §2.

57a. Cf. De Siena, *Commentarius Censurarum*, p. 26.

58. *Etiam effectu non secuto.* De Meester, *Compendium*, II, n. 1386, 1.

59. Vermeersch-Creusen, *Ep.*, III, n. 517, 2; Cappello, *De Censuris*, n. 230; De Meester, *l. c.*

60. *Jus Poenale*, n. 60, note 4.

61. *L. c.*

62. Cf. supra, p. 117 f.

customers who have permission).[63] Finally, public libraries are not affected by this censure.[64] The *retinentes* of a public library are not its employees or paid officials, rather they are the people or the community who pay for its maintenance and development, if not for its establishment. The community as a rule is made up not only of Christians but also of infidels or non-baptized persons, who are not bound by the laws of the Church. But, even though the components of a community were all Catholics, the responsibility of choosing the books for the public library is placed upon one or several persons, and, therefore, the community as a whole cannot be called to account for every evil book in the library. On the other hand, the persons selected for the management of the library are merely employees, guardians of those books but not keepers of them. Therefore, it cannot be proved that the censure of can. 2318, §1 against *retinentes* affects public libraries.

For one to incur the excommunication for *reading*[65] the books specified in can. 2318, §1, it is necessary that he read or keep such works "knowingly" (*scienter*).[66] Therefore, the

---

63. Cf. supra, p. 212.

64. Noldin, *De Censuris*, n. 62, c.

65. A person ordering, commanding, begging, advising another to read without permission some forbidden work for him, does not really *read* (A Coronata, *Inst. Jur. Can.*, II, p. 336; Badii, *Inst. Jur. Can.*, II, p. 159; Cipollini, *De Censuris Lat. Sent.*, p. 106), but is punishable just as if he actually read the work himself, in virtue of cann. 2209, §§1-3, and 2231. Cf. Cappello, *De Censuris*, n. 233; Marc-Gesterman-Raus, *Institutiones Morales Alphonsianae*, I, n. .1317. Cf. also Suarez, *o. c.*, n. 19; Schmalzgrueber, *o. c.*, nn. 47-50. If, however, the person who is commanded or begged to read a forbidden book by another has permission to keep or read it, he sins against the law of nature and even the Church law (can. 1398, §1), but neither he nor his *mandans* incur the censure (Cf. Pistocchi, *I Canoni Penali del Codice Ecclesiastico*, p. 36; Sole, *De Delictis et Poenis*, n. 328, 2) : not he, because he reads *with* permission; not his *mandans*, because he is not asking the reader to commit a crime which is forbidden under pain of excommunication, i. e. "to read without permission". Can. 2318 does not include the case of one who, having permission to read evil books, reads them to another who is not entitled to hear them. Cf. also supra, p. 115 f.

66. St. Alphonsus, *Theol. Mor.*, VII, n. 296; Suarez, *De Fid. Div.*, disp. 20, sect. 2, n. 17; Schmalzgrueber, *Jus Eccl. Un.*, lib. V, pars I, tit. XIX, n. 38; De Meester, *Compendium*, III, n. 1386, 2; Cappello, *De*

transgressor of this law must know from personal or public knowledge, or from a trustworthy person; a) that this book was written by an apostate, a heretic or a schismatic and that in it apostasy, heresy or schism are advocated or that it was forbidden through an Apostolic letter; b) that it is forbidden under pain of excommunication. Knowledge of the reservation is not necessary,[67] but ignorance of the law or of the punishment, even though crass and supine, excuses one from this penalty; not, however, affected ignorance.[68] The legislator uses the word "knowingly" (*scienter*) only for *legentes* and *retinentes*, not for *editores* or *defendentes*. The consequence is that if editors and defenders of works, forbidden in this canon, violate the law through crass and supine ignorance, they incur the censure.[69]

This penalty does not fall upon one who has permission to read and keep prohibited books, even though he should abuse his permission and violate the natural law (can. 1405, §1);[70] nor is it contracted by one who presumes permission because of an urgent necessity.[71]

The excommunication is incurred only when the work has been published, i. e., has been put on sale or offered for public circulation, as the words *opere publici iuris facto* of can. 2318, §1, clearly indicate.[72] This is in keeping with the nature of all punishments *latae sententiae* which are not incurred unless the crime is complete or consummated in accordance

Censuris, n. 231; D'Annibale, *In Const. Apost. Sedis*, n. 40; Pighi, *Censurae Lat. Sent.*, n. 85.

67. Cappello, *o. c.*, n. 72.

68. Can. 2229. Thus, suppose a person doubts whether a book comes under can. 2318, §1. He can easily find it out, but does not wish to do so for fear that he may not be able to read the book. This is affected ignorance (Cf. Cappello, *De Censuris*, n. 50), and therefore the culprit is not excused from the censure.

69. Can. 2229, §3, n. 1.

70. Schmalzgrueber, *l. c.*, n. 39; D'Annibale, *o. c.*, n. 34 (note 3).

71. Supra, p. 214.

72. De Meester, *Compendium*, III, n. 1386, 2, a; Pighi, *Censurae Lat. Sent.*, n. 55; Woywod, *A Practical Commentary*, II, p. 469; Cerato, *Censurae Vigentes*, n. 70, 1, f.; Cappello, *De Censuris*, n. 224; Farrugia, *Comment. in Cens. Lat. Sent.*, n. 172, A; Cipollini, *De Cens. Lat. Sent.*, p. 103.

with the words of the law.[73] Therefore, no one is affected by the censure contained in can. 2318, §1 if only a few copies of the work are printed, or if a large number of copies are printed not for general publication but for a restricted number of persons (e. g., the pupils of a professor), or if all the printed copies of a work, intended for publication, are destroyed before they are published for any reason whatever (e. g., prohibition of the civil authorities).[74] Accordingly, neither editors, nor defenders, nor readers nor keepers of books specified in this canon are excommunicated unless these works have been published.

The Church punishes with a censure only crimes or sins which are grave or *mortal.*[75] Therefore a person who edits, reads, keeps or defends books of apostates, heretics and schismatics advocating apostasy, heresy or schism, or any other book prohibited by name through Apostolic letters, does not incur any excommunication, if his action is not a mortal sin because of the lack of full advertence, or perfect consent or grave matter. Authors do not agree as to what constitutes *grave matter* in reading or keeping[76] a book forbidden under pain of excommunication.

As for *reading,* St. Alphonsus[77] after enumerating certain opinions held by some before him, lays down the following rule. If one, upon opening a book, falls upon a heretical doctrine and keeps on reading, he is excommunicated even though he reads a few lines. If, however, the book of a heretic deals with something indifferent (not heretical), no excommunication is incurred unless he read more than an entire folio page (16 pages in octavo).[78] This opinion, with some slight changes,

---

73. Cann. 2228, 2242, §.

74. Cappello, *l. c.*

75. Can. 2242, §1.

76. No question is raised as to any parvity of matter in *editing* or *defending* a book because it is evident that in either case the whole book is edited or defended and therefore there is always mortal sin. Cf. De Meester, *Compendium,* III, n. 1386, a, c, γ.

77. *De Proh. Libr.,* V, n. 6; *Theol. Mor.,* VII, nn. 284, 292.

78. Suarez, *De Fid. Div.,* disp. 20, sect. 2, n. 20; Lugo, *De Virt. Fid. Div.,* disp. 21, sect. 2, n. 82; Schmalzgrueber, *Jus Eccl. Un.,* lib. V, pars I, tit. VII, nn. 32, 40, 41, practically hold the same doctrine. In

has generally been accepted by many recent authors.[79] Noldin,[80] however, considers as grave matter three or four medium-sized pages of a really harmful section of a book and thirty pages of a less objectionable section. This rule is based on the principle that grave matter consists in what is seriously dangerous for the average reader.[81] Other modern authors[82] hold that the amount of matter which is sufficient to propose and propound heresy is grave matter, even though in reality no heresy is defended therein. According to them, about six octavo pages constitute grave matter.[83] In this view no distinction is made between dangerous and harmless sections of a book.

In practice, one cannot be accused of mortal sin (as far as the positive law is concerned in connection with excommunication), if he reads only a few lines, even though of a very harmful nature.[84] However, if he reads six[85] pages or more of a very harmful nature or thirty[86] pages or more of a less serious character, he commits mortal sin and is excommunicated.

As for *keeping*, it is generally agreed that mortal sin is committed by keeping a book or a notable part of it for a considerable time.[87] The amount of a book required to constitute

---

fact they place grave matter between ten lines and one folio page. The exact amount in individual cases depends on the nature of what is read.

79. Bucceroni, *Inst. Theol. Mor.*, II, n. 1165; Arndt, *De Libr. Prohib.*, n. 166, 3; Cappello, *De Censuris*, n. 233, 3; Bouuaert-Simenon, *Man. Juris Can.*, p. 552. Cf. also Vermeersch, *De Prohib. et Cens. Libr.*, p. 101 f.; Boudinhon, *La Nouvelle Legisl. de l'Index*, p. 309 f.

80. *Summa Theol. Mor.*, II, n. 707. This view is accepted by Betten, *The Roman Index of Forbidden Books*, p. 35.

81. Noldin, *l. c.*

82. De Meester, *Compendium*, III, n. 1386, a, c, α; Santi-Leitner, *Praelectiones Juris Canonici*, V, p. 97; Cocchi, *Comment. in C. J. C.*, VI, n. 67.

83. Cf. also Vermeersch, *De Prohib. et Cens. Libr.*, p. 102.

84. Suarez, *l. c.*; Lugo, *l. c.*; Schmalzgrueber, *l. c.*

85. De Meester, *l. c.*

86. Noldin, *l. c.*

87. De Meester, *Compendium*, III, n. 1386, 2, c, β; Suarez, *De Fid. Div.*, disp. 20, sect. 2, n. 22.

grave matter in keeping is greater than that required in reading.[88] As to the lapse of time needed for mortal sin, some difference is found in the opinions of authors. Some consider it a mortal sin to keep a work for more than two[89] or three[90] days, unless there is a reasonable cause to justify a longer delay even to a month.[91] Others, however, hold that it is certainly a mortal sin only when one keeps a book more than a month,[92] unless there is a just cause for greater delay. A reasonable cause for delay in both views would exist if one were waiting for permission to read the work he is keeping, or for an occasion to give it to one who has permission. Meanwhile, every precaution must be taken to avoid scandal or danger of perversion.[93] Noldin adds that one must not extend this time much over the month.

IV. The **persons affected** by the censure in question are all those who are bound by the ecclesiastical prohibition of books and have no permission to read forbidden works nor an urgent reason to presume that permission.[95] Cardinals, Bishops, even though only titular, and all other Ordinaries are exempt, in virtue of can. 1401, from the Church prohibition of books.[96] Therefore they are not subject to the penalties attached to it.[97]

---

88. Schmalzgrueber, *Jus Eccl. Un.*, lib. V, pars I, tit. VII, n. 43; Arndt, *De Libr. Prohib.*, n. 174; De Meester, *l. c.*

89. Schmalzgrueber, *l. c.*; Lugo, *De Virt. Fid. Div.*, disp. 21, sect 2, n. 86.

90. De Meester, *l. c.* Cf. also Boudinhon, *La Nouvelle Legislation*, p. 311.

91. Vermeersch, *De Prohib. et Cens. Libr.*, p. 102; De Meester, *l. c.*; Boudinhon, *o. c.*, p. 312.

92. Cappello, *De Censuris*, n. 234; Cocchi, *Comment. in Cod. Jur. Can.*, VI, n. 67; Noldin, *Summa Theol. Mor.*, II, n. 707, c.

93. Cappello, *l. c.*; Cocchi, *l. c.*; Noldin, *l. c.*; Boudinhon, *l. c.*; De Meester, *l. c.*

94. *L. c.*

95. Supra, p. 73 ff. Cf. also can. 2226, §1.

96. Supra, p. 196 f.

97. Can. 2226, §1. "*Poenae adnexae legi aut praecepto obnoxius est qui lege aut praecepto tenetur, nisi expresse eximatur.*" Cf. also Farrugia, *Comm. in Cens. Satae Sent.*, n. 177. The opposite view held by Cerato, *Censurae Vigentes*, n. 70, a, and Leech, *A Comparative Study*, p. 20, is untenable.

V. **Remission** from this excommunication is obtained
through absolution granted by the Holy See, i. e., the Supreme
Pontiff himself or the Sacred Penitentiary[98] or by any one to
whom the Holy See has granted this faculty.[99] This faculty is
given to the Papal Legates,[100] to Ordinaries in missionary
countries[101] and to local Ordinaries[102] elsewhere. The faculty
of local Ordinaries in this matter reads thus:

> "Absolvendi a censuris et poenis ecclesiasticis eos qui
> libros apostatarum haereticorum aut schismaticorum,
> apostasiam, haeresim aut schisma propugnantes,
> aliosve per Apostolicas Litteras nominatim prohibitos
> defenderint aut scienter sine debita licentia legerint
> vel retinuerint; iniuncta congrua poenitentia salutari
> ac firma obligatione supradictos libros, quantum fie-
> ri, poterit, ante absolutionem, destruendi vel Ordi-
> nario aut confessario tradendi."

A local Ordinary can exercise this power over his subjects whether he or his subject or both are in the diocese or
outside of it. He can use it only *in foro conscientiae*, even
though it be outside of sacramental confession. Within the
limits of his diocese, the Ordinary may subdelegate it; habitually, if he so desires, only to the Canon Penitentiary and
to the Vicars Forane who are to use it *in foro conscientiae*
and in the act of sacramental confession. The Ordinary may
delegate this power under the same conditions but for a limited
time also to some confessors selected by him. Finally he may
empower confessors who in particular cases have recourse to
him for their penitents. No one to whom this power has been
subdelegated[103] by the Bishop can delegate it again; nor can

---

98. The Sacred Penitentiary can absolve from this censure, even
when the case is public or notorious, according to Cappello, *De Censuris*,
n. 122 f.: *"Nam, licet censura sit vinculum praesertim fori exterioris,
eius absolutio tamen imitatur absolutionem a peccatis, ideoque* qua talis
(nota verbum) est potius actus fori interni".

99. Can. 2253, n. 3.

100. Vermeersch-Creusen, *Ep.*, I, n. 813 (I, 4).

101. Vermeersch-Creusen, *Ep.*, I, n. 814 (28).

102. Vermeersch-Creusen, *Ep.*, I (1929), Appendix III.

103. Cf. Faculties which Ordinaries receive from the Sacred Penitentiary, in Vermeersch-Creusen, *Ep.*, I (1929), Appendix III.

the Bishop authorize such a further delegation.[104]

A simple confessor cannot absolve from this censure without special faculty except in danger of death[105] and in the other urgent cases covered by can. 2254. In ordinary cases, he must apply to the local Ordinary or directly to the Sacred Penitentiary for the necessary faculties to absolve from this censure. The Apostolic Delegate also could be approached for this purpose, as he has powers to absolve from censures reserved in a special way to the Holy See.[106]

Art. II. *Non-reserved Excommunication*

Authors or publishers who, without the necessary permission, cause books of Holy Scripture or notes or commentaries on them to be printed incur, ipso facto, a non-reserved excommunication.[107]

This censure affects only authors and editors. An author, however, does not incur the excommunication, if he simply gives or sells his manuscript, without concerning himself in any way about the printing of it.[108] For can 2318, §2, punishes authors, only when they *"cause* books of Holy Scripture or notes or commentaries on them *to be printed"*, without the required permission. The crime is committed as soon as the work is put under the press, with the intention to publish it.[109]

---

104. Can. 199, §5; Vermeersch-Creusen, *Ep.*, I (1929), Appendix III.

105. Can. 2252.

106. See faculties in Vermeersch-Creusen, *Ep.*, I, n. 813 (I, 4).

107. Can. 2318, §2. Cf. also Vermeersch-Creusen, *Ep.*, III, n. 517, II; De Meester, *Compendium*, III, n. 1387; Farrugia, *Comment. in Cens. Lat. Sent.*, p. 11; Boudinhon, *La Nouvelle Legislation de l'Index*, p. 316; Cocchi, *Comm. in Cod. Juris Can.*, VIII, n. 145; Cappello, *De Censuris*, n. 397 ff.; Noldin, *De Censuris*, n. 96; Hurley, *Index Legislation*, p. 250 f.; Pennacchi, *In Const. Apost. Officiorum ac munerum*, p. 353 ff.; Moureau, *La Nouvelle Legislation de l'Index*, p. 103; Gennari, "Circa la nuova disciplina, etc.", *Il Mon. Eccl.*, X, Part I (1897), p. 156 f.; Wernz, *Jus Decretalium*, III, p. 135 (118); Arndt, *De Libris Prohibitis*, n. 180.

108. De Meester, *o. c.*, III, n. 1387, 2; Vermeersch, *De Prohib. et Censura Libr.*, p. 110.

109. Vermeersch-Creusen, *Ep.*, III, n. 517, II; Cappello, *De Censuris*, n. 398; De Meester, *Compendium*, III, n. 1387, 2.

In fact, the law under consideration punishes directly the *printing* of a work and not the publication of it. However, the number of the copies printed must be sufficiently large to constitute an *edition.* The present law, then, does not refer to the printer nor to any one of his employees as such. Nevertheless, if these are equally responsible, with the author and the publisher, for printing the work, which, without their aid, would not have been printed, they incur the excommunication.[110]

Not all Scriptural works come under this law[111] but only: 1) *books of Holy Scripture*, whether there is question of the original text or of a translation, old or new, into a dead language or the vernacular; 2) *annotations* to or *commentaries* of any book or part of a book of Holy Scripture.[112] No matter how integral and faithful the text or the translation, no matter how orthodox and patristically correct the interpretation may be, any one of these works, lacking the necessary approbation, may not be printed. However, the work must be a book in the strict sense,[113] or, at least according to some,[114] it must consist of several numbers of a Scriptural periodical bound in one volume.

The approbation or permission required is that which is granted, after previous examination of a book, by the local Ordinary of the author, or by the Ordinary of the place in which the work is published or printed.[115] A religious needs also the permission of his major Superior.[116] In the case of a vernacular translation of the Holy Scripture the work must be published under the vigilance of the Bishop or Bishops

------

110.   Can. 2209, §§1-3.

111.   De Meester, *l. c.*; Boudinhon, *o. c.*, p. 319 f.

112.   *Anotations* accompany and elucidate the text, while a *commentary* constitutes a complete interpretation or explanation of a book of Holy Scripture or part of it. Cf. De Meester, *l. c.*; Vermeersch-Creusen, *l. c.*

113.   Supra, p. 221 ff.; De Meester, *l. c.*

114.   Vermeersch-Creusen, *l. c.*; Cappello, *o. c.*, n. 399, 3.

115.   Can. 1385, §1, n. 1 and §2.

116.   Can. 1385, §3.

and with notes taken chiefly from the holy Fathers of the Church and from other learned and catholic writers.[117] The permission of the Ordinary should be given in writing and should be printed at the beginning or at the end of the book.[118]

As long as permission has been obtained from any one of the three local Ordinaries mentioned, i. e., the Ordinary of the author or of the place where the work is published or printed, no excommunication is incurred. The mere lack of the additional permission from the religious Superior, if the author be a religious, is unlawful but does not make the author and the editor subject to the excommunication.[119] The same is true if the permission granted, at least orally, by the local Ordinary is not printed in the work.

Absolution from this censure can be given by any confessor because it is not reserved to any one.

THE END

---

117. Can. 1391.

118. Can. 1394, §1.

119. Cappello, *o. c.*, n. 398, 1; Vermeersch, *De Prohib. et Cens. Libr.*, p. 109.

BIBLIOGRAPHY

SOURCES

A. General

Acta Apostolicae Sedis, (*A A S*), (Rome, 1909—)
*Acta et decreta Concilii Provincialis Mechliniensis Quarti anno MCMXX
Mechliniae habiti,* (Mechlin, 1923).
Acta Sanctae Sedis, (*A S S*), 41 vols. (Rome, 1865-1908).
Ante-Nicene Fathers, The (American Reprint of the Edinburgh edition,
New York, 1903).
*Bullarum Diplomatum et Privilegiorum Sanctorum Romanorum Ponti-
ficum Taurinensis editio,* 24 vols. (Turin, 1857-1872).
Canones et Decreta Sacrosancti Oecumenici Concilii Tridentini, (editio
novissima, Turin: Pietro Marietti, 1913).
*Codex Juris Canonici Pii X Pontificis Maximi Jussu digestus Benedicti
Papae XV auctoritate promulgatus,* (Rome, 1919).
Codex Theodosii (ed. Mommsen-Meyer, Berlin, 1905).
Codicis Juris Canonici Fontes Cura Emi. Petri Card. Gasparri Editi
(Rome, 1923).
Collectanea Sacrae Congregationis de Propaganda Fide, (*Coll.*) 2 vols.
(Rome, 1907).
Concilii Plenarii Baltimorensis II Acta et Decreta, (Baltimore, 1894).
Concilii Plenarii Baltimorensis III Acta et Decreta, (Baltimore, 1884).
Corpus Juris Canonici, 2 vols. (2. ed., Richter-Friedberg, Leipzig, 1879).
Corpus Scriptorum Ecclesiasticorum Latinorum, (*C S E L*) (Vienna,
1866—)
*Decreta Authentica Sacrae Congregationis Indulgentiis Sacrisque Reli-
quiis Praepositae,* ab anno 1668 ad annum 1882 (Ratisbon, 1883)
Decreta Authentica Congregationis Sacrorum Rituum, 7 vols. (Rome,
1912)
Denzinger-Bannwart, *Enchiridion Symbolorum Definitionum et Declara-
tionum de Rebus Fidei et Morum* (15. and 16. ed., Freiburg, i. B.:
Herder & Co., 1922)
Mansi, J. D., *Sacrorum Conciliorum Nova et Amplissima Collectio,* 53
vols. (Paris-Leipzig, 1903-1927)
Migne, J. P. *Patrologiae Cursus Completus,* Series Latina (*M P L*),
221 vols. (Paris, 1844-1870). Series Greca (*M P G*), 161 vols.
(Paris, 1857-1864)
Monumenta Germaniae Historica — Auctorum Antiquissimorum, Tomus
IX, vol. I (Berlin, 1892)
Pii IX Pontificis Maximi Acta (Ex typographia Bonarum Artium)
Thesaurus Resolutionum Sacrae Congregationis Concilii, 168 vols. (Rome,
1745-1908)

B. Principal Roman Indexes

Index of Paul IV (Rome, 1559)
Index of the Council of Trent (Pius IV, Rome, 1564)
Index of Clement VIII (Rome, 1596)

Index of Alexander VII (Rome, 1664)
Index of Clement X (Rome, 1670)
Index of Innocent XI (Rome, 1681)
Index of Benedict XIV (Rome, 1752)
Index of Benedict XIV (Rome, 1758)
Index of Pius VII (Rome, 1819)
Index of Gregory XVI (Rome, 1835)
Index of Pius IX (Rome, 1877)
Index of Leo XIII (Rome, 1881)
Index of Leo XIII (Rome, 1900)
Index of Benedict XV (Rome, 1917)
Index of Pius XI (Rome, 1922)
Index of Pius XI (Rome, 1929)

WORKS OF REFERENCE

A Coronata, O. M. C., *Institutiones Juris Canonici*, 2 vol. (Turin: Marietti, 1928-1931)

Aertnys, J., - Damen, C. A., C. SS. R., *Theologia Moralis*, 2 vols. (Turin: Marietti, 1928)

Aichner, Simon, *Compendium Juris Canonici* (6. ed., Brixen, 1887)

Arndt, A., S. J., *De Libris Prohibitis Commentarii* (Ratisbon, 1895)

Avanzini, Peter, *De Const. "Apostolicae Sedis"* (2. ed., Rome: 1874)

Ayrinhac, H. A., S. S., *Administrative Legislation in the New Code of Canon Law* (New York: Longmans, Green and Co., 1930)

[Bachofen], Charles Augustine, *A Commentary on the New Code of Canon Law*, 8 vols. (2. ed., St. Louis: Herder, 1923)

Badii, Caesar, *Institutiones Juris Canonici*, 2 vols. (3. ed., Florence: Libreria Editrice Fiorentina, 1921-1922)

Bargilliat, M., *Praelectiones Juris Canonici*, 2 vols. (37. ed., Paris: Baston, Berche et Pagis, 1923-1924)

Baronii-Raynaldi-Ladarchi-Theiner, *Annales Ecclesiastici*, 36 vols. (Bar-le-Duc, 1864)

Bellarmine, Robert, S. J., *Opera Omnia*, 8 vols. (Naples, 1858)

Benedict XIV, *De Servorum Dei Beatificatione et Sanctorum Canonizatione*, 7 vols. (Prato: 1839)

Beringer, F., S. J., *Les Indulgences, Leur Nature et Leur Usage*, 15. ed. published by P. A. Steinen, S. J. (4th French ed. in 2 vols., Paris: P. Lethielleux, 1925)

Bethleem, Louis, *Romans à lire et Romans à proscrire* (9. ed., Paris: Revue des Lectures, 1925)

Betten, F. S., S. J., *The Roman Index of Forbidden Books* (Chicago: Loyola University Press, 1925)

Blat, Albertus, O. P., *Commentarium Textus Codicis Juris Canonici*, 5 vols. (Rome: Typographia Pontificia in Instituto Pii IX, 1921-1927)

Bohatta, Hanns, *Einführung in die Buchkunde* (Vienna: Gilhofer & Ranschburg, 1927)

Bouché, A. - Leclercq, *Histoire De La Divination Dans L'Antiquité*, 4 vols. (Paris, 1879-1882)

Boudinhon, A., *La Nouvelle Legislation de l'Index* (2. ed., Paris: P. Lethielleux, 1924)

Bouuaert-Simenon, *Manuale Juris Canonici* (2. ed., Ghent and Liège, 1926)

Bouix, D., *Tractatus De Curia Romana* (Paris, 1880).

Boyd, E. - Summer, J. S., *Debate on Censorship of books* (New York: The League for Public Discussion, 1924)

Brasichelli, Joseph Maria, *Indicis librorum expurgandorum in studiosorum gratiam confecti*, tomus I (Rome, 1607)

Brevi Considerazioni Sopra una Lunga Lettera di Massimo d'Azeglio (3 Aprile, 1847)

Bucceroni, Januarius, *Institutiones Theologiae Moralis* (5. ed., Rome, 1908)

Cappello, Felix M., *De Curia Romana Juxta Reformationem a Pio X Sapientissime Inductam* (2 vols., Rome: F. Pustet, 1911)

Cappello, Felix, M., S. J., *Summa Juris Canonici in usum Scholarum concinnata*, 2 vols. (Rome: Università Gregoriana, 1928-1930)

Cappello, Felix, S. J., *Summa Juris Publici Ecclesiastici ad norman Codicis Juris Canonici et recentiorum Sanctae Sedis documentorum concinnata* (Rome: Università Gregoriana, 1924)

Cappello, Felix, S. J., *Tractatus Canonico-Moralis De Censuris iuxta Codicem Juris Canonici* (Turin: Marietti, 1925)

Carroll, Lewis, *Feeding the Mind* (London, 1907)

Catalogue Alphabétique Des Ouvrages Candamnés (Paris, 1836)

Catalanus, J., *De Magistro S. Palatii Apostolici* (Rome, 1751)

Catalanus, J., *De Secretario Sacrae Congregationis Indicis* (Rome, 1751)

Catholic Encyclopedia, 16 vols. (New York, 1907-1914)

Cavagnis, Felix, *Institutiones Juris Publici Ecclesiastici*, 2 vols. (Rome, 1888)

Cavigioli, J., *De Censuris Latae Sententiae Quae in Codice Juris Canonici Continentur Commentariolum* (Turin: Libreria Editrice Internazionale, 1919)

Censura Generalis contra errores quibus recentes haeretici asperserunt (Pincia, 1554)

Cerato, Prosdocimo, *Censurae Vigentes* (2. ed., Pavia: Seminario, 1921)

Chelodi, Joannes, *Jus de Personis juxta Codicem Juris Canonici Praemisso Tractactu de Principiis et de Fontibus J. C.* (2. ed., Trent: Libr. Editr. Tridentum, 1927)

Ciccognani, H. J., *Commentarium ad Librum I Codicis* (Rome: Schola Typographica "Pio X", 1925)

Cipollini, Albertus D., *De Censuris Latae Sententiae iuxta Codicem Juris Canonici* (Turin: M. Marietti, 1925)

Conway, Bertrand L., C. S. P., *The Question Box* (new edition, New York: The Paulist Press, 1929)

Cronin, Michael, *The Science of Ethics*, 2 vols (Dublin: M. H. Gill & Son, 1909)

D'Angelo, Sosio, *La Esenzione Dei Religiosi* (Turin: Lega Italiana Cattolica Editrice, 1929)

D'Annibale, Joseph, *Summula Theologiae Moralis*, 3 vols. (Rome, 1897)

D'Annibale, Joseph, *In Constitutionem Apostolicae Sedis qua censurae latae sententiae limitantur commentarii* (Roma: Declee, 1909)

Dawson, Samuel Arthur, *Freedom of the Press* (New York: Columbia University Press, 1924)

D'Erbigny, M., S. J., *Theologia de Ecclesia*, 2 vols. (3. ed., Paris: G. Beauchense, 1927-1928)

De Meester, A., *Juris Canonici et Juris Canonico-Civilis Compendium* (new ed., Bruges: Desclée de Brouwer, 1921-)

De Siena, Pasqualis, *Commentarius Censurarum juxta Novum Codicem Juris Canonici* (Naples: F. Giannini, 1918)

Dieckmann, Hermannus, S. J., *De Ecclesia Tractatus Historico-Dogmatici* (Freiburg i. B.: Herder and Co., 1925)

Disraeli, Isaac, *Amenities of Literature*, 2 vols. (new ed., New York: Thomas Y. Crowell, 1881)

Ditchfield, P. H., *Books Fatal to Their Authors* (London, 1895)

Du Plessis D'Argentré, C., *Collectio Judiciorum de Novis Erroribus* (Paris, 1728)

El Retirado, *Importancia De La Prohibición de Malos Libros* (Mexico, 1832)

Ernst, Morris L. - Seagle, William, *To the Pure... A Study of Obscenity and the Censor* (New York: The Viking Press, 1928)

Eymericus, Nicolaus, *Directorium Inquisitorium Cum Commentariis F. Peniae* (Venice, 1595)

Eymieu, Antonin, *Le Government de soi-meme, Essai de Psychologie Pratique*, Premiere serie: *Les grandes lois* (20. ed., Paris: Perrin and Co., 1921)

Fanfani, L., O. P., *De Jure Religiosorum* (Turin: Marietti, 1920)

Fanfani, L., O. P., *De Indulgentiis*, 2. ed. (Turin: Marietti, 1926)

Farrer, James Anson, *Books Condemned to be burned* (London, 1892)

Farrugia, Nicolaus, O. S. A., *Commentarium in Censuras Latae Sententiae Codicis J. C.* (2. ed., Malta: Fortunato Mizzi, 1921)

Ferraris, Lucius, O. F. M., *Bibliotheca Canonica Juridica Moralis Theologica necnon Ascetica Polemica Rubricistica Historica* (editio novissima mendis expurgata, Rome, 1889)

Ferreres, Joannes B., S. J., *Institutiones Canonicae juxta Novissimum Codicem a Benedicto XV promulgatum* (2. ed., Barcelona: Eugenius Subirana, 1920)

Ferreres, Joannes, B., S. J., *Compendium Theologiae Moralis* (Barcelona: Eugenius Subirana, 1928)

Feije, *Tractatus de Libris Prohibitis*

Ford, John, *Criminal Obscenity, A Plea for Its Suppression* (New York: Fleming H. Revell Company, 1926)

Francus, Daniel, *Disquisitio academica de papistarum indicibus librorum prohibitorum et expurgandorum* (Leipzig, 1684)

Funk, F. X., *Didascalia et Constitutiones Apostolorum*, 2 vols. (Paderborn, 1905)

Funk, F. X., *A Manual of Church History* (Transl. from 5. German ed., by L. Cappadelta, 2 vols., London: B. Herder, 1910)

Gay, Jean, *Saisie De Livres Prohibés* (Turin, 1876)

Geisert, Henry A., *The Criminal* (St. Louis: Herder, 1930)

Genicot, Edwardus - Salsmans, I., S. J., *Casus Conscientiae* (Brussels: Alb. DeWitt, 1922)

Genicot, Edwardus - Salsmans, I., S. J., *Institutiones Theologiae Moralis* (10. ed., Brussells: Alb. Dewitt, 1922)

Gennari, Casimiro, *Quistioni Teologico-Morali di Materie riguardanti specialmente i nostri tempi* (Rome, 1907)

Gibbings, Richard, *An exact reprint of the Roman Index Expurgatorius* (Dublin, 1837)

Gibbons, James, *The Faith of Our Fathers* (Holy Name ed., New York: Holy Name Bureau, 1929)

Gigot, Francis E., *General Introduction to the Study of the Holy Scriptures* (Unabridged ed., New York: Benziger Brothers, 1900)

Gratius, Ortwin, *Lamentationes Obscurorum Virorum* (Cologne, 1518)

Gretser, Jacob, S. J., *De Jure et More Prohibendi, Expurgandi et Abolendi Libros Haereticos et Noxios*, contained in Gretser, Jacob, S. J., *Opera Omnia* (Ratisbon, 1739) tom. XIII *Miscellanea Polemica.*

Gury, J. P. - Dumas, H., *Compendium Theologiae Moralis* (6. ed., Lyons, 1899)

Gury, J. P. - Tummolo, P. R., *Compendium Theologiae Moralis*, 2 vols. (3. ed., Naples: Ufficio Succursale della Civiltà Cattolica, 1925)

Haebler, Von Konrad, *Handbuch der Inkunabelkunde* (Leipzig: Karl W. Hiersemann, 1925)

Hagedorn, Francis Edward, *General Legislation on Indulgences* (Washington: Catholic University, 1924)

Hannot, Jean Baptiste, *Index Ou Catalogue Des Principaux Livres condamnés et defendus par l'Eglise* (Namur, 1714)

Hart, N. H., *Index Expurgatorius Anglicanus* (London, 1872)

Hefele, Charles Joseph, *A History of the Christian Councils, from the Original Documents, to the close of the Council of Nicaea, A. D. 325.* Translated from the German and edited by William R. Clark (Edinburgh, 1871)

Heymans, A., *De Ecclesiastica Librorum Aliorumque Scriptorum in Belgio Prohibitione Disquisitio* (Brussels, 1849)

Hilgers, J., S. J., *Der Index der Verbotenen Bücher* (Freiburg i. B.: Herdersche Verlagshandlung, 1904)

Hilgers, J., S. J., *The Roman Index and Its Latest Historian, a Critical Review of "The Censorship of the Church of Rome" by George Haven Putman* (Techny, Ill.: Society of the Divine Word, 1908)

Hilgers, Joseph, S. J., *Die Bücherverbote in Papstbriefen* (Freiburg i. B., 1907)

Houben, Heinrich Hubert, *Verbotene literatur von der Klassischen zeit bis zur gegenwart; ein kritisch-historisches lexicon über Verbotene bücher, zeitschriften un theaterstücke, schriftsteller und verleger,* 2 vols. (Berlin: E. Rowolt, 1924-1928)

Hull, Ernest, R., S. J., *Man's Great Concern* (New York: Kennedy and Sons, 1920)

Hurley, T., *A Commentary on the Present Index Legislation* (New York: Benziger Bros., 1908)

Hyland, Francis Edward, *Excommunication* (Washington: Catholic University, 1928)

Index Auctorum Damnatae Memoriae (Lisbon, 1624)

Index Expurgatorius Librorum qui hoc saeculo prodierunt vel doctrinae non sanae erroribus inspersis vel inutilis et offensivae maledicentiae fellibus permixtis juxta Sacri Concilii Tridentini decretum: Philippi II Regis Catholici jussu et auctoritate atque Albani Ducis consilio ac ministerio in Belgia concinnatus anno MDLXXI (Antwerp, 1571)

Janssen, Johannes, *History of the German People at the Close of the Middle Ages,* 16 vols. (London, 1909)

Jerome, St., *De Viris Illustribus* (Leipzig, 1879)

Kirsch, Felix M., *Sex Education and Training in Chastity* (New York: Benziger Bros., 1930)

Kiselstein, G., *L'Index, Les lois de l'Eglise, Le devoir des Catholiques* (Liege: La Pensée Catholique, 1927)

Klotz, M. J. Christian, *De Libris Auctoribus Suis Fatalibus Liber Singularis* (Leipzig, 1768)

Knabenbauer, Jos., S. J., *Commentarius in Quattuor Evangelia Domini N. Jesu Christi* (Paris, 1897)

Koch-Preuss, *Handbook of Moral Theology,* 5 vols. (2. revised ed., St. Louis: Herder, 1921)

Konings, A., C. SS. R., *Theologia Moralis,* 3 vols. (3. ed., New York, 1877)

Leech, George, *A Comparative Study of the Constitution "Apostolicae Sedis" and the "Codex Juris Canonici"* (Washington: Catholic University, 1922)

Lega, M., *Praelectiones in Textum Juris* (Rome, 1910)

Lehmkuhl, Augustinus, S. J., *Theologia Moralis,* 2 vols., (12. ed., Freiburg: Herder, 1914)

Lenhart, John M., O. M. Cap., *The "Open Bible" in Pre-Reformation Times* (New York: The Paulist Press)

Lépicier, Alexis, O. S. M., *Indulgences, Their Origin, Nature and Development* (London: Burns Oates & Washbourne, Ltd., 1928)

Liguori, St. Alphonsus, *Theologia Moralis,* 4 vols. (new ed., of Leonard Gaudé, Rome, 1905)

Liljencrants, Johan, *Spiritism and Religion* (Washington: Catholic University, 1918)

Lord, Daniel A., S. J., *I Can Read Anything* (St. Louis: The Queen's
    Work Press, 1930)
Lugo, Joannes, De, S. J., *Disputationes Scholasticae et Morales* (Ed.
    nova Fournials, Paris, 1868)
Lynk, Frederick M., S. V. D., *Twelve Talks on the Art of Right Reading*
    (Techny, Ill.: Mission Press, S. V. D., 1919)
Malou, *De la lecture de la Bible en langue vulgaire* (Louvain, 1846)
Marc, C. - Gestermann, F. X. - Raus, J. B., C. SS. R., *Institutiones Mo-
    rales Alphonsianae*, 2 vols. (18. ed., Paris: E. Vitte, 1927)
Maroto, Philip, *Institutiones Juris Canonici*, 2 vols. (Madrid: Editorial
    del Corazón de María, 1919)
Martin, Victor, *Les Congregations Romaines* (Strasbourg: Librarie
    Bloud & Gay, 1930)
Melo, Antonio, O. F. M., *De Exemptione Regularium* (Washington: Cath-
    olic University, 1921)
Mendham, Joseph, *The Literary Policy of the Church of Rome* (London,
    1830)
Michiels, G., O. M. C., *Normae Generales Juris Canonici*, 1 vols. (Lublin,
    Poland: Universitas Catholica, 1929)
Milton, John, *Aroepagita: A Speech to the Parliament of England for
    the liberty of Unlicensed Printing* (London, 1819)
Mothon, J. P., O. P., *Traité Sur L'Etat Religieux* (Paris: Societé S.
    Augustin, Desclée, De Brouwer et Cie, 1922)
Mothon, J. P., O. P., *Institutions Canoniques*, 3 vols. (Paris: Societé S.
    Augustin, Desclée, De Brouwer et Cie, 1922-1924)
Moureau, *La Nouvelle Legislation de l'Index* (Lille, 1898)
Müssener, Theol. Hermann, *Die Kirchlichen Büchergesetze* (Düsseldorf:
    Von L. Schwann, 1928)
Neuberger, Nicholas J., *Canon 6 or The Relation of the Codex Juris
    Canonici to Preceding Legislation* (Washington: Catholic Univer-
    sity of America, 1927)
Noldin, H., S. J., *Summa Theologiae Moralis*, 3 vols. (16. ed., Innsbruch:
    Fel. Rauch, 1923)
Pallavicino, Sforza, *Istoria del Concilio de Trento*, 4 vols. (Rome, 1833)
Pastor, Ludwig, *The History of the Popes*, Edited by Frederick Ignatius
    Antrobus of the Oratory, 20 vols. (London, 1899-1931)
Pederzini, Fortunato Cavazzoni, *Ragionamento sopra il tema proposto
    dalla R. Accademia di Scienze, Lettere, ed Arti di Modena nei se-
    quenti termini: "Dimostrare co' migliori argomenti i mali della stam-
    pa licenziosa e i vantaggi della ben regolata; e quindi la necessità
    di una savia censura."* (Modena, 1843)
Peignot, G., *Dictionnaire Critique, Littéraire et Bibliographique Des
    Principaux Livres Condamnés au Feu, Supprimés ou Censurés*, 2
    vols. (Paris, 1806)
Pennacchi, J., *In Constitutionem Apostolicam Officiorum ac Munerum
    De Prohibitione et Censura Librorum a Leone XIII Divina Provi-
    dentia Papa XIII Latam Brevis Commentatio* (Rome, 1898)
Petzholdt, Julius, *Bibliotheca Bibliographica* (Leipzig, 1866)
Pighi, J. B., *Censurae Latae Sententiae et Irregularitates quas habet
    Codex Juris Canonici cum Brevi Commentario* (7. ed., Verona: Cin-
    quetti, 1922)
Pistocchi, Mario, *I Canoni Penali del Codice Ecclesiastico Esposti e Com-
    mentati* (Turin: Marietti, 1925)
Pope, Hugh, *The Catholic Church and the Bible* (New York: Mac Millan
    Co., 1928)
Popper, William, *The Censorship of Hebrew Books* (New York: The
    Knickerbocker Press, 1899)
Preuss, Arthur, *A Study of American Freemasonry* (St. Louis: Herder,
    1924)

Proal, Louis, *Passion and Criminality*, translated from the French by
A. R. Allison, M. A. (Oxon.) (London, 1905)

Putnam, G. H. Litt. D., *The Censorship of the Church of Rome*, 2 vols.
New York & London, 1906)

Putzer, Joseph, *Commentarium in Facultates Apostolicas* (New York:
Benziger, 1893)

Quigley, Joseph, *Condemned Societies* (Washington: Catholic University,
1927)

Raynaud, Theophilus, S. J., *Eretemata de Malis ac Bonis Libris deque
Iusta aut Iniusta Eorumdem Confixione* (Lyons, 1653)

Reiffenstuel, Anacletus, O. M. F. R., *Jus Canonicum Universum*, 4 vols.
(Editio novissima, Rome, 1831)

Retana, W. E., *La Censura De Imprenta En Filipinas* (Madrid, 1908)

Reusch, F. H., *Der Index der Verbotenen Bücher* (erster band, Bonn,
1883)

Roberti, F., *De Delictis et Poenis*, 1 vol. (Rome: S. Apollinare)

Roberts, William, *The Earlier History of English Bookselling* (London,
1889)

Roelker, Edward G., *Principles of Privilege* (Washington: Catholic University, 1926)

Sabetti-Barrett, S. J., *Compendium Theologiae Moralis* (New York: Fr.
Pustet, 1920)

Sanchez, Thomas, S. J., *Opus Morale in Praecepta Decalogi*, 2 vols.
(Parma, 1723)

Santi, F. - Leitner, M., *Praelectiones Juris Canonici* (New York: Pustet,
1904)

Schaffer, Kurt, O., *Die Leipziger Bücherkommission als Zensurbehörde
1800-1815* (Borma-Leipzig, 1911)

Schelhorn, J. G., *Amoenitates Historiae Ecclesiasticae et Literariae*
(Frankfurt, 1737)

Schmalzgrueber, F., S. J., *Jus Ecclesiasticum Universum*, 12 vols. (Rome,
1845)

Schroeder, T. - Ellis, H., *Witchcraft and Obscenity Twin Superstitions*
(New York: Free Speech League, 1912)

Schroeder, Theodore, *The Historical Interpretation of Unabridged Freedom of Speech* (New York: Free Speech League, 1910)

Scott, Martin J., S. J., *Religion and Common Sense* (New York: Kennedy and Sons, 1926)

Shearman, M. - Rayner, O. T., *The Press Laws of Foreign Countries
with an appendix containing the Press Laws of India* (London: His
Majesty's Stationery Office, 1926)

Sepp, Christiaan, *Een Drietal Indices Librorum Prohibitorum* (Leiden,
1889)

Shuster, George N., *The Catholic Church and Current Literature* (New
York: The Macmillan Company, 1930)

Slater, Thomas, S. J., *A Manual of Moral Theology for English-speaking
Countries*, 2 vols. (New York: Benziger, 1908)

Sleumer, Albert, *Index Romanus* (Osnabrück, 1911)

Socratis Scholastici et Hermiae Sozomeni, *Historia Ecclesiastica* (Paris,
1668)

Sole, Jacobus, *De Delictis et Poenis* (Rome: Fr. Pustet, 1920)

Solieri, F., *Juris Publici Ecclesiastici Elementa* (Rome, 1900)

Suarez, Franciscus, S. J., *Opera Omnia*, 26 vols. (Paris, 1856-1861)

Tanquerey, A., *Synopsis Theologiae Dogmaticae*, 3 vols. (Rome: Desclée
and Co., 1921)

Theodoreti et Evagri, *Historia Ecclesiastica* (Amsterdam, 1695)

Tixeront, J., *History of Dogmas*, 3 vols. (2. ed., St. Louis: B. Herder Book Co., 1921)

St. Thomas Aquinas, *Summa Theologica* (Editio altera Romana ad emendationes impressa et noviter accuratissime recognita, Rome: Forzani, 1923)

Toso, Albertus, *Ad Codicem Juris Canonici Benedicti XV Pont. Max. auctoritate promulgatum Commentaria Minora* (2. ed., Rome: Marietti, 1921)

Ubach, Joseph, S. J., *Compendium Theologiae Moralis*, 2 vols. (Freiburg, i. B.: Herder & Co., 1926)

Van Coillie, C., *Commentarius in Constitutionem SSmi Dni Leonis Papae XIII "Officiorum ac munerum"* (Bruges, 1899)

Vermeersch, Arthur, S. J., *De Prohibitione et Censura Librorum* (2. ed., Tours, 1898)

Vermeersch, Arthur, S. J., *Theologiae Moralis Principia, Responsa, Consilia* (2. ed., Rome: Università Gregoriana, 1927)

Vermeersch, Arthur, S. J., *De Castitate et De Vitiis Contrariis* (Rome: Università Gregoriana, 1921)

Vermeersch, Arthur, S. J., *De formulis Facultatum S. C. de Propaganda Fide commentaria* (Bruges: Bagaert, 1922)

Vermeersch, A. - Creusen, J., S. J., *Epitome Juris Canonici* (Vol. 1., 3. ed., Mechlin: H. Dessain, 1927; Vol. II-III, 2. ed., Mechlin: H. Dessain, 1925)

Von Dobschütz, Ernst, *Das Decretum gelasianum De libris recipiendis et non recipiendis in kritischem Text herausgegeben und untersucht* (Leipzig, 1912)

Vouaux, Léon, *Les Actes de Paul et Ses Lettres Apocryphes* (Paris: Libraire Letouzey et Ané, 1913)

Wehrlé, René, *De La Coutume Dans Le Droit Canonique* (Paris: Libraire du Recueil Sirey, 1928)

Wernz, Franciscus Xaverius, S. J., *Jus Decretalium*, 6 vols. (2. ed., (Rome, 1908)

Wernz, F. X. - Vidal, Petrus, *Jus Canonicum ad Codicis Normam Exactum* (Rome: Gregorian University, 1923)

Windle, Sir Bertram, C. A., *The Church and Science* (London: Catholic Truth Society, 1917)

Winslow, Francis Joseph, *Vicars and Prefects Apostolic* (Washington: Catholic University, 1924)

Woywod, Stanislaus, O. F. M., *A Practical Commentary on the Code of Canon Law*, in 2 vols. (New York: J. F. Wagner, 1925)

Zaccaria, F. A., *Storia Polemica delle proibizioni dei libri* (Rome, 1777)

Zaretzky, Otto, *Der erste Kölner Zensurprozess* (Koln, 1906)

PERIODICALS

Acolyte, The (Huntington)
American Catholic Quarterly Review (Philadelphia)
Ami du Clergé, L' (Langres)
Apollinaris (Rome)
Canoniste Contemporain, Le (Paris)
Catholic News, The (New York)
Catholic University Bulletin (Washington)
Civiltà Cattolica, La (Naples)
Conference Bulletin of the Archdiocese of New York (New York)
Ecclesiastical Review, The (Philadelphia)
Ephemerides Theologicae Lovanienses (Louvain)
Etudes Religieuses (Paris)
Homiletic and Pastoral Review, The (New York)
Irish Ecclesiastical Record, The (Dublin)

Monitore Ecclesiastico, Il (Rome)
Nouvelle Review Theologique (Paris)
Perfice Munus (Turin)
Periodica de re canonica et morali utilia praesertim Religiosis et Missionariis (Bruges)
Periodica De Re Morali Canonica et Liturgica (Bruges)
Supplement to the American Journal of International Law (New York: The American Society of International Law, 1907-)
Tablet, The (London)
Theologisch-praktische Quartalschrift (Linz)
Zentralblatt für Bibliothekswesen (Leipzig)

Universitas Catholica Americae

Washington, D. C.

Facultas Iuris Canonici

No. 72

1932

TITULI

QUOS

AD DOCTORATUS GRADUM

IN

JURE CANONICO

APUD UNIVERSITATEM CATHOLICAM AMERICAE

CONSEQUENDUM

PUBLICE PROPUGNAVIT

JOSEPH MARIA PERNICONE

SACERDOS ARCHDIOECESIS

NEO-EBORACENSIS

JURIS UTRIUSQUE LICENTIATUS

HORA III P. M. DIE XXVIII MAII A. D. MCMXXXI

TITULI

DE JURE CANONICO

XXXVII.	Canones 1732-1741	De Litis Instantia.
XXXVIII.	Canones 1742-1746	De Interrogationibus Partibus in Judicio Faciendis.
XXXIX.	Canones 1747-1769	De Probationibus.
XL.	Canones 1960-1992	De Causis Matrimonialibus.
XLI.	Canones 1993-1998	De Causis contra Sacram Ordinationem.
XLII.	Canones 2147-2167	De Remotione et Translatione Parochorum.
XLIII.	Canones 2168-2185	De Modo Procedendi contra Clericos non Residentes, etc.
XLIV.	Canones 2186-2194	De Modo Procedendi in Suspensione ex Informata Conscientia Infligenda.
XLV.	Canones 2214-2254	De Poenis et Censuris in Genere.

DE JURE ROMANO

XLVI.	Periods of Roman Law.
XLVII.	Personality.
XLVIII.	Citizenship.
XLIX.	The Roman Family.
L.	Cura and Tutela.
LI.	Adoption.
LII.	Roman Marriage.
LIII.	Modes of Acquiring Singular Things.
LIV.	Modes of Acquiring an Aggregate of Things.
LV.	General Character of Obligation.
LVI.	Classification of Obligations.
LVII.	General Principles of Contracts.
LVIII.	Real Contracts.
LIX.	Verbal Contracts.
LX.	Literal Contracts.

Vidit Facultas:

LUDOVICUS MOTRY, S. T. D., J. C. D., *a Secretis.*
VALENTINUS SCHAAF, O. F. M., J. C. D.
FRANCISCUS LARDONE, S. T. D., J. U. D.

Vidit Rector Magnificus Universitatis:

JACOBUS HUGO RYAN, Ph. D., S. T. D.

BIOGRAPHICAL NOTE

Joseph Maria Pernicone, born at Regalbuto, Italy, on Nov. 4, 1903, attended the public school of that place. On November 4, 1915 he entered the preparatory seminary of Nicosia. Thence he went to Catania to continue his ecclesiastical studies in the archiepiscopal seminary of that city. In 1920 he came to New York and, after one year in Cathedral College, entered St. Joseph's Seminary, Dunwoodie, N. Y. He was ordained to the priesthood on Dec. 18, 1926 by His Excellency, the Most Reverend John J. Dunn. In the fall of that year he entered the graduate School of Canon Law at the Catholic University of America, Washington, D. C. He completed the course of prescribed studies in June, 1928.

CANON LAW STUDIES

1. FRERIKS, REV. CELESTINE A., C. PP. S., J. C.D., Religious
Congregations in Their External Relations, 121 pp., 1916.
2. GALLIHER, REV. DANIEL M., O. P., J. C. D. Canonical Elections,
117 pp., 1917.
3. BORKOWSKI, REV. AURELIUS L., O. F. M., De Confraternita-
tibus Ecclesiasticis, 136 pp., 1918.
4. CASTILLO, REV. CAYO, J. C. D., Disertacion Historico-canonica
sobre la Potestad del Cabildo en Sede Vacante o Impedida del
Vicario Capitular, 99 pp., 1919 (1918).
5. KUBELBECK, REV. WILLIAM J., S. T. B., J. C. D., The Sacred
Penitentiaria and Its Relations to Faculties of Ordinaries and
Priests, 129 pp., 1918.
6. PETROVITS, REV. JOSEPH J. C., S. T. D., J. C. D., The New
Church Law on Matrimony, X-461 pp., 1919.
7. HICKEY, REV. JOHN J., S. T. B., J. C. D., Irregularities and Simple Impediments in the New Code of Canon Law, 100 pp., 1920.
8. KLEKOTKA, REV. PETER J., S. T. B., J. C. D., Diocesan Consultors, 179 pp., 1920.
9. WANNENMACHER, REV. FRANCIS, J. C. D., The Evidence in
Ecclesiastical Procedure Affecting the Marriage Bond, 1920. (Not
Printed).
10. GOLDEN, REV. HENRY FRANCIS, J. C. D., Parochial Benefices
in the New Code, IV-119 pp., 1921. (Printed 1925).
11. KOUDELKA, REV. CHARLES J., J. C. D., Pastors, Their Rights
and Duties According to the New Code of Canon Law, 211 pp.,
1921.
12. MELO, REV. ANTONIUS, O. F. M., J. C. D., De Exemptione Regularium, X-188 pp., 1921.
13. SCHAAF, REV. VALENTINE THEODORE, O. F. M., S. T. B.,
J.C. D., The Cloister, X-180 pp., 1921.
14. BURKE, REV. THOMAS JOSEPH, S. T. B., J. C. D., Competence
in Ecclesiastical Tribunals, IV-117 pp., 1922.
15. LEECH, REV. GEORGE LEO, J. C. D., A Comparative Study of
the Constitution "Apostolicae Sedis" and the "Codex Juris Canonici," 179 pp., 1922.
16. MOTRY, REV. HUBERT LOUIS, S. T. D., J. C. D., Diocesan Faculties according to the Code of Canon Law, II-167 pp., 1922.
17. MURPHY, REV. GEORGE LAWRENCE, J. C. D., Delinquencies
and Penalties in the Administration and the Reception of the
Sacraments, IV-121 pp., 1923.
18. O'REILLY, REV. JOHN ANTHONY, S. T. B., J. C. D., Ecclesiastical Sepulture in the New Code of Canon Law, II-129 pp., 1923.
19. MICHALICKA, REV. WENCESLAS CYRILL, O. S. B., J. C. D.,
Judicial Procedure in Dismissal of Clerical Exempt Religious,
107 pp., 1923.
20. DARGIN, REV. EDWARD VINCENT, S. T. B., J. C. D., Reserved
Cases According to the Code of Canon Law, IV-103 pp., 1924.
21. GODFREY, REV. JOHN A., S. T. B., J. C. D., The Right of Pa-
ronage According to the Code of Canon Law, 153 pp., 1924.

22. HAGEDORN, REV. FRANCIS EDWARD, J. C. D., General Legislation on Indulgences, II-154 pp., 1924.
23. KING, REV. JAMES IGNATIUS, J. C. D., The Administration of the Sacraments to Dying Non-Catholics, V-141 pp., 1924.
24. WINSLOW, REV. FRANCIS JOSEPH, A. F. M., J. C. D., Vicars and Prefects Apostolic, IV-149 pp., 1924.
25. CORREA, REV. JOSE SERVELION, S. T. L., J. C. D., La Potestad Legislativa de la Iglesia Católica, IV-127 pp., 1925.
26. DUGAN, REV. HENRY FRANCIS, M. A., J. C. D., The Judiciary Department of the Diocesan Curia, 87 pp., 1925.
27. KELLER, REV. CHARLES FREDERICK, S. T. B., J. C. D., Mass Stipends, 167 pp., 1925.
28. PASCHANG, REV. JOHN LINUS, J. C. D., The Sacramentals According to the Code of Canon Law, 129 pp., 1925.
29. PIONTEK, REV. CYRILLUS, O. F. M., S. T. B., J. C. D., De Indulto Exclaustrationis necnon Saecularizationis, XIII-289 pp., 1925.
30. KEARNEY, REV. RICHARD JOSEPH, S. T. B., J. C. D., Sponsors at Baptism According to the Code of Canon Law, IV-127 pp., 1925.
31. BARTLETT, REV. CHESTER JOSEPH, A. M., LL. B., J. C. D., The Tenure of Parochial Property in the United States of America, V-108 pp., 1926.
32. KILKER, REV. ADRIAN JEROME, J. C. D., Extreme Unction, V-425 pp., 1926.
33. McCORMICK, REV. ROBERT EMMETT, J. C. D., Confessors of Religious, VIII-266 pp., 1926.
34. MILLER, REV. NEWTON THOMAS, J. C. D., Founded Masses According to the Code of Canon Law, VII-93 pp., 1926.
35. ROELKER, REV. EDWARD G., S. T. D., J. C. D., Principles of Privilege According to the Code of Canon Law, XI-166 pp., 1926.
36. BAKALARCZYK, REV. RICHARDUS, M. I. C., J. U. D., De Novitiatu, VIII-208 pp., 1927.
37. PIZZUTI, REV. LAWRENCE, O. F. M., J. U. L., De Parochis Religiosis, 1927. (Not Printed).
38. BLILEY, REV. NICHOLAS MARTIN, O. S. B., J. C. D., Altars According to the Code of Canon Law, XIX-132 pp., 1927.
39. BROWN, BRENDAN FRANCIS, A. B., LL. M., J. U. D., The Canonical Juristic Personality with Special Reference to its Status in the United States of America, V-212 pp., 1927.
40. CAVANAUGH, REV. WILLIAM THOMAS, C. P., J. U. D., The Reservation of the Blessed Sacrament, VIII-101 pp., 1927.
41. DOHENY, REV. WILLIAM J., C. S. C., A. B., J. U. D., Church Property: Modes of Acquisition, X118 pp., 1927.
42. FELDHAUS, REV. ALOYSIUS H., C. PP. S., J. C. D., Oratories, IX-141 pp., 1927.
43. KELLY, REV. JAMES PATRICK, A. B., J. C. D., The Jurisdiction of the Simple Confessor, X-208 pp., 1927.
44. NEUBERGER, REV. NICHOLAS J., J. C. D., Canon 6 or the Relation of the Codex Juris Canonici to the Preceding Legislation, V-95 pp., 1927.
45. O'KEEFFE, REV. GERALD MICHAEL, J. C. D., Matrimonial Dispensations, Powers of Bishops, Priests, and Confessors, VIII-232 pp., 1927.
46. QUIGLEY, REV. JOSEPH, A. M., A. B., J. C. D., Condemned Societies, 139 pp., 1927.
47. ZAPLOTNIK, REV. IOANNES LEO, J. C. D., De Vicariis Foraneis, X-142, 1927.
48. DUSKIE, REV. JOHN ALOYSIUS, A. B., J. C. D., The Canonical Status of the Orientals in the United States, VIII-196 pp., 1928.

49. HYLAND, REV. FRANCIS EDWARD, J. C. D., Excommunication, Its Nature, Historical Development and Effects, VIII-181 pp., 1928.
50. REINMANN, REV. GERALD JOSEPH, O. M. C., J. C. D., The Third Order Secular of Saint Francis, 201 pp., 1928.
51. SCHENK, REV. FRANCIS J., J. C. D., The Matrimonial Impediments of Mixed Religion and Disparity of Cult, XVI-318 pp., 1929.
52. COADY, REV. JOHN JOSEPH, S. T. D., J. U. D., A. M., The Appointment of Pastors, VIII-150 pp., 1929.
53. KAY, REV. THOMAS HENRY, J. C. D., Competence in Matrimonial Procedure, VIII-164 pp., 1929.
54. TURNER, REV. SIDNEY JOSEPH, C. P., J. U. D., The Vow of Poverty, XLIX-217 pp., 1929.
55. KEARNEY, REV. RAYMOND A., A. B., S. T. D., J. C. C., The Principles of Delegation, VII-149 pp., 1929.
56. CONRAN, REV. EDWARD JAMES, A. B., J. C. D., The Interdict, V-163 pp., 1930.
57. O'NEIL, REV. WILLIAM, H., J. C.D., Papal Rescripts of Favor, VII-218 pp., 1930.
58. BASTNAGEL, REV. CLEMENT VINCENT, J. U. D., The Appointment of Parochial Adjutants and Assistants, XV-257 pp., 1930.
59. FERRY, REV. WILLIAM, A., A. B., J. C. D., Stole Fees, X-107 pp., 1930.
60. COSTELLO, REV. JOHN MICHAEL, A. B., J. C. D., Domicile and Quasi-Domicile, VII-201 pp., 1930.
61. KREMER, REV. MICHAEL NICHOLAS, A. B., S. T. B., J. C. D., Church Support in the United States, VI-136 pp., 1930.
62. ANGULO, REV. LUIS, C. M., J. C. D., Legislación de la Iglesia sobre la intención en la aplicación de la Santa Misa, VII-104 pp., 1931.
63. FREY, REV. WOLFGANG NORBERT, O. S. B., A. B., J. C. D., The Act of Religious Profession, VIII-174 pp., 1931.
64. ROBERTS, REV. JAMES BRENDAN, A. B., J. C. D., The Banns of Marriage, XIV-140 pp., 1931.
65. RYDER, REV. RAYMOND ALOYSIUS, A. B., J. C. D., Simony, IX-151 pp., 1931.
66. CAMPAGNA, REV. ANGELO, Ph. B., J. U. D., Il Vicario Generale del Vescovo, VII-205 pp., 1931.
67. COX, REV. JOSEPH GODFREY, A. B., J. C. D., The Administration of Seminaries, VI-124 pp., 1931.
68. GREGORY, REV. DONALD, J., J. U. D., The Pauline Privilege, XV-165 pp., 1931.
69. DONOHUE, REV. JOHN, F., J., J. C. D., The Impediment of Crime, VIII-110 pp., 1931.
70. DOOLEY, REV. EUGENE, A., O. M. I., J. C. D., Church Law on Sacred Relics, IX-143 pp., 1931.
71. ORTH, REV. CLEMENT RAYMOND, O. M. C., J. C. D., The Approbation of Religious Institutes, 171 pp., 1931.

9 780813 222615